THE
Athenian Gazette:
OR
CASUISTICAL MERCURY,

Resolving all the most

Nice and Curious Questions

PROPOSED BY THE

INGENIOUS:

From *Tuesday* March 17th, to *Saturday* May 30th, 1691.

The First Volume,

TREATING

On the several Subjects mentioned in the CONTENTS at the Beginning of the Book.

LONDON,

Printed for John Dunton, *at the Raven in the Poultry,*
MDCXCI.

Huntington Library Publications

ATHENIANISM was John Dunton's thought,
And in these features to Perfection brought;
For Knight and 'Gucht that Mystick Art did find,
To paint John's PROJECTS person, and his Mind.
They with the likeness, warmth and Grace do give,
And make his Picture seem to think and live:
And's Heraldry he from the Muses farms,
For PEGASUS shou'd be a Poets Arms.

THE ORACLE of the COFFEE HOUSE

John Dunton's

ATHENIAN MERCURY

BY

Gilbert D. McEwen

THE HUNTINGTON LIBRARY

San Marino, California

1972

Copyright 1972 by the
Henry E. Huntington Library and Art Gallery
Library of Congress Card Number 78–171109
Printed in the United States of America
by Kingsport Press
Designed by Mary Stoddard and Robert Shaw

Frontispiece: John Dunton. Engraved by M. Van der Gucht from a drawing by E. Knight. This engraving was the frontispiece for *The Life and Errors of John Dunton*, London, 1705.

For Cato

THE CONTENTS OF THE Fourth Volume.

WHAT Testimonies find ye in History (the Sacred Writ excepted) that can give us Assurance of such a Person as our Saviour and his Miracles? N. 1. q. 1.
Whether the keeping so many hundreds as are kept in Prisons n. 1. q. 2.
If a Man has a Brother by Nature or Affinity, n. 1. q. 3.
Whether there be a Species in Nature of which one Creature does only exist? n. 1. q. 4.
An Abstract of Mr. Rogers Book of Melancholy.
Whether the Vaudois, as is suggested, have maintained the Profession of the Christian Religion uncorrupted with the Errors of Popery from the Primitive Times? or if not, when did they reform? n. 2. q. 1.
Whether a Dissenter is a Schismatick? n. 2. q. 2.
Whether Moses had a real or visionary sight of Canaan from Mount Pisgah? n. 2. q. 3.
What Historical Account can you give of the Antiquity of Tyburn? n. 2. q. 4.
Was there ever any such Executions practis'd in England as Hanging in Chains alive? n. 2. q. 5.
Why should not a mutual Consent dissolve the Marriage Contract? n. 2. q. 6.
A person has a perverse contentious Wife, n. 2. q. 7.
How are those words to be understood, Heb. 6. 4, 5, 6. ——For 'tis impossible for those who were once enlightened, &c. if they shall fall away, to renew them again, &c? n. 2. q. 8.
Whether repeating the word, O God, in Discourse, n. 2. q. 9.
Who was the first Philosopher? n. 2. q. 10.
What Physical Difference is there between the pale Summer, Lightning, n. 2. q. 11.
Whether Bees make that humming sort of a Noise with their Mouths or with their Wings? n. 2. q. 12.
Whether when a Horse Neighs, is it a rejoycing, or because he is angry. n. 2. q. 13.
After what Manner should a Gentleman at the first Visit accost his Mistress? n. 3. q. 1.
What Behaviour and Carriage in the progress of an Amour will be most Winning, n. 3. q. 2.
What Expression's fittest for a Lover to make use of to declare his Passion? n. 3. q. 3.
Whether Tears, Sighs, and earnest Entreaties be of greater force to obtain a Ladies Favour than a moderate Degree of Zeal with a wise and manly Carriage? n. 3. q. 4.
Whether Interrupting Discourse by repeated Kisses ben't rude and unmannerly, n. 3. q. 5.
How far may Singing and Musick be proper in making Love? n. 3. q. 6.
Whether would it be greater Prudence, n. 3. q. 7.
You tell us in one of your Mercuries, in your Definition of Love, that 'tis a little pretty soft thing that plays about the Heart, n. 3. q. 8.
Whether the Answers of the Oracles of old, n. 4. q. 1.
Whether the word ברא, which we Translate Created, n. 4. q. 2.
I have oftentimes heard and read of the Life of Man being divided into several parts, as Infancy, Childhood, &c. n. 5. q. 1.
A Maid at Windsor dreamt that her Father was killing her Mother, n. 5. q. 2.
Concerning this following Query, there has been several hot Disputes, n. 5. q. 3.
Whose Daughter was Cain's Wife? n. 5. q. 4.
Was Adam a perfect Man? n. 5. q. 5.
Whether there be such a Serpent as an Amphisbena? n. 5. q. 6.
What think you of the Millennium? n. 6. q. 1.
Gentlemen, for the sake of a disconsolate Gentlewoman, n. 7. q. 1.
It was observed in this City, upon the Night for the Publick Rejoycing about the surrendring of Lymerick, n. 7. q. 2.
One of a Sanguine Complexion being married to a Husband, n. 7. q. 3.
An Homunculne, &c. n. 7. q. 4.
I want to be resolved what kind of Creature that is which the Scripture calls a Dragon? n. 7. q. 5.
Upon my Wifes Conception I am immediately sick, and so continue every Morning, n. 7. q. 6.
There being a strange Story of an Apparition, n. 7. q. 7.
It hath been my misfortune to be seduced, n. 7. q. 8.
What ought one rightly to think of such Dissenters, n. 7. q. 9.
Gentlemen, there's a young Woman has set her Affections upon a Young Man, n. 7. q. 10.
Whether the Delivery of a Gate and Fort, n. 8. q. 1.
I Vowed, without any other Witness than God and my own Conscience, n. 8. q. 2.
A Young Gentleman falling in Love with a young Lady, n. 8. q. 3.
Whether

CONTENTS

Preface *page ix*

1. The Great Question Project *page 3*
2. The Athenian Itch *page 23*
3. Bouquets and Brickbats *page 33*
4. Fringe Benefits *page 49*
5. "A Decay'd Gentleman" *page 59*
6. Compassion and Comedy 1693 *page 67*
7. Dunton Invites the Muse *page 89*
8. Science for Everyman *page 113*
9. Money and Matrimony *page 141*
10. Faith for Everyman *page 163*
11. "Fuimus Troes, fuit Ilium. . . ." *page 191*
12. Athenianism: the Final Years *page 209*

Index *page 243*

PREFACE

John Dunton's importance as a bookseller and chronicler of bookselling in Augustan England has long been recognized, but no full-length study has ever been made of his greatest project, a question-and-answer periodical, the *Athenian Gazette: or Casuistical Mercury,* which flourished from 1691 to 1697. Among critics, there have been many allusions to the *Mercury,* and Walter Graham devoted more space to it than to any other single periodical in his *English Literary Periodicals* (New York, 1930). The quaint emblem of the anonymous Athenian Society stands as frontispiece in his book.

The *Mercury* is not readable in the way of its great successors, the *Tatler,* the *Spectator,* Defoe's *Review,* and Swift's *Examiner,* which impressed the reader with their literary qualities and the timeliness of their comment. Rather, the *Mercury* set out to engage the reader by means of its novel feature, the question, and then to keep him as a reader by educating, informing, and entertaining him. In publishing twice weekly for over five years, the *Mercury* laid the groundwork for those later periodicals that epitomize English society just after the turn of the century.

I have not attempted an exhaustive bibliographical study of the *Mercury.* There remains much to be learned about the printing and distribution of periodicals in the late seventeenth century. Rather, I have concentrated upon the people involved and the contents of the periodical.

Most of my work has been done at the Henry E. Huntington Library, San Marino, California. I am grateful to the staff of the Library for unstinting help and encouragement, and particularly to Miss Mary Isabel Fry, Miss Constance Lodge, Miss Ann Hyder, Mrs. Betty Leigh Merrell, Mrs. Dorothy Heninger, Mrs. Jane Evans, John S. Pomfret, Director of the Library, now retired, and James Thorpe, present Director. I am also indebted to the William Andrews Clark Library, Los Angeles, for use of resources; to the Bodleian Library, Oxford, for permission to use Dunton manuscript items; and to Harvard University for the use of T. M. Hatfield's unpublished dissertation, *The True Secret History of John Dunton* (1926).

A grant from the American Philosophical Society in 1963 was of great assistance to me in carrying my work forward. My colleagues at Whittier College, especially Albert Upton, have been helpful in a hundred ways, and I am grateful to the College for financial assistance.

Professor Richmond P. Bond of the University of North Carolina gave me excellent advice and encouragement, and his colleague, Professor Robert Haig read early chapters and steered me to valuable Dunton materials. Professor James Sutherland's penetrating questions were of great help. To Professor George Mayhew, of the California Institute of Technology, and Professor Paul Zall, of California State College at Los Angeles, I owe more than I can ever repay for the many hours they spent in reading and criticizing my work and in encouraging me at times of most need. They helped make possible whatever good qualities the work has and are in no way responsible for its flaws.

Sally M. Cosgrove, Sheila Stephens, and Jan Takahashi typed the many rough drafts of my manuscript and Ann Farmer typed the final version and prepared the index. Their help was invaluable.

My wife has been the greatest help of all, never herself doubting and never letting me doubt that the Athenian Project would someday be finished.

Gilbert D. McEwen

Whittier, California
17 January 1970

THE
ORACLE of the COFFEE HOUSE
John Dunton's
ATHENIAN MERCURY

1

The Great Question Project

As he walked with two friends over St. George's Fields one memorable day in 1691, young John Dunton fell unusually silent, his mind strangely uneasy over some *"flaming Injury."* In this sensitized state he was struck by a thought which he told his companions he would "not exchange for Fifty Guineas." They teased him to disclose it, but could get from him only its "first rude *Hint . . . a confused Idea of concealing the Querist and answering his Question."*[1]

Thus was born the best-known and longest-lived of all seventeenth-century literary periodicals, *The Athenian Gazette, or Casuistical Mercury, Resolving all the most Nice and Curious Questions proposed by the Ingenious.*[2] However legendary this account may be, set down as it was more than a dozen years after the project was launched, Dunton did in fact begin a weekly periodical of questions and answers on Tuesday 17 March 1691. Within two weeks it changed to semiweekly publication on Tuesdays and Saturdays, and continued so for the most part until it ceased publication on 14 June 1697.[3] For a very brief period in 1692 the *Mercury* appeared three times a week in order to forestall a rival publication.[4] There were two suspensions, one forced by order of the Licenser in 1692,[5] and another voluntary, for business reasons, in 1696–97.[6] In all, Dunton printed the answers to nearly six thousand questions in the twenty volumes and five hundred eighty numbers of his periodical. The whole undertaking was, for the 1690's, a great success, surviving all threats to its existence until newspaper competition and Dunton's own personal difficulties combined to send it under. Had these unfavorable circumstances not risen almost simultaneously, the *Mercury* might have gone on even longer.

The way in which Dunton's earlier career led to the outstanding achievement of his life, the *Athenian Mercury,* is told in his autobiographical work, the *Life and Errors of John Dunton.* Stuffed with minute details of his eventful life from his birth in 1659 to about 1703, this gossipy, inaccurate and opinionated work relates the "stages" of the author's life, each "stage" followed by a chapter explaining what Dunton would do if he could live it again. "Stage III," for example, is that of "BATCHELOURSHIP . . . *from the time of his freedom* [from apprenticeship], *to the Day of his Marriage"* (LE,pp.69–85), followed by "THE IDEA OF A NEW LIFE: OR, The Manner how I'd Think, and Speak, and Act, might I live over the Stage of Batchelourship again" (LE,pp.86–94). He wrote the book in "retirement" in the country, estranged from his second wife over the marriage settlement, out of bookselling because of debts, and in the mood to settle scores against enemies, praise his friends, and let the world know of his own importance.

Dunton was born in 1659 at Graffham in Huntingdonshire, the son of John Dunton, an orthodox clergyman.[7] Destined for his father's vocation, he would have been the fourth in his line to occupy the pulpit. But he was an inattentive scholar and perhaps also a rejected child, for when John's mother died his father left his little son, only three years old, in a foster home and went to Ireland for several years.[8] The boy was apprenticed at fifteen to Thomas Parkhurst, a Presbyterian bookseller and a distinguished member of the Stationers Company. He ran away from Parkhurst once and returned home on foot, but his father brought him back, Parkhurst received him once more into his apprenticeship, and he had fulfilled his articles on 5 December 1681, when he was twenty-one years old.[9]

Upon the advice both of his father and of Parkhurst, he then looked for a convenient shop in a convenient place (LE,p.70). Dunton's "Sign of the Black Raven" identified his shop at three different locations, all in the Stocks Market quarter, between 1681 and 1697.[10] Eager to marry, he first sought to find whether his trade "wou'd carry Two, and then to proceed upon a safe Bottom" in courting, being aware of "the Ruine and the *Unhappiness, that other Apprentices have run 'emselves into, by a too early Engagement in the Affairs of Love,*" and in particular of one who married secretly and, made conscious of his folly and disgrace, "pin'd away *Piece-meal* to his Grave" (LE,p.59).

Mere chance brought him to his first wife, Elizabeth Annesley, daughter of the Rev. Samuel Annesley (1621–1696),[11] for he strolled one Sunday into her father's meeting place. There, he related,

> instead of engaging my Attention to what the Dr. said, I suffer'd both my Mind and my Eyes to run at Random, and 'tis very rare but Satan can throw in a Temptation when the Sinner lies empty for't. I soon singled out a Young Lady that almost charm'd me Dead; but . . . I found to my Sorrow she was pre-ingag'd: However, my Friends . . . advis'd me to make an Experiment upon her Elder Sister . . . and the Hint they gave me, as Providence would have it, made a deeper Impression upon me than all the Recommendations they had given me before. (LE,pp.75–76)

Dunton transferred his attentions to Elizabeth, and soon came "to mention the Matter first of all" to Dr. Annesley, who, as the father of two dozen children, was understandably nothing loath. The minister prudently sent for Thomas Parkhurst, however, who gave Dunton "a Character that was favourable enough" (LE,p.76). Of the letters of courtship that passed between Dunton, who signed himself "Philaret," and "Iris," as he always called Elizabeth, his exemplify his usual ebullience, hers a prudence learned from her father, with which she cautioned, *"At present please to deny yourself a little Luxuriance in your Letters, lest my Father should find them, and be offended with them."*[12]

Their marriage, which took place on 3 August 1682, was symbolic of the grounds upon which Dunton built his career as a bookseller, for his father-in-law was one of the most distinguished Dissenters in London (LE,p.81). In publishing, Dunton preferred the Dissenters' copy to that of London's hack writers, whose "great Concern lay more *IN HOW MUCH A SHEET*, than in any generous respect they bore to the *COMMONWEALTH OF LEARNING*" (LE,pp.70–71). His father in apprenticing his son to Parkhurst, "a Religious and a Just Man," had also ensured the influence of Dissent (LE,p.34). The schoolmasters of the Dissenters' academies became known to Dunton through Parkhurst, and for fifteen years works of controversy, morality, and piety by Dissenters were a substantial part of Dunton's catalog.

Before Dunton met Elizabeth Annesley, an astute friend recommended that he ask for the hand of Sarah, daughter of the Rev. Thomas Doolittle, pointing out that she would bring as a dowry her father's copies for nothing, "and his *Book* on the *Sacrament* . . . has sold to the Twentieth Edition, which would have bin an Estate for a *Bookseller*" (LE,p.74).

"This Design was quite lost in the Novelty of another," wrote Dunton; but Doolittle, master of a Dissenters' academy at Islington, let Dunton publish his book, the *Lord's Last Sufferings*. Copy was entered in the *Term Catalogue* in November 1681, and upon its publication in 1682, Dunton, following a common practice of the day, exchanged copies with other booksellers to furnish his shop with a variety of books for sale.[13]

At about this time Dunton met Samuel Wesley, who was later to become his brother-in-law and his most important associate in the publication of the *Athenian Mercury*. Wesley, a student at Mr. Veal's dissenting academy in Islington, was already "much celebrated for his Vein at Poetry."[14] He was soon to become the first poet to be published by Dunton. *Maggots: or, Poems on Several Subjects, Never before Handled,* "By a Schollar," appeared in 1685. The sense of *maggot* as an original and obsessive idea appealed so much to Dunton that the word became a familiar one in his vocabulary. In the duodecimo volume of poems that sense is borne out in such poems as "A Pindarique On the Grunting of a Hog," "To my Gingerbread Mistress," and especially in "An Anacreontique on a Pair of Breeches." This last was plagiarized by the writers, probably including young Jonathan Swift, of a Tripos entertainment at Trinity College, Dublin, not long afterward.[15]

Dunton's story of his life from 1682 to the end of 1688 begins with a confusion of chronology and continues with many assertions of events almost impossible to verify. In broad outline, the verifiable chronology is as follows: independent bookselling in Stocks Market, early 1682 to about October 1685 (LE,pp.69–100); a voyage to the Massachusetts Bay Colony to sell books and collect debts from patrons, October 1685 to August 1686 (LE,pp.101–196); and in the remaining twenty-eight months, ten months in hiding from bailiffs in London (LE,pp.197–198), a period of about a year entirely unaccounted for, and a trip to Holland, Flanders, and Germany from which Dunton alleged that he returned on 15 November 1688 (LE,pp.198–215).

Some of his experiences were certainly not typical for a bookseller, but they were not unusual for one who leaned toward Dissent, and especially for one who might also have dabbled in the Monmouth plot. He was not important enough at first in his trade to be in any great danger, but in May 1685, as soon as James II gave Sir Roger L'Estrange extraordinary powers to enforce the regulations concerning treasonable, seditious, and scandalous publications,[16] Dunton ceased publishing.

Four months later he set sail for that haven of Dissent, the Massachusetts Bay Colony, with a stock of books which he described to his father-in-law as *"very proper for that place"* (LE,p.102). He gave as reasons for his voyage the "Universal Damp upon Trade" caused by the defeat of Monmouth in the West, and five hundred pounds that were owing him in New England (LE,p.101), but commented quite unashamedly, after citing his wife's obedient consent and Dr. Annesley's encouragement for the trip, "I was very glad of any Excuse that wou'd make my Friends more indulgent to my *Rambling Humour*" (LE,p.103).

Once in Boston, Dunton wrote to Dr. Annesley asking

whether he should sell his "venture" at retail or wholesale (LE,p.119). Half the venture, worth £500, had gone down with another ship in the convoy; Dunton had to "admire the good Providence" that had kept him from trusting himself to that ship (LE,p.113). Annesley's reply, dated almost two months later, was really no answer at all, for it proffered the advice only that "Present Providences upon present Circumstances must be observ'd" (LE,p.119). The young bookseller seems to have undertaken both methods of merchandising and to have made a good profit, although he complained about the scarcity of cash payments: "He that trades with the Inhabitants of *Boston,* shou'd be well furnished with a *Grecian Faith;* he may get Promises enough, but their Payments come late" (LE,p.125).

Dunton called upon the clergy, whom he regarded as his best customers everywhere, whether in London, Dublin, or Boston; and he made his acquaintance with the booksellers of Boston (LE,pp.124–128). Then, leaving his warehouse in charge of Samuel Palmer, his servant, he went on carefree junkets about the Colony, often with such a fair companion as the Widow Brick, "The Flower of Boston," up behind him on his mount, but he was careful to remark, in bookseller's metaphor, that the virtues of his female friends in Boston were all to be found in his dear Iris, "as 'twere in a NEW EDITION, more Correct and enlarg'd" (LE,p.143).

His most significant visit in respect to his publishing career was to the Mathers, father and son, in Boston. Of Cotton Mather, just then finishing his *Magnalia Christi Americana,* he remarked: "His Library is very large and numerous; but, had his Books been fewer when he writ his History, 'twould have pleas'd us better" (LE,p.125). Yet he obtained permission to print Cotton Mather's books in England, and in his letters praised Mather's company as "Heaven," his library as "the best sight that I had in Boston."[17]

Dunton also visited the Rev. John Eliot in Roxbury, for the venerable missionary to the Indians was an old friend of Dr. Samuel Annesley, Dunton's father-in-law. Eliot gave his visitor a dozen Indian Bibles, and a dozen dying speeches of converted Indians.

Dunton left Boston 5 July 1686, even though he had not settled his affairs there. Mr. Richard Wilkins, his agent in Boston, to whom he addressed the last of his *Letters from New England,* was admonished to collect for him the £500 outstanding by dunning the "Dull Payments of Connecticutt. . . . and some in Boston will bear the Spur."[18] As for the large orders for books for his friends in Boston, Salem, and Harvard College, they were all to be sent back on the same ship in which Dunton made his return voyage.

When he returned to England he left behind him in Boston his man Samuel Palmer, who "had not the Courage to see *Old England* again, for he had been dabbling in *Monmouth's* Adventure" (LE,p.182). There was some danger for Dunton himself in a return to England, even though he found a temporary relaxation of attitude toward Dissenters and those who had supported Monmouth. If we are to accept his word, the threat was due to his continuing surety for a sister-in-law's debts, an obligation which caused him to go into hiding for ten months immediately upon his return to England (LE,p.197). But either his recollection was inaccurate or he had been quickly persuaded to risk surety again upon his return, for he stated that he had been threatened with arrest for the same reason *before* he embarked for America and that in his absence his wife had paid the fifty pounds required to clear the sister-in-law, Bethia Bishop, that his bail might receive no damage (LE,pp.106,122). In one of her letters to her husband in New England, Elizabeth Dunton wrote: *"I am not able to express how great a Trouble it has been to me this Winter, that you should be brought into so many Troubles and Bondships, by Marrying of me.*

If there is any Encouragement for settling in New-England, *I will joyfully come over t' ye; but am rather for your going to* Holland, *to trade there"* (LE,p.122).

In the same letter Elizabeth Dunton protested that it was the highest demonstration of her husband's love that he entrusted her with his secret affairs. Except during this long absence, she was clerk and bookkeeper for her husband and, as calm as he was mercurial, probably served in other ways to keep both the business and its proprietor on an even keel (LE,p.100).

Upon the ground that *"Excess of Joy might prove fatal to Iris,"* Dunton had a message sent to her upon his return to London that there was a gentleman at the Queen's Head Tavern in Spitalfields who could give her news of "Philaret." The fancy pleased him because he thought his own condition "did not a little resemble the Fate of *Ulysses* at his Return from the *Trojan War"* (LE,p.196). Like Tennyson's Ulysses, however, Dunton soon found cause for taking another ramble, this time to Holland. Although he averred that going surety once more for Elizabeth's sister, and her defaulting once more, forced the trip,[19] a political motivation should not be discounted altogether. His absence from England was for most of the period between September 1685 and November 1688; his accounting for the time he did spend in England was sketchy; and he published no books and entered no titles for publication during the period. All this could have been the behavior of a man who feared more than debtors' prison.

His trip to Holland is credible, for he alluded to a brother-in-law, husband of still another Annesley daughter, with whom he stayed in Rotterdam,[20] and to a reunion in Amsterdam with "Captain" Benjamin Alsop, a former bookseller who had left London to follow Monmouth.[21] He told also that in Amsterdam he met the astrologer Partridge, Swift's future victim, who was predicting the fall of James and his replacement by William of Orange (LE,p.210). Dunton went with Alsop to visit two Dissenting ministers, Matthew Mead, whose works were published by Parkhurst, and John Shower, some of whose works Dunton published, both before and after this time. In Rotterdam, another Dissenting minister, John Spademan, gave him two volumes on the Edict of Nantes, which he also published later in London.[22]

Dunton found the Netherlands a congenial environment.

He stayed four months in Amsterdam, visiting with the many Englishmen there who hoped soon to return triumphantly to England with William as their new king. By some happy coincidence he returned to London on 15 November 1688, just in time to welcome William to London. The weary traveler found his wife in good health and all his affairs in peace, and as for himself, "The Humour of *Rambling* was now pretty well off . . ." (LE,p.215).

For the next ten years Dunton's rambles were purely fictional, but during this time he flourished as a bookseller in London, learning, in the comparatively favorable climate of William and Mary's reign, all the new ways a bookseller could turn a profit and inventing some ways of his own. His *Life and Errors,* with its long lists of booksellers, printers, bookbinders, clergymen, and patrons, bears witness to his busy, gregarious existence, and the *Term Catalogue* more reliably supplements the record with the titles of his numerous publications.

After returning from Holland, he did not resume publishing under his own imprint until Easter term, 1689. The intervening six months was a reasonable length of time for him to establish his business once more after an absence of over three years. The books he published in 1689 and 1690 were of much the same sort he had published before the Monmouth rebellion, and some were by authors he had published during the earlier period. Such works as the *Joy of Faith,* by Samuel Lee; the *Tragedies of Sin,* by Stephen Jay; *Poetical Fragments,* by Richard Baxter; and the *Soul's Return to its God in Life, and at Death,* by Samuel Slater, made up the bulk of Dunton's entries in the *Term Catalogue* in 1689.[23]

There were significant changes, however. Aside from pious publications, there were three new sorts of enterprise within the two-year period, 1689–1691, that culminated in the launching of the *Athenian Mercury.* Most nearly related to his specialty of Dissenters' works were two books first published and advertised separately and then together; the first and second collections of the *Dying Speeches, Letters and Prayers . . . of those Eminent Protestants who suf-*

fered in the West of England . . . (1689); and the *Bloody Assizes: or, a compleat History of the Life of George Lord Jefferies* (1689). These were so successful that a fourth impression of "the Dying Speeches" was contemplated in 1692, information being invited in the pages of the *Mercury* for "a new martyrology."[24] The combined edition of the life of Jeffreys and the speeches was advertised in its third edition as completing "the whole *Western* Transactions for the Year 85," the reader being warned that any other book must be an imperfect abridgement of the contents, "seeing the Gentlemen from whom the Bookseller bought the Copy . . . were the only Men in the West, whose curiosity led them to observe all my Lord Jefferies proceeding throughout his whole Western-circuit, the truth of which they are ready to attest upon Oath."

The author of both parts was John Tutchin (1661?–1707), son of a Nonconformist minister and son-in-law of another one, John Hicks, executed at Taunton in 1685 for complicity in Monmouth's rebellion. Tutchin was afterwards editor of the Dissenting *Observator* (1702–1707). He shares a couplet with Defoe in the *Dunciad,* ii, 146–147:

>Earless on high stood unabashed Defoe,
>And Tutchin flagrant from the scourge below.

"Dying speeches" such as found in Tutchin's books were still popular fare in 1690 but soon began to suffer at the hands of satirists. Dunton received notice in Swift's *Tale of a Tub* as the publisher of the speeches made from the ladder by "ascending Orators." "These Speeches," Swift wrote with irony, were "the choicest Treasury of our British Eloquence," of which "that worthy Citizen and Bookseller, Mr. *John Dunton,* hath a faithful and painful Collection, which he shortly designs to publish in Twelve Volumes in Folio, illustrated with Copper-Plates. A Work Highly useful and curious, and altogether worthy of such a Hand."[25]

Dunton also published political biographies that criticized James II and elevated William III. An example of these is the *Popish Champion: or, a compleat history of the Life and Military Actions of Richard Earl of Tyrconnel,* a forty-six page work that appeared in 1689; to it was added, in eleven pages, *An Account of the Life and Memorable Actions of Father Petre the Jesuit.* Biographical data on Tyrconnel is scant in this volume, much of it being devoted to descriptions of Ireland and of the military campaign there. The additional work on Father Petre is even slimmer, a testimony to the elusiveness of its subject (who is not even recorded in DNB).

A third phase of Dunton's post-Revolution activities began with a little cluster of news sheets or newsletters of a kind plentiful between the departure of James from England and the conclusion of the struggle in Ireland. These show that Dunton was drawn gradually into the publication of news and periodicals. That memorable day in 1691 was preceded by several years of experience in testing the wants of the reading public in seventeenth-century London.

The earliest newsletter found with Dunton's imprint is *A Continuation of News From that part of His Majesties Fleet that now lies at High-Lake near Chester.* This double column folio half-sheet was licensed 20 August 1689 by "J. F." [James Fraser] and printed for John Dunton "at the *Black Raven* in the *Poultrey.* 1689." It bears "Numb. 2" in the upper right-hand corner, *recto;* no first number seems to be in existence.

The news detailed in this sheet came "From on Board the *Hannibal* Aug. 14. 1689." It is a factual first-person account of the English ship's movements in pursuit of privateers, with the frustration of being often anticipated by the Dutch, and with some humor, as that occasioned by their passing the group of islets called "the Bishop and his Clerks:"

> We found 'em very peaceable Rocks; they let us all go by without touching us, though had we had a fancy to try hard-heads with 'em 'tis ten to one we had got the worst on't.

A Continuation is an early example of Dunton's use of his periodicals to further his bookseller's trade, for it contains an advertisement for the *Bloody Assizes,* including the "dying speeches . . . Printed by the order of several of their Relations."

Another such newsletter appeared in the next year:

Good News from Ireland . . . of a Late Signal Victory Gain'd by our English Forces near Dublin . . . Printed for John Dunton at the Raven in the Poultrey [n.d.]. Although not dated, it describes some events of the first week of July 1690 surrounding the main event of the Battle of the Boyne.

On 6 November 1689, Richard Janeway, a Dissenting bookseller of Queen's Head Alley, Paternoster Row, entered in the *Stationers Register, "A Ramble Round the World . . . with The Irish Courant on the Same Sheet."*[26] No authorship is indicated in the entry, but Dunton's favorite word in the title is the first identifying mark. The running title then leads unmistakably to him:

> . . . the most Pleasant Travels, Voyages, & Adventures of KAINOPHILUS Throughout the Habitable Earth, &c. To which will be added, all the Authors Juvenile Rambles. The like Discoveries in such a Method never made by any *Traveller* before. The whole Work will be all along intermixt with *Essays both Historical, Moral, and Divine,* &c. and may properly serve (when finished) as a compleat help to *Discourse* upon all Occasions.

The major portion of *A Ramble Round the World,* the periodical, consists of a connected series of travel episodes, all of which appeared in 1691 in the third volume of a three-volume novel by Dunton, *A Voyage Round the World . . . which contains the rare adventures of DON KAINOPHILUS . . . Done into English by a Lover of Travels,* published by Richard Newcome.[27] In both publications Dunton's pseudonym of Kainophilus, "lover of novelty," is suggestive of Athenianism, then on the verge of creation. Prefaced to the *Voyage,* among half a dozen poetical compliments to the author, are twenty-four quatrains of doggerel, "A Poetical explanation of the frontispiece," clearly parallel to autobiographical episodes in the *Life and Errors,* and further marked by the various grammatical forms of *ramble.* (The frontispiece is an elaborate zodiacal emblem.) Seven of the doggerel stanzas describe Dunton's sea voyage to Boston, six more his adventures there, and three his trip to Holland, before he returned, a "faithful Ulysses, / . . . Casting Anchor i' th' arms of his beautiful Iris." In conclusion, "When the Earth he had viewed, and described to a wonder, / When hee'd Rambled all over't here at last he creeps under."

The vein of humor running through *A Voyage Round the World* is like that in the *Life and Errors*. Irrepressible, self-centered but observant of his surroundings, Dunton poured his words into the loosely containing form of a journey. He appears as a vain but friendly man, quick to complain against suspected enemies, extravagant in praise of loyal friends.

The Introduction in Number 1 of *A Ramble Round the World* has the nervous, whimsical style found also in the *Voyage,* the Prefaces to the *Athenian Mercury,* and the *Life and Errors;* it has also Dunton's characteristic vocabulary.

> I have been a Rambler ever since I was 14 Years Old, and have Travelled through all Countries in the World; Whether it were a Maggot in my Head, or a Breeze in my Tail, or Quick-Silver in my Feet, I know not; but I could never be at rest long in one place, spurr'd on by an insatiate Desire of Novelties; I was always moving from one Stage to another, rummaging every corner and neuke of the World, till after Seventeen Years Travels, I returned to my Native Country again, as to my Center, where I intend to fix, till they have found out the way to the Moon; . . .

Dunton's introduction has in it the germ of the *Mercury.* He asserts that there are many "unwilling to lay out a Shilling or a Crown on a Journal of Travels bound together, who will not grutch to part with a Penny at a time for a single Sheet." The penny sheet will neither cloy the mind nor frighten the pocket.

Dunton continued his life's story in Number 2 of *A Ramble Round the World* and later reproduced it exactly in *A Voyage Round the World.* Below the date line of the paper the topics to be dealt with were spread out across the page; the first five drawn from the novel, the last, "An Irish Oration in praise of the Church-Ceremonies," continued a comic Irish dialect monologue begun in Number 1 as "an Elegant Sermon of one of their Mountain Kernes, to the Rabble, his Brethren, on occasion of the late Eclips of the Moon, on the 19th of September last."

Perhaps further numbers of *A Ramble* were published, for both parts of Number 2 end in an effort at suspense: "How we disposed of our selves that Evening I will relate in the next," and, "Having Copies of this and the former Irish Sermon, I was willing to Insert them, but in the Irish Court and Army. . . ."

The effort to maintain a level of interest that would make people buy future numbers of the news sheets was also an experiment in the practices that later supported the *Athenian Mercury* throughout its five hundred and eighty numbers. There was not enough news, as news was written at that time, to keep alive an *Irish Courant,* but the laconic style of news writing forced by official restrictions left room for Dunton's playful rambling. There is a personal quality in the writing, however trivial or foolish its subject, a genial assumption that the reader will be refreshed by the writer's easy flow of narrative interspersed with pious reflections. Of equal importance is the element of suspense, not breathtaking but sufficient to coax a penny for the next issue.

Dunton's voyage-ramble found its more appropriate completion in a book, but its appearance in periodical form was one of the early signs of what became the author's jealously guarded specialty, the periodical with questions, designed to entertain and inform in such a way as to hold the reader's interest from one issue to the next.

Before launching the *Mercury* of Mercuries, Dunton assisted in the publication of two other periodicals, both of which had *Mercury* in their titles: the *True Protestant Mercury,* chiefly political, ran weekly from 6 December 1689 to 7 February 1689/90; the *Coffee House Mercury,* another weekly, lasted only three weeks, from 11 to 25 November 1690. Richard Janeway, printer of the *Ramble Round the World,* was also printer of the *Protestant Mercury . . . an Impartial History of the Times.* The *Coffee House Mercury* resembles its famous successor in having items of historical or literary interest, such as "Reflections on the Ancient Courage of the British" and "A Rare Passage Relating to Dr. Sherlock's New Book."

Dunton's publishing activities during the two years preceding the *Athenian Mercury* indicate his Whiggish political position, a position certainly solidified when he was paid for the propaganda of the news sheets and the books about Jeffreys continued to sell. His attitude remained apparent in the *Mercury* though in milder form—for example, in his support of William's published desire for moral reformation. In the earlier publications he also gained a taste for periodical publication. Even though repeated attempts at maintaining regular publication failed, they encouraged the development of the idea that finally struck the fancy of the public happily enough to permit a stabilization of its form and content. His bent toward innovation often led him into downright foolishness, but it also revealed prime examples of social and intellectual attitudes that would otherwise have remained obscure during that transitional decade before the turn of the century. Among these were practical treatment of scientific questions, a generous attitude toward intellectual women, especially writers, a belief in a single standard of morality for men and women, a sympathy for imprisoned debtors, a moderate attitude toward all brands of Protestantism, and a fair regard for the Jews in England. The entire "Athenian Project" was motivated by the wish to promote popular education. Like some of the exhibits of P. T. Barnum and some of the plays on the Chautauqua stage, the *Mercury* had its meretricious features, but it shared another more desirable feature with its more modern channels for popular education, a basically sincere motivation.

Only one other journalist of the 1690's went significantly beyond the ephemeral news sheet; Peter Motteux, the Huguenot translator and journalist, published the *Gentleman's Journal: or, The Monthly Miscellany* for almost three years, January 1692 to November 1694. It was a work of great variety and the first magazine to have "departments," such as literary criticism, and even the words and music of popular songs. The actualization of Dunton's "rude Hint," however, contained even more variety than the *Gentleman's Journal* and was not aimed at any such exclusive readership as the gentlemen of London. It took all knowledge for its province, and within certain self-imposed moral limitations undertook to find the answer to any question that could be asked. In striving to fulfill this aim, the *Athenian Mercury* became an instrument of popular education and a worthy forerunner of the "improving" works characteristic of the next century. The story of this pioneer periodical provides knowledge essential to an understanding of its better-known successors of the following decade, such as the *Weekly Review,* the *Tatler* and *Spectator,* the *British Apollo,* and the *Examiner.* The *Mercury* has a simpler basic concept, with relatively slighter emphasis upon the personality of its writers, and less political motivation than its successors. From an examination of its publishing innovations, of its ways of expressing opinion, and of the subjects with which it dealt there also emerges an understanding of the times in which it flourished.

NOTES TO CHAPTERS

CHAPTER 1

[1] John Dunton, *Life and Errors* (1705), p.249. [THE / LIFE and ERRORS / of / JOHN DUNTON / Late Citizen of *London:* / — / *Written by Himself in S O L I T U D E.* / — / With an Idea of a New Life; / Wherein is Shewn / How he'd Think, Speak, and Act, might he / Live over his Days again: / — / Intermix'd with the / NEW DISCOVERIES / The Author has made / In his Travels Abroad, / And in his / Private Conversation at Home. / — / Together with the LIVES and Characters of a Thou- / sand Persons now Living in *London,* &c. / — / Digested into *Seven Stages,* with their Respective Ideas. / — / *He that has all his own Mistakes confest, / Stands next to him that never has transgrest, / And will be censur'd for a Fool by none, / But they who see no ERRORS of their own.* / Foe's *Satyr upon himself,* P.6 / — / *L O N D O N*: Printed for S. Malthus, 1705. 12mo. 6½ in. by 4. / Frontis. portrait of Dunton, drawn by E. Knight, engraved by M. Van der Gucht. Emblem of *Pegasus With News* in lozenge at bottom center of portrait, page 7¼ in. long to accommodate verses: ATHENI-

ANISM *was John Dunton's thought, / And in these features to Perfection brought; / ˚For Knight and Gucht that Mystick Art did find, / To paint John's* PROJECTS *person, and his Mind. / They with the likeness, warmth and Grace do give, And make his Picture seem to think and live: / And's Heraldry he from the Muses farms, / For* PEGASUS *shou'd be a Poet's Arms.*]

A new edition of the *Life and Errors,* together with a number of Dunton's other writings, edited by J. B. Nichols (1779–1863), was published in two volumes, with continuous pagination, in 1818, by J. Nichols, Son, and Bentley, London. All references are to the 1705 edition (LE) unless otherwise noted.

[2] Referred to henceforth as the *Mercury.* Published in nineteen volumes of thirty numbers each (17 March 1691–8 February 1696), and a twentieth volume of only ten numbers (14 May–14 June 1697). The first two numbers were issued weekly on Tuesday. Thereafter, through Volume VI, the first eighteen numbers of each volume were issued semiweekly on Tuesday and Saturday, the remaining twelve all at once, undated, a few weeks after Number 18, to make up a bound volume sold at Dunton's shop. Volumes VII through XIX were issued in thirty numbers semiweekly on Tuesday and Saturday.

A supplement (abbreviated as *Supp.*) of about thirty pages was issued with each of the first five volumes (1691–92). In references to the *Mercury,* volume, number, question number, and date are abbreviated in the following form, e.g. (V.1.3). Date, (Tue 1 Dec 91) is occasionally added for clarification.

[3] Monday and Friday were the publication days for Volume XX.

[4] Volume VI, Numbers 10 and 12, were extra numbers issued on Friday 4 March and Monday 7 March 1692, in response to the rival *Lacedemonian Mercury* (See Chapter 4).

[5] See Chapter 5.

[6] See Chapter 11, pp.198–201.

[7] LE,p.6: "I was born at *Graffham* in *Huntingtonshire* [sic], the 14th of *May,* 1659." But Dunton's father and his first wife "had only *one Son,* who was Born on the 4*th* of *May,* 1659." "The Holy Life and Triumphant Death of . . . Mr. John Dunton Late Minister of Aston Clinton. . . ." *Dunton's Remains,* London, 1684, p.19.

[8] Dunton implies that his father was in Ireland for as long as seven years (LE,pp.9,14), but Thomas M. Hatfield, in the *True Secret Life of John Dunton,* unpublished dissertation, Harvard, 1926, p.7, notes that the father was made rector of Aston Clinton, Bucks., in 1663, when his son was only four years old. The father may have been a Dissenter who, like Jonathan Swift's grandfather, sought refuge in Ireland at the Restoration, but who, unlike grandfather Swift, soon returned to England and orthodoxy. Young John, however, remained with his uncle, William Reading, near Chesham, until he was ten, when his father remarried, to Mary Lake of Aston Clinton, who bore her husband four children, a son, Lake, and three daughters, Elizabeth, Mary, and Sarah. The father died in 1676.

[9] LE,pp.33ff. The dates of the bond of apprenticeship are from the unpublished Books of the Stationers Company, as given by Hatfield, p.8.

[10] At the date of his marriage, he was situated *"at the Black Raven in Prince's Street,"* LE,p.101. The imprint of *Dunton's Remains* (1684) is "at the *Black Raven* in the *Poultrey* over against the *Stocks-Market.*" The volume contains an engraving, "The Arraignment Tryall and Execution of Christ . . . for John Dunton at ye Black Raven in the Poultrey, 1683." On 18 Sept 1694, the imprint of the *Mercury* (XV.5) changed from "in the *Poultrey"* to "in *Jewen-Street."*

[11] Samuel Annesley is much better known as the minister who exercised a benevolent influence upon Daniel Defoe through his sermons, first at Little St. Helen's in Cripplegate and later when he had been deprived of his living there and set up a private meeting house.

[12] LE,p.80. Among twenty-six quatrains of doggerel autobiography prefacing the text of Dunton's *A Voyage Round the World* [1691] is one devoted to the courtship of Elizabeth Annesley:

> But now for the Ramble of Rambles contriving,
> For he's out of his Time, and he Rambles a Wiving;
> Nine Lasses run squeeking, tho there nothing to fear is,
> Let 'em go where they will now he had caught his dear
>   Iris.

[13] *T.C.* I.458. Michelmas Term [Nov.] 1681. The Harvard Library copy of this work gives Thomas Parkhurst as publisher, suggesting that copies traded were given a new title page by the bookseller who received them.

[14] LE,p.72. Dunton's chronology is not accurate. Wesley entered Veal's academy in 1678. In 1680, Veal gave up the academy because of harassment, and Wesley entered the academy of the Rev. Charles Morton at Newington Green, where he remained until 1683; either the duel took place some two years before publication or Dunton was mistaken about Wesley's whereabouts at the time. See Luke Tyerman, *Life and Times of Samuel Wesley* (London, 1866), pp.66–70.

[15] See George P. Mayhew, "Swift and the Tripos Tradition," *Philological Quarterly,* XLV, 1 (Jan. 1965), 85–101.

[16] *Historical Manuscripts Commission (Seventh Report)*, p.409a.

[17] John Dunton's *Letters from New-England* (Boston, 1867), p.75. C. N. Greenough long ago pointed out Dunton's unacknowledged indebtedness to Overbury's *Characters,* Fuller's *Holy and Profane State,* Earle's *Microcosmography,* and other works for at least eighty-four items, mainly "characters." Most of the data on Indians came from Roger Williams' *A Key into the Languages of America,* 1643, and Dunton may not even have set foot in Natick. See "John Dunton's Letters from New England," *Publications of the Colonial Society of Massachusetts,* Vol. XIV (March 1912) 213–257.

[18] Quoted from Bodleian MS Rawl D. 72 in T. M. Hatfield, *True Secret Life,* p.32.

[19] "At last, purely to oblige my Sister, I took a Trip over to *Holland, Flanders, Germany,* &c. Tho' she has now forgot every Circumstance of it; for the Memories of most People are something slippery in such Cases, unless they be refresh'd" LE,p.199.

[20] "Mr. *Richardson,* (a true *Nathaniel*) who was marry'd to my Wife's

Sister . . . I took Lodgings with him, for the Time I stay'd there" LE,pp.199–200.

[21] Dunton said he took over Alsop's shop in the Poultry when Alsop left for the West and a commission in Monmouth's army, and that in Amsterdam, Alsop gave him "a Noble Treat," with the *Secret History of Monmouth's Adventure for the Crown of England,* LE,p.211.

[22] LE,p.201. Announced in XI.26 (Sat 7 Oct 93).

[23] *T.C.* II.246; II.283; II.294; II.297.

[24] "*The third Impression* of the Book entituled, *The New Martyrology,* Or *Bloody Assizes,* being quite sold off, a *4th* Impression of the said Book is speedily design'd. This is therefore to desire all those Countrey Gentlemen, and others who had Friends that suffer'd in the West of *England* . . . under the Cruelty of *George* Lord *Jefferies,* to send to *John Dunton* . . . by the tenth of *February* next" V.12 (Sat 9 Jan 91/92).

Dunton must have maintained a connection in Holland, for the combined works were published there in 1689 by A. D. Oossaan as *De Bloedige Vierschaar, of een volkomene history van het leven en bedryf van George Lord Jefferies . . . Uyt het Engelsch vertaald.* [A copy is in the British Museum.]

[25] *A Tale of a Tub* (ed. Guthkelch and Smith), second edition, Oxford, 1958, p.58.

[26] The two numbers are dated, Number 1, "Mac-land, October the 16th, 1689," and Number 2, "Friday November the 8th. 1689."

[27] Dunton later repented having published this work, classing it with six others as "NOVELTIES," of which he wrote: "I heartily wish I had never seen 'em, and *advise all that have 'em to burn 'em*—" LE,p.223.

2

The Athenian Itch

> . . . 'tis not without great importunity we have undertaken a task of this Nature, which at first sight appears to be a Subject chosen out and calculated on purpose for *Objections;* but yet a Consideration of those advantages a great part of the World may reap by it, has superseded that Difficulty. The Design is briefly, to satisfy all *ingenious and curious Enquirers* in to *Speculations,* Divine, Moral and Natural, &c. and to remove those Difficulties and Dissatisfactions, that shame or fear of appearing ridiculous by asking Questions, may cause several Persons to labour under, who now have opportunities of being *resolv'd in any Question* without knowing their Informer. (I. 1)

With this happy expression of concern for the general good, the *Athenian Gazette* was launched as a weekly periodical on 17 March 1690/91.[1] Dunton and a brother-in-law, Richard Sault (1660?–1702), wrote the first two numbers "without any more Assistance." Sault was the first person to whom Dunton unfolded his plan in any detail—"over a Glass of Wine I unbosom'd my self to him"—but almost immediately John Norris, (1657–1711), the Oxford Platonist, through a chance meeting with Sault, "very generously offered his Assistance *gratis,* but refused to become a stated Member of Athens" (LE,p.256).

The impatience of their readers and "the Curiosity of their Questions," however, soon required "a Third Member of Athens." Samuel Wesley, by now an ordained priest of the Church of England but without any ecclesiastical position when Dunton started the *Mercury* was free to write as much as his brother-in-law could use and happy to do it to support his wife and child.² On 10 April 1691, Wesley and Sault signed an agreement with Dunton, according to which the bookseller would pay them ten shillings for every number in print.³

Although scornful of hack writers in general, Dunton had found in Wesley and Sault two men unusually well qualified to furnish him *"Speculations,* Divine, Moral, and Natural" (I.1). Wesley was a polymath and a poet; Sault was a mathematician, small poet, and translator. With the addition of Wesley, wrote Dunton, "we found ourselves to be Masters of the whole Design, and thereupon we neither lessen'd nor increas'd our Number" (LE,p.257). The new and novel literary periodical was therefore a family enterprise, with brothers-in-law bound to brother-in-law by an agreement that the principals respected through the prosperous years of publication.

The Athenian Society as a public image did not exist at the very beginning. There was no mention in the *Mercury* of a learned society until the periodical had existed for over a year, and then only after two "outsiders" had provided the basis for it. The first was Jonathan Swift, whose *Ode* to the Athenian Society he sent to Dunton on St. Valentine's Day, 1692; it was published in the *Fifth Supplement,* most probably on All Fool's Day.⁴ The second was Charles Gildon, whose anonymous *History of the Athenian Society,* published late in May 1692, expanded and ornamented the myth of an all-knowing Athenian Society, first celebrated by Swift's *Ode* as the "great Unknown . . . far exalted Men," Protean in the *"Variety of Shapes"* they assumed "to please and satisfie Mankind."

For the first year, however, Dunton and his two principal writers worked anonymously, not yet having been "identified" as the Athenian Society. Neither questions nor answers were signed. In the columns of the *Mercury* Dunton was referred to as "our Bookseller," and at the bottom of the *verso* page the publisher was indicated as "P. Smart," from Volume One, No. 1, through Volume Two, No. 15.⁵

The periodical first mentioned the qualifications of its

writers on Tuesday 5 May 1691 (I.13), when it was announced that *"We have now taken into our Society a Civilian, a Doctor in Physick, and a Chyrurgeon, on purpose to be more serviceable to the Age; wherefore we think fit to give Notice that all the most nice* Physical, Chyrurgical, Anatomical, *and* Law Questions . . . *shall also have their Answer either in* Single Numbers, *or at the end of every Volume."*

Medical and legal questions never became numerous, however, and seldom required or received a highly technical answer. The original three writers were certainly "masters" of this part of the design, as well as of their obvious specialties, and the legal and medical Athenians were most probably fictitious.

To Wesley fell questions on religion, history, "chronology," and literature; to Sault, those on mathematics, surveying, physics, and astronomy. Questions on courtship, marriage, and social behavior were no one's special domain, nor were those on apparitions, witchcraft, and other manifestations of the supernatural and the marvelous. Contributions by Dunton himself are sometimes recognizable by their style and subject. He was sympathetic toward the problems of apprentices, and interested in all kinds of social questions.

There were some very practical provisions in the agreement, such as item 4, that each volume should contain thirty numbers with a preface and an index, "the preface to be written by the sd Wesley and Sault for which they shall have 10s betwixt 'em."[6] Another item provided that Dunton would not take any additional writers into the project without the consent of Sault and Wesley, and that neither of them would "engage in the like undertaking for any other person but the sd Dunton" so long as he paid them as agreed. There was to be

> a meeting every Fryday in the afternoon in some Convenient place betwixt the sd Wesley and Sault to consult of what they have done and to receive new Questions for the next week and the party not coming before 3 of ye Clock is to forfeit one Shilling to be spent and

the party that has not finisht his paper by that time excepting Corrections shall forfeit one shilling to be likewise spent.

The agreement, signed by the three principals, also bears the signatures of James Smith and Mary Smith, "Her Mark," as witnesses. The Smiths' coffee house was the "Convenient place" adjacent to Dunton's shop in the Stocks Market, and its proprietors became prospective beneficiaries from late arrivals and late papers.

In the first number questions were invited by means of the following notice:

All Persons whatever may be resolved gratis *in any Question that their own satisfaction or Curiosity shall prompt 'em to, if they send their Questions by a Penny Post Letter to Mr.* Smith *at his Coffee-house in* Stocks-Market *in the* Poultry, *where orders are given for the Reception of such Letters, and care shall be taken for their Resolution by the next Weekly Paper after their sending.*

In the second number, a week later, the editors acknowledged the encouragement of a great many letters to continue their *"Gazett"* and promised to answer whatever questions or objections were sent them "consistent with Modesty and pertinent for Information." Further emphasizing propriety, they offered "to answer only what is a *fitting Entertainment for the Ingenious,* or what does consist with Faith and Good Manners. . . . As to the *Objections* which we receive from time to time, we design to answer them every *three Weeks;* for by that time we suppose we shall have enough to fill one Paper."

In this number, the second and last of the weekly issues, appeared the first of many requests to the readers to wait for further notice before sending any more questions, hinting that there was a backlog of four thousand. Three weeks and six numbers later, new questions were once more invited (I.8, Sat 18 Apr 91). Whether the editors were actually so swamped at such an early date cannot be ascertained, but their request gave the impression of a wide circulation and great public interest.

The writer of the Preface to Volume One, who signed himself "Unknown," answered a charge that the *Mercury* was *"a Mercenary Design to get a Peny"* by asking whether the Stationers Company expected to gain by printing the Holy Bible. Those writing the *Mercury,* he continued, were "not very ambitious of the name of *Authors"* and could protest safely that *"they never had, nor ever expected one Sixpence for their Pains, nay scorn any such thing; and would even go near to desist from their share therein were it once offered: Though not at all condemning those who do otherwise if their* Circumstances *require it, and think he may be as* Honest *and* Brave *a Man who writes a* Peny-Sheet *to supply His Necessities, as he that buys and reads it for his satisfaction or Diversion."*

The protest of a scholarly disinterest was in keeping with another mark of "Athenianism," its implied connection with the Universities. Almost twenty years before, Dryden, in his Prologue to a revival of *The Silent Woman,* addressed an Oxford audience as "Athenian Judges." Even earlier, the Puritan Nathanael Culverwel, in *A Discourse of the Light of Nature* (1646), addressed Cambridge students as Athenians, plainly suggesting that his audience there was, like Paul's in Athens, seeking novelty (pp.8, 198).

For Dunton, too, Oxford was the Athens of England, and Wesley was his live specimen of an Oxford scholar. When Dunton boasted that the Society included *"several* Cambridge and Oxford *Scholars"* (VI.7, Tue 23 Feb 92), he meant Samuel Wesley. The frontispiece to the *Young Students Library,* a collection of essays and articles which Dunton published in May 1692, is a folio-size emblem of the Athenian Society, picturing at its four corners Athens, Rome, Oxford, and Cambridge. References to "a Member of our Society," which began to appear in 1692, implied that no higher accolade could be awarded.

In the *History of the Athenian Society* (p.6), Gildon associates Dunton's choice of the word *Athenian* with Acts 17.21: *"For all the Athenians and Strangers which were there spent their time in nothing else, but either to tell, or to hear some News."* For Dunton, if not for his collaborators, the scriptural emphasis upon novelty was appropriate. The notion of answering questions without revealing who had asked or answered them was truly unique in a periodical. Commonplace as it is today, in Dunton's time it was an innovation to be guarded jealously, and as we shall see, "Athenian" Dunton scolded Tom Brown and Daniel Defoe for their exploitations of the idea.

The word *Mercury* did not appear in the title on 17 March 1691. Apparently without knowing that he was flouting authority, Dunton headed the first number in large roman type, "The Athenian Gazette, / Resolving WEEKLY all the most / *Nice and Curious Questions* / Propos'd by the INGENIOUS." Between parallel rules below the title the date, Old Style, was placed, and "Numb. 1." in black letter appeared in the upper right-hand corner.

Number 2 bore mute testimony that Dunton had made a mistake, for the title had become "The Athenian Mercury." Between the rules with the date were the words *"Licensed and Entred according to Order."* The *London Gazette,* published weekly by the office of the Secretaries of State, had objected to Dunton's appropriation of the "official" part of its title. Dunton admitted, probably correctly, in the *Life and Errors* that the change was made "to oblige Authority" (LE,p.256), although in May 1691 he answered a question about the change quite differently:

> Gaza signifies a Treasury, and therefore we reserve it for the general Title of our Volumes, designing to intitle 'em the *Athenian Gazette,* or *Casuistical Mercury:* And *Mercuries* signifying a Messenger, 'tis the more proper Title for the single Papers, which run about to Coffee houses and elsewhere, to seek out *Athenians.* (I.12.1)

ii

From the very first the *Mercury* reflected a variety of interests. Number 1 answered seven questions, three about the soul, and one each about good and bad angels, wife-beating, and the origin of the spots on the moon. Number 2 squeezed in thirteen questions, no two on the same subject, besides a list of twenty-two to be answered next time, and a comment on "some *Questions* which we think not proper to take any notice of, our Design being to answer only what is a *fitting* Entertainment for the Ingenious, or what does consist with *Faith and good Manners.*" Number 3, the first semiweekly issue, answered fourteen questions.

Occasionally a number was devoted to a single subject, such as a philosophical or religious concept, or some natural phenomenon. Editorializing was inconspicuous and infrequent, occurring most often as an advertisement at the foot of the *verso* page, but occasionally declaring a political or religious position in a question and answer. It was unlikely that such declarations were paid propaganda, although in their use of hyperbole they hark back to the journeyman political writing found in Dunton's news sheets of 1689–90. A question in Number 2 illustrates the vigorously expressed and thoroughly safe political sentiments of the *Mercury:*

Quest.2. *What can Prompt that Monster of a Man, that calls himself by the Name of Protestant, to bring in the* French, *and restore King* James?

Such a man, replied the Athenians, was a greater monster than Polyphemus, "to whom Nature gave but one Eye," not to see "the peculiar Hand of God in the late happy Revolution, and the particular Guardian Care of Heaven towards the Instrument, his Sacred Majesty, in his first Attempt, his Action at the *Boyne,* and his late Voyage into *Holland.*" Such "Opposers of Heaven" would find out their error "if they took half the pains in unprejudic'd thinking, as they do in an unaccountable acting."

The absolute physical limit on the length of questions was the double-column format of the folio half-sheet; a somewhat more flexible limitation was in the sizes of type chosen for a particular issue. Number 6, a very full number set in brevier, has 2700 words in answer to *"What is* the Soul of Man, *and whether Eternal?"* There was still room for 850 words on judicial astrology and two more short answers.

In contrast to the uniform type size of the *London Gazette,* the *Mercury* appeared usually in mixed dress, a combination of pica and brevier with the *recto* set in larger type and the *verso* dwindling into the smaller size to accommodate all the copy. All questions and most advertisements were set in italic with proper nouns in roman; answers were in roman, with proper nouns, quotations, and emphases in italic. Black letter was used sparingly in the *Mercury* even though Dunton used it to excess in many of his books. Cuts, which seldom appeared, usually illustrated answers to questions on astronomy, optics, or geometry.

The *Mercury* had a characteristically sober appearance, unadorned and devoid of esthetic appeal, for Dunton's gift of innovation was limited to the basic idea of a respectable, informative periodical that would appeal to Londoners who frequented the coffee houses and to country gentlemen interested in the town. The *Mercury* succeeded upon the positive merits of its varied matter and vigorous style, and stayed out of trouble by expressing Williamite political sentiments and moderate religious views.

William and Mary could do no wrong. Louis XIV was a monster. The Athenians' religion was "Church of England," but there was good in the Dissenters and even the Quakers were honorable and fair-minded adversaries. The *Mercury* did offend the High Flyers in 1692 and was suspended for three months. The hypersensitivity of this Jacobite faction, however, rather than the effrontery of the *Mercury,* was to blame. No other periodical of the 1690's, except the *London Gazette,* lasted as long.

The *Mercury* encouraged belief in the reliability of the Society's answers in a number of disarming ways. If the members did not know an answer, they said so; if experiment or investigation was required to find out an answer, they volunteered to carry it out; if they doubted the validity of data submitted to them, they asked for proof. But they did not make assertions of infallibility and so could not reasonably be charged with falling short of an impossible aim.

Especially in the early stages, however, they modestly let it be known that no self-respecting coffee house would be without the *Mercury,* that only by reading the *Mercury* could a country gentleman remain informed, and that the apprentice, the servingmaid, and the ordinary citizen needed the *Mercury* to become educated and to rise in the world.

In this undertaking Wesley and Sault played different roles. Wesley was a very learned man who took pleasure in the breadth of his knowledge. He had been fortunate in his early experience as a student in Dissenting academies, for these were the only schools where scientific education was accorded much importance. Defoe's temperament was undoubtedly more compatible with such instruction than Wesley's, but both of them, once exposed to Charles Morton's *Compendium Physicæ,* a syllabus in manuscript,[7] had a modern concept of the natural world and more than ordinary respect for experimental learning.

During his sojourn at Oxford as a student in Exeter College (1683–1688), Wesley turned to the study of theology and ancient languages. His answers to religious and philosophical questions in the *Mercury* follow his two sorts of education.

Richard Sault answered the mathematical questions, many of which were meant to confound the Athenians. He advertised his services as a mathematics tutor in the *Mercury,* and his answers provided the reader with a demonstration of his skill. Questions on astronomy and physics may also have been his province, although Wesley had learned enough about these subjects at Morton's academy to have answered the questions printed in the *Mercury.* All the answers to scientific questions (except some few into which fancy was allowed to creep) are modest, reasonable, and matter-of-fact, and in them demonstration, rather than authority, is essential.

The several categories of questions will be discussed in later chapters and more specific consideration will be given to the contributions of the three writers responsible for the vast array of information, exposition, and opinion in the *Athenian Mercury.*

CHAPTER 2

[1] The *Athenian Mercury* was one of the earliest to adopt New Style dating, beginning the practice with VI.1, Tue 2 Feb 92. The following year the change was made in IX.10, Sat 14 Jan 93. Beginning the fourth year of publication, the change was made at the earliest date possible, in XII.21, Tue 2 Jan 94. In 1695 the change was made on New Year's Day, in XVI.5, and in the last year in which there was a January publication, XIX.20 was dated 4 Jan 96.

[2] H. A. Beecham, "Samuel Wesley Senior: New Biographical Evidence," *Renaissance and Modern Studies,* University of Nottingham, VII (1963) 87.

[3] Bodleian Library, MS. Rawl. D. 42 f.118.

[4] VII.2 (Sat 2 Apr 92) announced that the *Fifth Supplement* containing Swift's *Ode* was "now publisht."

[5] The title page to Volume One carries Dunton's name as publisher. The completed volume was published on 8 June 1691, but "P. Smart" made his last appearance on 14 July. "P. Smart" was also the publisher of *Religio Bibliopolæ* (1691), an imitation of Sir Thomas Browne's *Religio Medici,* written by Benjamin Bridgewater with some possible additions by Dunton himself. (Cf. A. C. Howell, "John Dunton and an Imitation of the *Religio Medici,*" *Studies in Philology* XXXIX, 3 (1932) 442–462.)

[6] The reason for deciding upon thirty numbers is obscure. Dunton may have projected six volumes for the first year, for VI.18 came out on 26 March 1692, a little over a year after I.1. In the second year of publication only four volumes appeared, slowed by suspension and the change beginning with VII to dating all thirty numbers; in the third and fourth years, three and a half each; in the remaining ten months before voluntary suspension there were three volumes.

[7] First published as *Compendium Physicæ,* Vol. XXXIII, *Publications of the Colonial Society of Massachusettes,* Boston, 1940. See Chapter 8, pp.123,132 and n. 12.

3

Bouquets and Brickbats

Dunton's efforts to maintain a mystery about the composition and publication of the *Mercury* paid off unexpectedly in February 1692. An unsolicited laudatory ode to the Athenian Society, written by "Mr. *Swift,* a Countrey Gentleman," came to him accompanied by a letter in which the author related how his earlier misgivings about the Society had been set at rest. He had heard more from his cousin Thomas Swift at Oxford, where he saw "two or three" of the bound volumes in mid-December 1691, and from Sir William Temple at Moor Park, where he saw all the four volumes and Supplements which had been published by Christmas of that year.[1]

Sir William had for some time been so interested in the *Athenian Mercury* that he had submitted at least one lengthy contribution concerning talismans and two other subjects.[2] Although this item did not appear in the periodical until Tuesday 22 December 1691 (V.7.1), an apology accompanied it, *"that the great numbers* (of questions) *that lye upon our hands have hitherto prevented our answer to 'em."*

Swift's cautious inquiries before his acceptance of the Athenians as a *bona fide* Society are evidence that the initial success of the periodical was due partly to its novelty, and not just to its service as a medium of information. Swift and his intimates wanted to be sure that the *Mercury* was not a vehicle for dangerous political opinions, not a covert means for attack upon the Church, and not a practical joke on those who might take it seriously only to be revealed later as dupes.

The *Ode* was Swift's first poem to be published in England. The author's connection with Sir William Temple could be easily surmised from the "Moor-park" date line of the letter, as well as the allusion in it to *"a Person of very great Learning and Honour."* It was Dunton's good fortune that the *Mercury* had such an attractive reputation that Sir William encouraged Swift to make his contribution. Swift wrote early the following May to Thomas Swift that his patron had exercised the final and decisive influence upon the project: "S^r W^m T^s speaking to me so much in their [the Athenians'] Praise, made me zealous for their cause for really I take that to be a part of the Honesty of Poets that they can not write well except they think the subject deserves it."[3]

Swift's admiration for the Athenian Society and his pride in his own accomplishment appeared in the same letter when he told his cousin that

> . . . the Poem I writt to the Athen. Society . . . is so well thought of that the unknown Gentlemen printed it before one of their Books, and the Bookseller writes me word that another Gentleman has in a book calld the History of the Athen. Society, quoted my Poem very Honorably (as the fellow calld it) so that perhaps I was in a good humor all the week. . . .

The good humor of Swift's attitude disappeared later when he discovered that the "great Unknown" were in the pay of John Dunton, the same bookseller who had backed out of an agreement to bring out a history of England planned by Sir William Temple, and which Sir William had hoped Swift would execute. Swift never again could find anything good to say about Dunton.

Swift's praise came at a moment when others were mounting an attack on the Athenians. A rival publication, the *London Mercury,* undertaken by Tom Brown, William Pate, and Charles Gildon, had appeared on Monday, the first of February, offering to answer all questions submitted to the *Athenian Mercury* and to supply the Athenians with queries. Tom Brown, who wrote most of the new periodical, had already established his reputation as a humorous writer. William Pate, a prosperous woolen draper and later a friend of Swift's, furnished financial backing. Gildon, who was just beginning his career as a writer, defected within a couple of weeks and served as the anonymous author of the *History of the Athenian Society,* a work in fulsome praise of the Athenians, published in May 1692.

The Athenians responded to the *London Mercury* the very next day. Volume 6, Number 1 (Tue 2 Feb 92) carried the following notice:

> *Yesterday Morning was publisht a Paper interfering with our Athenian Project,* . . . *we therefore here give publick notice, That those Questions which he pretends to answer shall be answer'd again by us, that so neither our Querists, the* Booksellers, *nor the* London-Coffeehouses *may be imposed upon by buying Questions twice answered, for they shall always find in our Papers the best of his Thoughts, and our own Improvements upon all* Questions *whatever, together with Remarks upon his* Errors. *We shall now change one of our days of publishing into that of his, and oftener if he gives any further occasion.*

Tom Brown (1663–1704) was ideally suited for an attack on the *Mercury.* Broadly speaking, he was Samuel Wesley's opposite number, for he had a university education, was a competent classicist and linguist, and was the sort of poet who could write easily for almost any occasion. His religion was orthodox and uninfluenced by Dissent. His first published work, provoked by the *Hind and the Panther,* was the *Reasons of Mr. Bays Changing His Religion* (1688), a defense of orthodoxy that demonstrated what his modern biographer recognizes as one of Brown's greatest skills, "the borrowing of a plan from another author, to be refashioned, expanded, infused with new ideas, and made expressive of his own peculiar point of view."[4] In a much less serious and intense way, that is the skill Brown applied to his satire of the *Athenian Mercury.*

The *London Mercury* was designed to look like the *Athenian Mercury* in almost all details: canon-size title, volume and number indications, dateline, double column, questions in italics, answers in roman, folio half-sheet, advertisements on its *verso* right-hand column, and a notice that questions would be received at a coffee house, Welsh's, "without Temple Bar." It was published on Mondays and Fridays to anticipate the *Athenian Mercury*'s Tuesday and Saturday editions.[5]

In the opening number the writer relates that the night before, suffering from insomnia, he took up a copy of Aristophanes and laughed over that part of "The Clouds" in which Socrates and Chaerophon measure the leap of a flea from one's beard to the other's. Now terribly awake and *"destitute either of* Opium *or* Poppy-water," he chanced to take up a copy of the *Athenian Mercury* and before he had read a paragraph was asleep and dreaming. In his dream Aristophanes came to him and asked for news of the town, not affairs of state,

> *. . . but as to what related to the* Beaux Esprites, *and Men of Thought and Over-Thought, the Brothers of the Quill and the like: Whether the Soul of the Virtuosos of our Age were agreeable to that of his* Socrates, *&c. I assur'd him the very same extravagant whims were still in Being, and every Day reviv'd . . . . We have had . . . Pumps, Looms, and Machines which you never dreamt of in your earlier days; and the Virtuosos of the Athenian Society have found out that a tunnel revers'd is full as good for the Eyes as Spectacles.*[6]

Aristophanes was amazed to hear that there were *"any of that Nation yet in Being, whose Noddles are cast in the same projecting Mould they were in* [his] *Days."*

Brown assured him that the present Athenians were only a company of unknown nameless undertakers who tried to answer all questions sent them, especially by women, *"for whom they have a most profound Veneration . . . from the Lady in her cock's Commode, to the Oyster-wench in her lawful occupation at the Tavern-Door."* They called themselves Athenians because they resembled the owl, the bird of Athens, but really they *"only emulated the modern*

Athenians, selecting the silly and trifling Queries of the Blue and Green-Apron Men, and Casting aside the ingenious and witty, as alien from their Design and Purpose;" when they were reprimanded, they thought it wise enough to answer, "that they who sent those Queries thought them as wise as any." If one pointed out to them their gross errors, *"this grave Assembly say for an Answer, That a Dart of a pen will mend them. . . ."* The Athenians, Brown continued, *"busy the Press with impertinent Questions of Apprentices and Chamber-maids; and instead of enquiring into the Solution of witty and judicious Points, relating to History and Philosophy, which have been sent them, they have everlastingly stuff'd their Papers with Receipts for Fleas &c. and such like wise Lectures."*

Aristophanes thought that such writers should have a gold piece for each of their few good lines, a buffet for each bad one, but Brown persuaded him this would be too severe since the modern Athenians would get nothing but buffets.

Brown attacked the Athenians because he simply could not stand their solemn academic tone and was irked to see Dunton claiming as his exclusive property an idea that Brown considered far from original. During the four months of attack he parodied the style of the Athenians with considerable skill, giving caricatures of Dunton and his writers. He was especially eager to demonstrate that none of the Athenians were Latinists and repeated again and again the charge that the Latin verse in the *Mercury* was full of false quantities. He could be both scurrilous and witty, as when he seized upon a question in Latin verse which the *Mercury* had for the sake of decorum answered in Latin. Brown wrote in burlesque style:

> For a frolick we'll answer this question a l'Athenienne—Faith and troth, dear sir, we believe you are a naughty Man, and if the truth were known, a dealer in the Mathematicks, a Virtuoso in Natural Philosophy, —a Wag, a meer Wag, no doubt on't,—nay, we fancy you have red hair and a long nose [Brown has been described as red-haired] . . . Unde Martiali &c. it is

nothing in the World but downright Bawdry and Obscenity . . . you have indeed, Sir, wrapt up your present in a clean Handkerchief, and so forth; but . . . you have mistaken your Men, Sir; you have gone to the wrong House—We Athenians are a set of morose startch'd Fellows; some of us are already in the State of Matrimony, by the same Token, that one of us has a Wife, that never long'd but she knew the Person. The next are in a fair way to it; very pretty Rogues, and Swinging Fortunes let me tell you . . . So much to the Gentlemen, to excuse ourselves from answering him in the scurvy language call'd Latin, which is ten times worse than Hebrew;—As for the English Reader, he may satisfie himself that it is a prophane and wicked Question, and let the Lacedemonians do what they will, we for our parts will sow none of your what d'ye call'm, your Cushions to the Elbows of Iniquity. (LM I.1)

Brown aimed at two targets: at Dunton for the pretentiousness of his scheme and his "dog in the manger" attitude, and at Wesley for his pompous and self-conscious display of academic learning.

In the second number of the *London Mercury,* the writer observed that although the Athenians complained in every number of the thousands of questions they had to answer, "yet they will allow none to come in to their relief and speedier satisfaction of the curious, without accusing them as guilty of interfering . . . with their design, their project I mean. . . ." His bookseller had received a note of reprimand "from a learned member of that Society J——D—— I mean the undertaker, who specified the abusing of HIS paper: Alas poor paper!"

Dunton announced prematurely in the *Mercury* of 6 February (VI.2) that all interference had been suppressed. Brown retorted in a way that anticipated Swift's treatment of Partridge:

The undertaker (himself an Athenian) having, to no purpose, endeavoured to suppress this paper, thought he would at last perswade the world he had not laboured in vain, and therefore very formally declares in Saturdays Mercury, that all attempts to interfere with [us] in the Athenian Project were wholly suppressed, the publishing of this today is as effectual a proof of the falsity of his foolish boast, as if we spent a whole column upon him. (LM I.3)

"But we fancy," concluded Brown, "this was but the last clap of thunder he had in store, for just after he begins to clear up in friendly accommodation, promising to answer the ladies queries tomorrow. . . ."

When Gildon left Brown after only four numbers of the *London Mercury* had been published, Brown was forced to suspend publication for ten days. In Number 5 Brown attacked "C. G." for accepting a bribe to desert him. Gildon had in the meantime written a *mea culpa* "to the Gentlemen of the ATHENIAN SOCIETY," which Dunton published on 16 February [misdated 15] (VI.5). The letter sounds as if Dunton himself had dictated it:

> Being at length convinc'd that the Design I was *lately engag'd* in did not reach up to that *Morality* which I aim at, I thought my self oblig'd to desire you to insert this short Letter in your *Mercury,* to satisfie the World of the *injustice,* as wel as *fruitless* endeavour of such an Undertaking: . . . I believe no Man that is the *first Designer* of any thing that by his Industry only has turn'd to account, will say he wou'd be content to have another make use of his Project. . . .

In the first number to bear the new title of *The Lacedemonian Mercury,* Brown asked, "Why do the Athenians pretend to the sole privilege of answering questions under a reign that has been so severe against monopolies; and why do they call the Londoners Interlopers, since they have neither a patent nor an act of Parliament for their Mercury?" (LM I.9).

Brown argued that the town had better plays when both theaters were open, and the players had better audiences, so why might not all querists expect better satisfaction and the booksellers better encouragement with the two Mercuries?

Dunton was threatening Brown meanwhile with the publication of some "Memoirs" which he asserted would discredit all three undertakers of the rival periodical. He advertised that he was being importuned "to publish the *stifled Memoirs* . . . relating to the Life of—" and that if the occasion arose for it "these *Memoirs,* together with those that are promis'd me by another hand relating to his Friend the *Atheist,* and Mr. *Urinal,* (being all well attested) will make a most surprizing History."[7]

The course of the rivalry was tortuous. Each periodical undertook to answer both its own questions and those of its rival. On the first of March, a Tuesday (VI.9), Dunton even announced that the *Athenian Mercury* would increase to four numbers weekly, "for more speedy Answers." He published numbers the following Friday, Saturday, and Monday, after which the periodical reverted to Tuesday and Saturday publication.

The Lacedemonians scoffed at the propriety of the Athenians, but the latter maintained a pose of moral superiority. To a question put in Latin verse that appeared in both periodicals, the Athenians responded that they dared not answer in Latin because the lines were so good, but must not translate into English because they were so bad. They contented themselves "with letting the Learned understand their meaning, and the Ladies guess at it by the Answer," given in English (VI.13.1).

The low point of the rivalry came when the Athenians implied that all Lacedemonians since the days of Lycurgus were sons of whores (VII.10.6) and the Lacedemonians retorted that the Athenians were sons of whores for saying so, "for by the Fundamental Constitution of *Billingsgate* (in the language of which refined place we must own them to be mighty proficients, though in no other) Son of a whore sounds full as Prettily and Emphatically out of one Mouth as another . . ." (LM I.26.6).

The Lacedemonians scorned to notice another query in

the *Athenian Mercury* as to *"Whether Mr.* Pate *is not as likely to be the Beast mention'd in the* Revelations, *as any private Person whatever?"* (VII.10.8). The Athenians' affirmative answer was accompanied with the following numeralogical computation, in which 666 signifies the Beast of the Apocalypse:

To		
V. V. Pate	X	10
Woollen	C	100
Draper	D	500
just by	vi	6
Fleetstret.	L	50
	DCLXVI	666

The character of the rivalry suggests that Dunton and Brown put their heads together to prolong it as a "battle of the books." There was the excitement of having both journals answer the same questions, competing vigorously for the reader's attention and his penny as they jeered at each other's answers and threatened to publish more often to put each other out of business. Dunton's insistence upon unique rights to a "question project" was motivated by cupidity more than by pride, and if the rivalry sold more copies he would not be averse to it. In relating the end of the affair, however, he insisted that Brown came to him "with all the CIVILITY imaginable" to make peace, and that Brown, after Sault threatened to draw upon him, "cry'd *Peccavi,* and promis'd very faithfully that he'd never meddle any more . . ." (LE,p.257).

The rivalry had continued for three months when Gildon finished work on "The History of the *Athenian Society.* . . . By a Gentleman, who got Secret Intelligence Of their Whole Proceedings. . . ." Undated, the volume was "printed for James Dowley" in London.[8] It was noted in the *Athenian Mercury* for Saturday 30 April 1692 (VII.10.1), as "publisht this Week." Who, an inquirer wanted to know, was the author of this work prefixed by poems from such "Ingenious Men" as Mr. Tate, Mr. Motteux, and Mr. Richardson?

The Athenians denied "being concern'd with writing the *History*;" in fact, "they heard nothing of it till the 9*th* Sheet was going to Press," and then one of them sent a letter expressing "our utter dislike of the Undertaking." The author had uncivilly inserted the letter in his *History*, "with Remarks upon it." They were forced to say that "tho his Writings shew him to be a very *witty Person,* in being able to say so much on so barren a Subject, yet we cannot think he has done by us in this Affair as he would have been served himself, neither has that Person who secretly gave him Intelligence of our Proceedings acted less ungenerously."

The Athenians' protest was false, however. A month earlier, Dunton had obliged Gildon by publishing for him on the last page of the *Fifth Supplement* a long list of *errata* from Gildon's *Nuncius Infernalis; or, a New Account from Below*. Thomas Jones, the first printer of the *London Mercury*, had printed the book, but when Gildon asked that a list of *errata* be included with it, Jones and the bookseller, "fearing such a vast number of Errors, would spoil the Sale of the Book, prevail'd with him to defer it a while." To vindicate himself, Gildon eventually picked out the most material mistakes for publication, to "attribute the false Printing, and false numbers to the intollerable neglect of the *Printer* and *Corrector*."[9]

The latest questions and answers that Gildon quoted from the *Mercury* had first been published in March, but Swift's *Ode,* from which he also quoted, was published on the first of April.[10] The *History,* printed with pages the same size as the *Mercury*'s, is only thirty-six pages, plus a leaf containing a dedicatory epistle by one "R. L." and poems by Tate, Motteux, "D. F." [Daniel Defoe], "D. T.," and Charles Richardson. The presence of these encomiastic verses suggests that the whole work was commissioned by Dunton, for he would have had a much stronger claim than Gildon on the friendly services of these contributors, especially Motteux and Defoe, both Dissenters.

In mid-May the Athenians attacked Brown, ostensibly in reply to the Lacedemonians' review (LM I.27, Mon 9 May 92) of the *History:*

As we have already publickly disown'd our Consent to any such History, or so much as our *Knowledge* of it till 'twas almost printed, so we are not at all oblig'd to concern ourselves further about it; but since by reason of this History, and some other passages whereby we have oppos'd the impious and Atheistical Assertions of some persons, we are styl'd *malicious, ignorant, impudent Blockheads, that we know nothing of the Tongues but what we steal, That we are Sons of Whores, if* &c. and such-like scandalous Treatment; we hear that the Author of the *said History* will next week fully consider these things. (VII.14)

In the same issue "that Gentleman who writ the *History of the Athenian Society*," was informed "that his Letter which so well characterizes those persons who misrepresented him, shall according to his desire be inserted in our next Mercury."

The "next Mercury" turned out to be a poetical number, with no letter in it from Gildon. In vain one looks for a letter in the succeeding numbers for May. The issue was closed with a threat and a challenge. On 28 May, Dunton threatened Brown: "There are *certain Memoirs* come to our Hands about the Lives of Mr. *B.* and his Friend, which our next *Saturdays* Advertisements shall tell the World what use is design'd to be made of 'em" (VII.18).

In a signed postscript in the last *Mercury* for May, however, Dunton accused "A Late Hackney *Author*" of sneaking attacks, and challenged him to make a forthright reply, signed, "and not to act so covertly with me as he did with Mr. *Jones,* in his *Scandalous Libel* upon him" (VII.19). Since this challenge coincided in date with the last number of the *Lacedemonian Mercury,* it never received a reply in print.

Between "Resumption *Osborn*" and "*Hoary Egglesfield*" in one of Dunton's cryptic catalogues of fellow Londoners in *Life and Errors* is "Mercury *Taylor* (deceased)" (p.364), the one-inch grave of Randal Taylor, who published the *Lacedemonian Mercury* after Brown's break with

Jones, and who, after suspension of the *Lacedemonian Mercury* at the end of May 1692, issued the *Moderator*. This double-column folio half-sheet came out on four successive Thursdays, beginning 9 June and ending 30 June. The *Moderator,* more restrained than its predecessor, yet bears several marks of Tom Brown's hand and pen; for example, in the first number, concerned mainly with the subject of libels against the Church, the writer specifically abjured Jacobitism but identified his motives as "the Sence of what he owes to the Publick, and to his Conscience, and the Consideration of some small Present from the Bookseller."

Number 3 of the *Moderator* announced that *"The Author designs in his next Examen to inspect the first Volume of the* Athenian Gazette, &c." The attack upon the Athenians in the next number was really an attack upon Wesley as a poet. As putative author of occasional poems in the *Mercury,* he had inspired the *Moderator*'s wish for no more royal victories because of the bad poetry they would bring forth: " 'twas really God's mercy, and the Lacedemonian's great Kindness, that secur'd our Ears from the dinn of Poetry on the late Naval-occasion: In case of another Victory, or raising the Siege of Namur, the Publick Magistrate ought to send betimes to forbid them."

The Athenians were singled out for special comment as writers of Panegyric,

> whom the least Victory, with the help of both her wings, will never be able to escape. They are the most calm peaceable Writers you ever read; they never disquiet your passions with the least concernment; but still leave you in as even a temper as they found you. They are the very Levellers in Poetry; for they creep along with ten little words in every line, and help out their numbers with *for to* and *unto,* and all the pretty expletives they can find, till they drag them to the end of another line, while the sence is left tired half way behind it. They doubly starve all their Verse, for want of thought; and then, of expression.

Anticipating criticism of his sharp remarks on Athenian poetry, the author provides evidence of the popularity of the *Athenian Mercury* with a certain class of reader, those who "have bought more of their *Athenian Gazettes* than would lie under all the Pies at my Lord Mayor's *Christmas.*" These are the same ones who, when the *Mercury* first came out, could be seen "reading 'em in the midst of Change-time; nay, so vehement were they at it, that they lost their bargain by the Candle's end." The *Moderator* wished "that such who love their writings may still admire them . . . their Elegy on Mr. *Boyle,* their panegyric on His Majesty's Expedition; and, above all, their famous Latin Epigram, are ample Testimonials" of their poetic skill. In fact, he concluded, "I believe there is no Man who writes well, but would think himself very hardly dealt with, if their Admirers should praise any thing of His."

A facetiousness, and also a familiarity with literary criticism and anecdote characteristic of Tom Brown, appear in the *Moderator's* citation of Rapin's story of the Venetian nobleman who every year sacrificed a Martial to the *manes* of Catullus, and of Dryden's finding himself indignant enough to offer up a Bussy D'Ambois to the *manes* of Ben Jonson:

> In imitation of this Frolick (since the modern ceremony of offering up one Author on the Altar of another is likely to advance into a fashion, as having already the authority of two such great Men to recommend it) the Courteous Reader may be pleased to take notice, the Author is resolv'd, as long as he lives, on the Festival of the *Seven-Sleepers,* to sacrifice a Volume of the *Athenian Mercuries* to the memory of Mr. *Quarles* and *John Bunyan.*

A final remark harks back to the earlier quarrel: "I expect in their next *Saturday's* Paper to be call'd *Son of a Whore* for the liberty I have taken with them in this."[11]

In its next number the *Moderator* proposed to consider the morality and physics of the Athenians with the same liberty the author had taken with their poetry. No more numbers appeared, and no notice of the fourth number was taken in the *Athenian Mercury*.

Brown was too witty to outlast Dunton. When he attacked, Dunton not only responded but also continued to inform and educate, absorbing Brown's punishment without giving up his principal service to readers. The signs of rivalry were no doubt of great interest to the frequenters of the coffee houses, particularly those who patronized Turner's, Welsh's, Smith's, or the Rotterdam, where the questions came in. But while Brown's attack was at its sharpest, Dunton began publishing all thirty numbers dated for the convenience of country readers, and launched both the *Compleat Library* and the *Young Students Library*, digests and notices of books, having in them only the faintest echoes of the journalistic quarrel.

The *Philosophical Transactions* had just been revived under the editorship of Richard Waller, but Dunton's somewhat less ambitious pieces of scientific and antiquarian information appealed to a wider circle of readers, many of whom were only dimly aware of the Royal Society's existence. For these there was no other printed source of information. It was to their interests that the *Mercury* now devoted itself. Never again did it engage in the sort of subterranean warfare it waged against the Lacedemonians.

CHAPTER 3

[1] *Supplement to the Fifth Volume of the Athenian Gazette,* pp.1–5; also in the *Poems of Jonathan Swift* (ed. Williams), Oxford, Clarendon Press, 1958, I, 14–15. *Ode* first advertised in VI.2 (Sat 2 Apr 92).

[2] "The late Sir *William Temple,* a Man of clear Judgement, and wonderful Penetration, was pleas'd to Honour me with *frequent Letters* and Questions, very Curious and uncommon; in Particular, that about the *Talismans* are his" LE,p.261.

[3] The *Correspondence of Jonathan Swift,* second edition (ed. Williams), Oxford, Clarendon Press, 1963, I,8.

[4] Benjamin Boyce, *Tom Brown of Facetious Memory,* Cambridge, Harvard University Press, 1939, p.21. Brown was interested in the *Athenian Mercury* from its inception, as indicated by an advertisement (I.11, Tue 28 Apr 91): "*The several Nice and Curious Questions sent us this last Week by Mr.* Tho. Brown *and others, shall be Answered at the* End of the Vollume [sic]."

[5] With No. 9, Monday 7 March, the *London Mercury* became the

Lacedemonian Mercury. Randal Taylor had succeeded T. Jones as printer three days earlier, with No. 8.

⁶ The Athenians had suggested cones of black paper with small apertures for a correspondent troubled with weak eyes.

⁷ VI.13 (Tue 8 Mar 92). "Atheist" must refer to Gildon, who had become a disciple of the Deist, Charles Blount, whose works he published in 1695. I have not been able to identify "Mr. *Urinal.*"

⁸ Dunton ingenuously admitted, much later, that one James Dowley "published for me *The History of the Athenian Society,* and was as Zealous to oblige me as any Binder in *London*" LE,p.344.

⁹ *Supp.* V, p.28.

¹⁰ Gildon quoted: *"How strange a Paradox is true! / That men who liv'd, and dy'd without a Name / Are the chief Heroes in the Sacred List of Fame." History of the Athenian Society,* p. 15.

¹¹ *Moderator,* No. 4, 30 June 1692.

4

Fringe Benefits

A shrewd business man, Dunton saw from the start that additional profits could come from the sale of the *Mercury* in bound volumes. In the second number, even before making a formal business agreement with Wesley and Sault, he announced that every thirty numbers would make up a volume, to be published with a preface and an index, both innovations for the English periodical. His agreement with Wesley and Sault stipulated that his associates would write both preface and index, "for which they shall have 10s betwixt 'em."

The bound volumes, together with the Supplements, and the *History of the Athenian Society,* printed so as to be bound up with the *Mercuries,* were frequently advertised. They sold so well that in 1707, when Dunton undertook a collected edition for Andrew Bell, he had to borrow volumes Eighteen and Nineteen from Narcissus Luttrell, putting up a surety of three guineas for their safe return.[1]

After Volume One, the volume number appeared to the left of the title; the serial number, as always, was at the right. Few periodicals of that day lasted long enough to require volume numbers. Of those that did last for some time, the *London Gazette* stayed with serial numbers, and the *Gentleman's Journal,* a monthly, used month and year dates only. At the outset only the first eighteen numbers of each volume of the *Mercury* were dated. The additional twelve could therefore be composed more at leisure, to be joined with the first eighteen for publication as a single volume. Beginning with Volume Seven, all thirty numbers were dated. Announcing this change in the Preface to Volume Seven, the Athenians said it was done to oblige *"Several*

Gentlemen *that live in the* Countrey *still complaining that they can never see the* Answers *given to their* Questions *in our* Twelve Numbers *or* Supplements *to 'em. . . ."*

The practice of publishing twelve additional issues all at once was defended by "the Interested Bookseller," upon the Athenians' invitation, in the fourth number of Volume Two (Sat 6 Jun 91). He wrote specifically to answer the objections that *"the Coffee-houses must take in 12 Numbers by the Lump."* Seven reasons for the practice, stressing the trade it brought to the coffeehouse, were listed in the most prominent place in this issue—the entire left-hand column, *recto.* For one thing, "those Gentlemen . . . not finding the *Mercury* there, go out again to seek it elsewhere," but if they are "accommodated without *further search* . . . spend their Moneys where they find it." New customers will come, too, and those who have sent in questions "will come *two or three times* to look for an Answer, we having *many,* and therefore without great partiality cannot limit a Day." Besides the curious, *"Generous Lovers* (who spend liberally) will throng the Coffee-houses every *first Tuesday* in the Month to read the *Female Questions."*[2] Before the Athenians dismiss the bookseller to attend to a coffee-man who "waits for a dozen Sets" of the *Mercury,* they allow him to make his last point: "That the *Youth will learn to be sober* and drink coffee, on purpose to make use of the Opportunities, which will make 'em Disputants, and fit Company for their Seniors."

Besides publishing undated numbers to bring in extra trade, Dunton also got out a Supplement of about thirty pages to go with each of the first five volumes of the Mercury.[3] As an early example of guaranteed income for a writer, the agreement with Wesley and Sault provided that Dunton, to make up the Supplements, would have translated "by another hand the Acta Eruditorum Lipsiae the Journall de Scavans the Universall Bibliotheque the Giornali de literati printed at Rome or any other pieces translated and added to every volume in as many distinct Numbers as he pleases provided still that all such translation doe not prevent what they otherwise should write of the weekly paper."

Although he showed concern for his own writers, Dunton pillaged the learned journals listed in the Agreement in order to fill the Supplements and the successors to them that he was to undertake in 1692. His chief source was the *Bibliothèque Universelle et Historique,* a pioneering journal begun by the Arminian scholar Jean Le Clerc at Amsterdam in 1686. A truly serious scholar interested in preserving freedom of the press by providing an open forum for ideas, Le Clerc began to publish a monthly containing abstracts and analyses of current books, both Protestant and Catholic. He felt that unsound beliefs were much easier to refute by being made public. Le Clerc numbered John Locke and Bishop Burnet among his good friends, and had many other correspondents in England. Over a fifth of the reviews in the *Bibliothèque Universelle* during its seven years of publication were of English books.

Le Clerc was at first assisted by Jean Cornand de La Crose, one of the new wave of refugees driven from France by the revocation of the Edict of Nantes in 1685. La Crose was an aggressive young journalist, contemptuous of Le Clerc's wise desire to preserve anonymity in reviewing such a wide selection of books. Both writers contributed to the first few volumes, but when La Crose, without Le Clerc's permission, had both their names printed at the head of the fourth volume, work in common became difficult and Le Clerc decided that each would do half of each volume. Even this was unsatisfactory to Le Clerc. He wrote the tenth volume himself and allowed La Crose to do the eleventh. La Crose made his volume an apology for William of Orange, prefaced by a signed epistle dedicatory to Princess Mary, in which he expressed passionate admiration for the future queen of England. Deeply offended by such a flagrant breach of anonymity, Le Clerc dismissed La Crose, and carried on the work through 1693 with other help.[4]

In the meantime La Crose had established a similar periodical in England, its title, not much different from

Le Clerc's, the *Universal and Historical Bibliotheque.* It was the first literary review to be licensed in England. Robert Midgely gave it an *imprimatur* in January 1687, but it lasted only three months. Soon after William and Mary were crowned, La Crose established himself in England to make a career of pilfering the journals of Le Clerc and other continental scholars. In 1691 he found himself at odds with John Dunton because of a monthly he started in July, called the *History of Learning,* "By one of the Two Authors of the *Universal and Historical Bibliotheque."* He boasted that this new periodical contained real abstracts of books, and not mere translations, *"as one lately Published."*[5] The slurring reference was to Dunton's first Supplement, published the last day of June.[6] Two weeks before the Supplement appeared, Dunton had gotten wind of La Crose's new project, for he immediately fulminated, in a long advertisement (II.7), against "an *Undermining Attempt"* with which "no Bookseller of Credit will concern himself," and promised to publish the *Mercury* three times a week and the Supplement more than once a month if necessary to keep his readers from buying answers to questions twice over. With the second number, in August, La Crose changed the name of his periodical to the *Works of the Learned.*

Dunton made no more attacks upon La Crose until December, but at the end of October in "Proposals" for the *Young Students Library,* printed in *Supplement III,* he indicated that he was going to strengthen his competition against La Crose's monthly by publishing yet another volume based upon the continental journals.[7]

In prospect was a volume of 120 sheets, *"in a very fair Letter,"* on paper the same size as the *Mercury*'s, at a price of ten shillings, payable in two instalments, *"which considering the excessive dearness of Paper, and Charge of Procuring* the Foreign Journals, *is not dear."* Whoever bought six copies would get a seventh free. If the number of subscriptions should *"arise to any* competent Number," the work would be finished by next Lady Day, 25 March. It was to contain a large alphabetical table *"which shall Comprehend the Contents of this Volume, and of all the* Athenian

Mercuries *and* Supplements *Printed in the Year 91."* Other attractions held out to the subscriber were "An Essay upon all sorts of Learning," by the Athenian Society and "an Emblem of the whole Athenian Society."

By December of 1691, Dunton was again in full cry after La Crose for attempting to take away his readers. The Preface to *Supplement IV* is a full page of diatribe against the *Works of the Learned,"A Piece . . . that the Learned will be very little obliged to."* Dunton asserted that he was *"the* First Undertaker, *and that the Forreign Journals are* no Frenchman's property, when Translated into the English Tongue." He accused La Crose of inaccuracy and laziness. *"Nay, so general the Complaint has been of the* False *and* Trifling Account *he gives of Books . . . no wonder he was continued no longer as an Assistant to* Monsieur Le Clerk." La Crose's pretense that Le Clerc had anything to do with the *Universal Bibliotheque* in London was *"an Encroachment upon our* English Liberties." Having no desire to expose La Crose, Dunton asked the reader only to compare the extracts of books in the Supplement with La Crose's work. As for the translations in the *Young Students Library,* recently proposed by Dunton, they would be no encroachment upon La Crose's translations, for *"we will take special care to have it well Translated, and revised by several Learned Persons. . . ."* Few or none of the pieces La Crose did for Le Clerc would be used, for the public had been promised that only the extracts of the most valuable books would be printed.

In the *Life and Errors,* Dunton pictured himself as the most generous and forgiving of men, unable to hold a grudge for long, and it is true that his quarrels almost always were resolved by some sort of treaty. His jealous opposition to La Crose ended in an agreement with the French journalist and his bookseller, Thomas Bennet. By the first week of February 1692, the three decided that they could not continue to publish extracts of books "without interfering with each other," and had agreed therefore to print "all the Extracts of Books hereafter made . . . in the same Journal entitled, *The Works of the Learned,* written by Mr. *de la*

Crose, a late Author of the *Universal Bibliotheque.*"⁸ The Supplements to the *Mercury* were to be limited to reporting "Natural and Artificial Rarities"—that is, their contents would be supplied by correspondents and no longer involve the cost of translation.

The Preface to *Supplement V,* published two months later, went into much more detail concerning the new model Supplement. The design, *"greedily embraced"* by the Athenians, was to give a history of the country by the best authors, and to add to it "all such informations *which any Ingenious Persons shall from time to time communicate* to our Society, *of whose Truth we can receive any Tolerable Assurance."* Not only would natural history be included, but also *"all* Artificial and Civil Things Remarkable in *England* and *Wales, Scotland, Ireland, and all the Forreign Plantations depending on them, &c."* Very little, in fact, was to escape their notice. They would present accounts of strange lights and noises in the heavens, the natural growth and improvements of the soil, minerals, *"and Things Dug,"* local history, such as battles and sieges, the various sorts of fowls and fishes, *"the* Murders that *have been formerly or lately committed in every County, and by whom, and when discovered. Princes, Famous and Great Men who have been Natives of each Province, County, Shire, Hundred, Town,* &c. *Immemorial Customs. In short, . . .* whatever is Curious & Entertaining *on every Subject. . . ."* In all, it was to be a combination in popular form of the main features of the *Philosophical Transactions* and antiquarian history. As if this gave an insufficient prospect, the reader was referred to the *"PARTICULAR DRAUGHT, which will suddenly be made Publick"* of a design "so much for the Honour and Profit of the English Nation."

The plan for a miscellany was altered within a month, however. In May, the Preface to Volume Six announced that Dunton had purchased full rights to the *Works of the Learned,* and gave a description of its successor, to be called the *Compleat Library; or, News for the Ingenious.* The monthly journal, to be carried on by *"a London Divine,"* would consist of nine sheets allotted to original pieces, four to historical accounts, and two to notes on *"the MEMORABLE PASSAGES happening Monthly; as also of the STATE of Learning in the World."* The first number, in May, was to include *"an Original Piece concerning the Integrity and Purity of the Hebrew Bible."* Articles on scriptural interpretation made up a third of the *Compleat Library* and were written for Dunton by the Reverend Richard Wooley, "a universal Scholar," whose reason was "fierce and cogent," but whose style was as "gentle and natural as his Mien, . . ." (LE,p.227).

The *Young Students Library,* originally promised for Lady Day 1692, had not yet appeared when the *Compleat Library* commenced publication. It had been delayed, first by extreme weather, and then because inclusion of two original pieces written by the Athenian Society had enlarged it by several sheets more than planned (VII.7). On 31 May the *Mercury* announced that the new work would be ready by 6 June "and not before" (VII.9). The following Tuesday it was published in one hundred and twenty-four sheets, including not only the alphabetical tables to the first five volumes of the *Mercury,* the five Supplements, and its own contents, but also a table for the *History of the Athenian Society,* now tacitly acknowledged to belong to Dunton.

"Our Bookseller," wrote the author of the Preface to the volume, "has been extremely harasss'd about a Speedy Publication, which, above all Men, he has least deserv'd; for there's no body more diligent, in his Employ, than himself, as every body of his Acquaintance will acknowledge."

Six presses had been at work on the book, another collection was in the press at the same time, and six weeks' frost had hindered the printers. No reasonable person could think that Dunton was careless in the matter or "responsible for things out of his power."

The *Young Students Library* was an expansion of the serious and scholarly parts of the *Athenian Mercury.* Wesley's hand is plainly evident in it, especially in a sort of "Syntopicon" entitled "An Essay upon all Sorts of Learning, Written by The Athenian Society," in eighteen folio pages, double column, at the beginning of the volume, and "A Discourse Concerning the Antiquity, Divine Original and Authority of the Points, Vowels, and Accents, That are placed to the Hebrew Bible."[9] The second of these had been promised for the *Compleat Library,* but it was forty-seven pages long, far too much copy for the monthly.

The discourse on Hebrew was somewhat controversial for its time. In the Preface to the volume, which may also have been written by Wesley, questions about the piece were invited by the notice that *"the Author of the* Hebrew *Punctuation, has retir'd into the Countrey, where his necessary business will take up a great part of his time; yet whatever Letters, Objections, &c. shall be sent to him about his Performance, if they be directed to our Bookseller, they will come to his hands, and he will notwithstanding his business, set apart so much time as to maintain what he has advanc'd, and to Answer all Objections whatever."*

Wesley's "necessary business" was that of another curacy in addition to the one at South Ormsby in Lincolnshire, which he had held since the summer of 1691. The living was small and his family was growing by yearly additions, from his wife's "lying in about last Christmass & threatning to do the same the next. . . ."[10]

In spite of his pastoral duties, however, Wesley wanted to defend his thesis that Hebrew was the perfect, God-given language. In his article and also in the prefatory essay to his long poem, the *Life of Christ* (1693), he maintained that Latin was a corruption of Greek, which in its turn had come from Phoenician and before that, Hebrew. The modern languages were "the adulterous mixture of 'tis hard to say how many languages."[11]

The Preface to the *Young Students Library* shows how strongly Protestant the Athenians were. Those articles in divinity taken from *"the Republick of Letters"* [Bayle's *Nouvelles de la république des lettres*], *"which pass'd through the hands of the French Divines,"* were regarded as *"very unsafe to publish in a Protestant Nation; where 'tis impossible not to find some who are weak and unsettled in our Religion."* Other works by scholastics abstracted in the

Continental journals they had found to be *"so much Jesuitiz'd"* as to be unrecognizable beyond their titles, the rest being *"what the Papal Interest was pleas'd to make 'em speak."* As a substitute for the "Jesuitiz'd" Fathers, the Athenians gave abstracts of *"the learned Dupin's Works"* and "Dr. Cave's Lives of the Fathers."[12]

Aside from these substitutions made to protect the young reader, there were contributions by Wesley and abstracts of works on religion, philosophy, and history. The *Young Students Library* also provided an impressive array of short scientific articles, which make up almost a fifth of the volume. Where attributions are made, the names of Boyle, Halley, Hook, Huygens, and Locke shine forth. There is a five-page abstract of the *Essay on the Human Understanding,* a shorter one of Sprat's *History of the Royal Society,* and several pages of *"Observations on* Mr. Boyle's *Specifick Remedies."*

These intelligent choices are not all directly attributable to the Athenians, however. Le Clerc had been interested in English books from the very start of his *Bibliothèque Universelle,* and sometimes printed notices of new ones before they appeared in the *Stationers Register.* So forehanded was Le Clerc, in fact, that in 1688 he secured from John Locke an extract from the *Essay on the Human Understanding* which he published immediately in the *Bibliothèque Universelle* as "Extrait d'un livre anglais qui n'a pas encore paru. . . ."[13] French and English readers alike had to wait until 1690 for the publication of the complete work. Some of his abstracts underwent a sea change, being translated into French and out again, before they appeared in Dunton's volume. Dunton took others directly from the *Philosophical Transactions.* Some of the scientific explanations had already appeared in shorter form in the *Mercury.*

For a year the *Compleat Library* maintained its character as a learned journal and then dwindled into an advertising medium for the bookseller. In April 1694 it expired. The *Gentleman's Journal* of Peter Motteux, a much more imaginative undertaking, also begun in 1692, was able to outlast the *Compleat Library* by only seven months. No new literary periodicals of any significance were to be undertaken until after the turn of the century, but the *Athenian Mercury,* much less literary than the others, still had several years of life left.

The *Young Students Library* appeared one time only. The *Compleat Library,* not nearly as complete, treated the same subjects, but in a different proportion, for two-thirds of its articles had to do with divinity. The short life of this publication in comparison with the *Mercury* is convincing proof that popular taste required frequent numbers offering a wide variety of subjects, not too much theory or speculation, but explanations of natural phenomena and advice for the solution of personal problems.

CHAPTER 4

[1] See Chapter 12, p.223 and n. 15.

[2] A fixed day for answering "female Questions" was first announced in I.18 (Sat 23 May 91), to oblige "the *fair Sex* . . . as knowing they have a very *strong party* in the world."

[3] Each of the five Supplements came out, undated, shortly after its companion volume of the *Mercury, Athenian Gazette* being used as the title for the bound volumes. An advertisement of the contents of each of the last three Supplements appeared beforehand in the *Mercury.*

[4] Annie Barnes, *Jean LeClerc et la république des Lettres,* Paris. Librairie E. Droz, 1938, pp.116–117.

[5] Pref. A3.

[6] Advertised in II.11 (Tue 30 Jun 91).

[7] Title page, *verso;* also issued separately.

[8] VI.2 (Sat 6 Feb 92). Dunton did not enter the title as his in the *Stationers Register* until 22 February.

[9] Luke Tyerman, *Life of Samuel Wesley,* pp.150–151, says unequivocally that these two long pieces are Wesley's, and also six short pieces upon various editions of the Bible, Hebrew grammars, lexicons, and poems.

[10] Samuel Wesley, Letter, 22 Aug 1692, Bodleian Library, MS Rawl. D. 406, printed in H. A. Beecham, "Samuel Wesley Senior: New Biographical Evidence," *Renaissance and Modern Studies,* Vol. VIII (1963) University of Nottingham, 108.

[11] *Life of Christ* (second edition), p.v.

[12] Cave's works were *Ecclesiastici* (1683) and *Scriptorum ecclesiasticorum historia literaria,* 2 Vols., (1688–89).

[13] *Bibliothèque Universelle et Historique,* VIII. (Jan 1688), 49–142.

5

"A Decay'd Gentleman"

A seemingly innocent question about a "Decay'd Gentleman," and the answer to it, published on 5 July 1692, very nearly cost the *Mercury* the great success it had begun to enjoy. If Dunton had had any political sense, he would surely have used it to keep out of trouble at such a sensitive time. July, which closed with William's crushing defeat by the French at Steenkirk, was the poorest time imaginable for an indiscretion in print.

While the king was in Flanders, Queen Mary, assisted by a cabinet of nine, attempted to manage affairs of state. As secretary of state, the Earl of Nottingham chose or dismissed licensers of the press, his deputies being approved also by the Archbishop of Canterbury and the Bishop of London for the books they were authorized to license. The status of the king and queen as joint and equal rulers with clear title to the throne was still a sensitive subject on which few had the temerity to comment openly in print. The licensers were expected to prevent the expression of divisive opinions on the subject.

The Athenians failed to see the danger in printing a question which by innuendo alluded to the queen, and James Fraser, a licenser since 1689,[1] gave his tacit approval to the number of the *Mercury* in which the following question appeared:

> *A Gentleman some Years since having two Daughters at Womens estate, marries 'em both to Persons of Quality, and gives 'em a large Dowry out of his Estate; after which being a Widdower, and having a plentiful Estate left, he Marries a second Wife, by whom he has*

one Son living, since which it has pleased God to bring this Gentleman into a low Condition, he not having now a Competency for himself or Family—on which he's despised by his two Daughters who live in great splendor, and forsaken by his Friends almost in general, only he's at present supported by a Gentleman, of whom he did not expect any such Friendship, who Promises to provide for him and his Family while he lives—The Question on the Case is—How this Decay'd Gentleman ought to behave himself to his Friend, with whom he now lives, to his two Daughters, their Husbands, and the rest of his pretended Friends, that he may end his days like a good Christian, and dye in Charity with all the World? (VII.29.18, Tue 5 Jul 92)

In their answer the Athenians urged the gentleman "to enquire how he behav'd himself towards his own Parents? whether he lost not his remaining Estate by his Extravagance or Folly? whether his *Second Match* was not below him, and other things of that Nature, the last of which may *mitigate,* tho' not *excuse* the *Behaviour* of his *Friends* towards him, the rest he ought to get clear off with Heaven."

Thus far the Athenians could have been proceeding in all innocence to advise some private person. Their further advice, too, did not do much more toward revealing the identity of the unhappy father and his daughters. The father was to ask whether there were real causes for his being slighted by his daughters, though "it's certain they are guilty of inexcusable *Ingratitude* and *Disobedience.*" He should find some way of letting them know their fault, "that they may . . . be brought to beg his *Blessing* and *Pardon.*" If they refuse, he is yet to forgive them, "but we are not so sure he's bound to give 'em his *Blessing,* a *Legacy* we think only due to *Obedient Children.*" He is "to slight and forgive" his other *"cold Friends"* and "for that *true, fast, only Benefactor* under Heaven, he's to pay him, next to the *Original Giver,* all the *Gratitude* and *Blessings* he's capable of . . . and if he does thus, we think he'll end his dayes as he desires, like an honest Man and a good Christian."

Had the matter been dropped here, the answer might have caused no more than an amused smile among those who thought they could identify the figures in the historical allegory. The Athenians' moralizing response betrays no wish to reveal identities, and most likely was given in ignorance of them. But the subject was not dropped. Four days after the first question was published, there appeared a second, from *"several"* who wished the Athenians *"to consider farther upon the Question of the Decay'd Gentleman"* (VII.30.10, Sat 9 Jul 92).

A marked change of sympathy is exhibited in the second answer. The father is not to think now of his daughters and friends "as if they were the Cause, or Poysoned in their Principles, and so disregarded him." He is to think upon "the Stroke from Heaven," and to remember "that the first Command in Paradice was the *Love* and *Obedience* of *Husbands* and *Wives,* and his Daughters as Married are under that immediate Obligation." Furthermore, the provocation he has given his relations and friends "is not Couched in the Question, as it ought to have been." His condition, however, "may be the imperscrutable Method of Punishment that God has taken to reward his Folly."

The Athenians not only deserted the "Decay'd Gentleman" but unwisely went on to hazard a "guess," the implied answer to which left no doubt that James II, living at Versailles as a poor pensioner of Louis XIV and spending his days at prayer, was the unhappy father: "if he be a *Papist,* (altho' that is omitted in the question) his best way is to *Cover his Condition with a Monastery,* where he may bewail the JUST JUDGMENT that has befallen him."

James's own feeling that God was punishing him for his personal sins was well known, as were his penitential visits to the great monastery of La Trappe, begun soon after he fled to France. The Athenians' suggestion, far from being original, was a thought that James himself had seriously entertained.

If any doubt of identity now remained, however, it was dispelled completely by the next consideration in the answer, of the legitimacy of the Decay'd Gentleman's "second

Wife's Son," in which it is observed that "a Father ought (as he is in a Publick Capacity) to have his Wife brought to Bed with such Persons about her as by *Custom* and *Law* ought to be at that time." If not, then even if the child was legitimate, "yet they must take it for their Pains, (if he lose his Publick Station) if no Body will believe them."

From this point on, the Athenians spoke out boldly against James, drawing the conclusion that "his acting so illegally in this and in all his other Proceedings, have given a just occasion for their disbelief, and for his Friends forsaking him." No other cause, they wrote in conclusion, had been suggested in the question, "(as there wou'd have been, had not the Querist been a SENSELESS BIGOT)." It was, therefore, "forborn to add more."

The discussion of the illegitimacy of James's child by Mary of Modena, the cause of much scandal and vicious talk in June 1688, was plainly gratuitous in the context of the questions asked. As phrased it made easy the positive identification of James, Mary, and Anne. Such transparency came from a false sense of security that was soon to be shattered.

One more appearance of the topic, in the next number of the *Mercury*, suggests that Dunton had become aware of danger and was trying to divert criticism by means of a petulant attack on the Jacobites. Asked *"Why do the Jacobites dislike your Answer last* Saturday?" the Athenians accused the Jacobites of imposing "the wrong sence" upon the first answer to the question about a *"private Gentleman despised by his Relations and friends,"* and of wresting the question from the private to "the most Publick and *Culminant."* The Jacobites were simply doing what they "in Concert with their ROMAN BRETHREN do by the News, *Jacobite it,* that is, *give it a false turn."*

The concluding sentences of this answer not only courted but won disaster. If the Jacobites

> will needs have it a Publick Case, tho' no Circumstances concurr thereunto, then three apparent *Absolute Falsities* are in the Question, *Viz. So despised, so sup-*

ported by a real Friend, and one that it could not be expected from: We might fling down the Glove to the most cunning, or the wickedest of that sort of Men, to try to make it true and hang together: They might as well instance in the Fallen Angels, as in the *French* King's being indued with pure Friendship, they both acting from the same Principle of Generosity. (VIII.1.11, Tue 12 Jul 92)

Volume Seven was advertised in this same number as due to be published the following Monday, but the reappearance of the notice on 19 July (VIII.3) indicated a delay. On Saturday, 23 July (VIII.4) Volume Seven was advertised as "now Publisht." All but the last of the offending questions were now available at Dunton's shop. Only one more number of the *Mercury* was to appear that summer, on Tuesday 26 July (VIII.5); the sixth number of Volume Eight is dated Saturday, 17 September 1692, and to the right of the date stands the name of the new Licenser, Edmund Bohun.[2]

There is evidence that Dunton knew by the last week in July that he was in for trouble. He tried to head it off by printing "Licens'd, *J. F.*" to the right of the date in the last two numbers he was allowed to publish, on 23 and 26 July. These were the first numbers of the *Mercury* ever to bear the licenser's initials, the sudden use of which raises the question of whether James Fraser had even seen the offending numbers before they were published. His initials, however, could save neither the *Mercury* nor the licenser, who was already in more serious trouble himself.

In April Fraser had licensed *"A true accompt of ye author of . . .* Εἰκον βασιλικη, *with an answere to Dr Hollingsworth."*[3] Written by Anthony Walker, D.D., of Fyfield in Essex, and published by Nathaniel Ranew, the book questioned Charles I's authorship of the personal prayers that most High Churchmen believed authentic. Walker's book was published in May, but its author had died in the meantime; an angry retort by Hollingsworth, published in June, referred to "the rude and undutiful Assaults of the late

Dr. *Walker* of *Essex*."⁴ The controversy raised by Walker lasted for years, overshadowing the suspension of the *Mercury*, but the two episodes were similar in their relation to the Stuart family.

Although Fraser had thus let slip past him two aspersions upon the Stuarts, his earlier mistake was the immediate cause for his removal. His name was last recorded in the *Stationers Register* on 4 July 1692, as having licensed a book, *The English Man's Phisitian*, on 21 June,⁵ more than a month before the "Decay'd Gentleman" made his unfortunate appearance. Dunton's description of the licenser also suggests that by July Fraser was already a marked man: "Diligent and Impartial in all the Parts of his Duty, but (notwithstanding these qualifications) the *High-Flyers* were continually hunching at him, and at last, he surrender'd his *Deputation*" (LE,p.350).

The "High Flyers" or High Church faction would certainly have resented a slur upon the Stuart family, but those around the queen picked up the imputation that she had been a disobedient daughter. Princess Anne had sent a penitent letter to her father in December 1691,⁶ but Mary remained unforgiven and unforgiving to her death. It was a contrast not to be commented upon publicly. Although suspension of the *Mercury* demonstrated how little freedom of the press there was, yet it is no wonder that Nottingham took prompt action. The whole effect of this and similar episodes in the control of the press was to discredit the licensing system and help initiate a very gradual move toward more liberal treatment of booksellers and authors.

Although there was no immediate notice given to the suspension of the *Mercury*, a play by Elkanah Settle, *The New Athenian Comedy*, never acted, but published in 1693, shows a knowledge of some of the details. The character of Stuff, i.e. John Dunton, refers to the time when the Athenians had their mouths stopped and it cost the "head-venturer . . . near thirty Guineas for a Golden Court-key to unlock 'em agen."⁷

With an air of injured innocence, Dunton gave his own version of the episode in *Life and Errors:*

The Earl of —— [Nottingham] was once pleas'd to Frown upon the *Athenian Mercury,* and forc'd us into silence; but when Men are pleas'd to make *personal Application,* (for the Offence was only taken at a Question that was sent us, of a *Father that had two Daughters*) 'tis a Sign there's a *sore Place,* else they'd never Wince for the Matter; however Captain *M—al* procur'd us Liberty to proceed and had Twenty-Five *Guineas* for that Service. (p.258)

When publication of the *Mercury* was resumed, there was no break in the sequence of numbers, and no immediate mention was made of the hiatus in their dating. In order not to forfeit the popularity of the *Mercury,* however, Dunton had placed an advertisement in the *Compleat Library* for August 1692:

This is to give Notice to all Querists, that the Members of the Athenian Society have not been idle in this Interval of Silence, but have prepared Answers to many Ingenious Questions sent 'em, of which you may speedily expect a further Account from the first Undertaker and Proposer of the Athenian Project. (p.282)

The appointment of the new Licenser Bohun, a Tory, came under attack by the Whig majority in the House of Commons within a few months, and he was removed in February 1693 for having licensed *King William and Queen Mary Conquerors,* a book published by Richard Baldwin and probably written by Charles Blount, the Deist.[8] Bohun had failed to see that the title would inflame those who believed in the hereditary right of the royal couple.

Dunton said of Bohun that he used "great Freedom of Speech, as one that wou'd neither seek, nor dread the power of any—He once took *the shortest way with Dissenters,* and was noted as a Furious Man against 'em." Yet Dunton admired him as "a pretty Author," had no trouble with him over licensing, boasted that Bohun "was wont often to visit" him, and concluded that "were it not for his former

Carriage towards Dissenters, [he] wou'd call him the *Phœnix* of the Learned Licensers—" (LE,p.352).

Dunton's own peace of mind had at least been achieved by December 1692, when an "all clear" was signaled in the Preface to Volume Eight of the *Mercury:*

> *The many encouraging Letters and repeated Thanks which we have received since our Second Appearance, gives us reason enough to hope that our design is still generally approv'd of, which is a sufficient Motive for us to prosecute it, and we shall endeavour to acquit our selves in it with the utmost Care and Impartiality that the Publick may expect at our hands.*

CHAPTER 5

[1] First in *Stationers Register,* III.348 24 March 1689.

[2] Appointment recorded in *State Papers Domestic, William and Mary,* p.438.

[3] Entered 19 April 1692. *Stat. Reg.* III.400; published in May, *T.C.* II.404.

[4] "Dr. Hollingworth's defence of K. *Charles* the First's holy and divine book. . . ." *T. C.* II.413. The same subject gave rise to vigorous debate in the twentieth century. Cf. "Milton's God" (letters to the editor from Peter Alexander, William Empson and others) London *Times Literary Supplement,* Nos. 3129 (16 Feb 1962) –3141 (11 May 1962).

[5] *Stat. Reg.* III.405.

[6] James Macpherson, *Original Papers*: containing the Secret History of Great Britain, London, W. Strahan and T. Cadell, 1776. I.241–242.

[7] *New Athenian Comedy,* p.3. See also Chapter 6.

[8] Edmund Bohun, *Diary and Autobiography* (ed. S. Wilton Rix), privately printed at Beccles, by Read Crisp, 1853, pp.101–120.

6

Compassion and Comedy
1693

> Let your Opposers *Trifling* Jests pursue;
> They write for MINUTES, but for AGES You.
> Charles Richardson, "Panegyrick upon the Athenian Society"

By 1693, the Athenian Society was firmly entrenched, its name on many a title page, its answers breathing more authority than ever. During the first two years of the *Mercury's* existence there had been little time for additional projects; producing two sheets weekly and a Supplement every couple of months monopolized the time of Dunton, his part-time mathematics tutor, and his part-time clergyman. From 1693 on, however, an increasing number of publications bore Dunton's imprint. Sault was engaged in tutoring and Wesley was writing the poetical *Life of Christ*, his magnum opus. John Norris, their incognito advisor, kept up during these years his steady output of moral and philosophical works.

Among the many works printed for Dunton, however, the one which aroused the greatest public interest had the least to recommend it as a literary work. A cheaply gotten up little book of less than sixty pages, the *Second Spira*, was printed from copy which Dunton said was put into his hands by Richard Sault on 26 December 1692, sixteen days after the alleged death of the atheist whose story it relates (LE,p.218). Its history is closely linked with that of the *Mercury*. Its publication was the kind of pious hoax which a sedulous follower of Dunton could easily produce, and its discovery reacted upon the Society with long-lasting effect.

The basic narrative which Sault used had survived, like

a bit of germ plasm, from the sixteenth century, when it was first published in German and Latin, the latter edition having a preface by John Calvin. The story is of the physical and mental torments endured by an Italian lawyer of Padua, a Catholic who had turned Protestant and later recanted under hierarchical pressure.[1] A ballad, ". . . *of master Ffrauncis an Italian a Doctor of Lawe who denied the Lord Jesus,*"[2] and a comedy by Nathaniel Woodes, *The Conflict of Conscience* (1581), are further evidence of early interest in the story in England. John Greenwood, a Puritan observer of the times, commented upon the story in a letter, noting that "thoughe God did pardon Cranmer for making that vile book, and his being metropolitaine, yet he condemned Francis Spira for denieng Christe and sinning agaynst the Holye Ghost. Thus you may see God doth that it pleaseth his majestie to do."[3]

There were at least thirteen editions during the seventeenth century of an expanded English version, a translation that first appeared in 1637 but was dated 1638: *A Relation of the Feare-full Estate of Francis Spira, in the yeare, 1548* (S.T.C. B1178). A duodecimo, as were almost all the seventeenth century editions of the work, it bore the initials of N. B. as the author, and is generally attributed to Nathaniel Bacon (1593–1660).[4] It was published again in 1665, 1672, 1678, 1681, 1683, 1688, and in Edinburgh in 1695. Benjamin Harris, who was in Boston at the same time as Dunton, had published the work in London, with additions, in 1683, and "the widow Harris" brought it out in 1688, a time when it would have served as good anti-Jacobite propaganda.

The story of Spira was published, from 1549 to 1820, as an avowed instrument of reform. An undated reprinting of the sixteenth-century English translation is recommended "chiefly to be used when the deuill dooeth assaulte us most fiercely, and death approacheth nighest."[5] "M. B." puns grimly in his preface to the 1683 edition: "Dum spiras, spera; *so maist thou take good, and no hurt, by the reading of this terrible Example."*

The *Feare-full Estate* and the *Second Spira* are approximately the same length, but Sault made a special effort to convince the reader that the story was true, and placed much stronger emphasis upon the reforming or evangelical power of the story. (It is not strange that John Bunyan should have earlier been impressed with "that dreadful story of that miserable mortal, Francis Spira.")[6] The title page of the *Second Spira* displays both features that Sault stressed in his text:

> The Second / SPIRA: / Being a fearful Example of / An Atheist, / WHO / Had Apostasized from the Christian / Religion, and dyed in Despair at / *Westminster, Decemb.* 8. 1692. / With an Account of his Sickness, Convictions, Discourses with Friends and Mini- / sters; and of his dreadful Expressions and / Blasphemies when he left the World. / As also a Letter from an Ac- / quaintance, with his Answer to it. / Publish'd for an Example to others, and recom- / mended to all young Persons, to settle them in / their Religion. / By J.S. a Minister of the *Church* / *of England,* a frequent Visitor of him du- / ring his whole Sickness. / The Second Edition, well Attested, / *London,* Printed for *John Dunton* at the *Ra-* / *ven* in the *Poultry.* 1693.[7]

The "Preface" is a further effort to enlist belief. The author, J. S.,[8] "Being often importuned" by his friends to publish the account as "very useful to the Publick," has "at last yielded to give the Papers and Notes which [he] took during the whole Visitation, to a Friend . . . to put 'em in some kind of Method and Order for the Press." He protests perhaps too much for the truth of his account, in a way that later became familiar through the usage of both Defoe and Swift. (One would like to imagine that Sault received professional advice from Defoe.)

> But as to what that Miserable Gentleman delivered himself (who is the Subject of this Relation) both I and the METHODIZER of my Notes have been superstitiously Critical as to give them as near the Truth, and very Expressions, as we could. . . .

Any doubter might consult Mr. Dunton. Cooperation with the bookseller is emphasized in a boast for the conciseness of the work. Some authors and booksellers, it is observed,

> clog the Matter of Fact with long and tedious Observations . . . only to make the Volume swell; here he will find no needless or trifling Digressions, but unmixt Relation, barely and purely deliver'd, so that the Reader all the while he reads, will be upon his Subject; and not perplex'd with an Expectation of it.

Facing the first page of the text is "The Attestation of Athens," which repeats that *J. S.*'s notes were given to a member of the Athenian Society. Below this solemn statement is added "The Attestation of Mr. Wolley" ("editor" of Dunton's *Compleat Library*):

> The Methodizer of this History being a Person of great Integrity, the Reader has not reason to question the truth of this printed Attestation here given concerning it; . . . I heartily wish those pious Gentlemen that have Estates would be instrumental in dispersing of 'em throughout the whole Kingdom, that so all ranks of Men, especially the Youth of this Nation, might reap some advantage by this extraordinary and amazing Instance.
>
> R. Wolley, M.A.

A description of the atheist's associates implies their kinship with the libertine character found in the comedies of the period; but as members of the Inns of Court they were a slightly different breed. They influenced the atheist, once an innocent and God-fearing country gentleman, who had gone to the Inns to study law in order to care for his estate. He became

> one of the CLUB which within these last seven Years met together constantly, *To lay down such Rules and Methods as that they might be critically wicked in every thing that they could, without the Laws taking*

hold of them; and therefore the law itself was more particularly examined, What Fallacies might be put upon it. (p.6)

A major difference from the earlier version is that the atheist fell sick precisely because of his dissolute life, whereas Francis Spira's affliction partook of the miraculous in stemming directly from his insincere recantation. The atheist's friends assured him that the soul would dissolve when the body died, but *J. S.,* dropping in for the first of many visits, disputed the assumption, citing the very latest authorities: "That the Soul is not Matter (said I) Descartes has prov'd in his Method, by shewing that the Soul is independent of Matter. That Matter itself cannot think neither in the Whole nor its Parts, is evident enough from Mr. Lock of HUMAN UNDERSTANDING" (p.10).

The atheist's melancholy reply to *J. S.* is also an early example of Locke's pervasive influence: "You have now sealed my Damnation, by giving me an Earnest of it, I mean an awakened Conscience . . ." (p.13).

The difference in approach is further underlined in the atheist's lament that "The Devil has nothing to do with the Torture I undergo; 'tis . . . the just Judgment of God upon me" (p.15). In contrast, Francisco Spira's relatively old-fashioned plight is shown in his assertion: "I have a whole Legion of Devils that [take] up their dwelling within me, and possess me as their own; and justly too, for I have denied Christ."[9] In the new Spira, calm philosophical discussion replaced the spectacular demise of the old Spira and his spiritual heir, Doctor Faustus.

By his familiar practice of dramatizing the events of his life with himself cast as the hero, Dunton made of the circumstances surrounding the *Second Spira* a most implausible fabric. Writing fully ten years after the event and a year after the death of Sault,[10] he listed the work as one of the seven of his publications that he should have committed to the flames. He was waited on in 1693 by clerical deputations who asked embarrassing questions about the facts of the atheist's case, an experience that seems to have rankled enough to make him forget his boast that he sold thirty thousand copies of the book within six weeks (LE,p.221). At any rate, he later advanced the belief that not only had Sault fabricated the story, but also that he had been in real life the unfortunate protagonist. He wrote of "the Methodizer" that

> a little before he writ the *Narrative,* he was under the severest Terrors of his own Conscience; his Despair and his Melancholy made him Look like some *Walking-Ghost;* and I heard several such broken Speeches as these, fall from him, I AM DAMN'D! I AM DAMN'D! I remember he came one Time into my Chamber in the *Poultry* in this Condition; and his Complexion and his Looks, were quite altered, and his Discourse run all upon Despair.
>
> After he was gone, *Dear Iris* came to me, and said *she was very much afraid Mr.* Sault *would do himself some mischief*—And the Truth is, there is such deep Despair in every Page of the *Second Spira,* that 'tis hard to conceive how any Man could write such a DISMAL NARRATIVE, that did not himself feel what he there relates. (LE,pp.218–219)

Dunton's suspicions were strengthened by the fact that Sault could give him no particular account of where Mr. Sanders lodged, yet if Sanders existed, Sault must have had to consult with him. In a turn-about from his offer in 1693 to answer all questions about the book, Dunton announced in 1705 that he had all the original copy of the *Second Spira* in his possession, "that the *Letter* and the *Preface,* which Mr. *Sault* pretended to receive from the *Divine,* are no more than *Counterfeits* of his own writing," and that "any *Gentleman* shall have the liberty to compare, for their own satisfaction, if they think it worth their while to call upon Mr. *Larkin,* at the *Half-moon* in *Hand-Alley*" (LE,p.219).

There follows a transcription of an undated letter to Sault from his wife on the subject of his unfaithfulness and setting forth conditions for a reconciliation.[11] Dunton alleges that Sault's penitent reply expressed the wish that he and his wife might meet in heaven. Again and again Dunton insists that he himself was an innocent party to the hoax, "willing to swear . . . upon *all the Bibles in the Queen's Dominions*" that he is telling the truth (LE,p.220). (In 1719 in the "Thirtieth Edition" of the *Second Spira,* Dunton updated his additions to the account given in the *Life and Errors* by then offering to swear upon all the Bibles "in the King's Dominions.") As for his detractors, ". . . all the Revenge I shall take upon these and my other Enemies is to forgive them; for if *Second Spira* be a *Forgery,* it is none of my making, nor *contrivance,* nor is there a Bookseller in *London* would have refused the Copy upon the like Information" (LE,p.221).

Fourteen years after the publication of the *Life and Errors,* Dunton sought to squeeze just a little more profit from the *Second Spira* by means of a "THIRTIETH EDITION," published for him by Sarah Popping. Introducing the whole work, he asserted that "this VALUABLE NARRATIVE is now greatly enquired after, and grown so extraordinary scarce (it being out of Print near Thirty Years, though above One Hundred Thousand of 'em were sold in a few Weeks) as are not to be purchased either in London, Dublin, Edinburgh, or in any other City in the British Dominions." (In fourteen years Dunton's recollection of the early sales of the work seems to have undergone a change, for the figure is more than tripled!)

Two of the five new items prefixed to the text of the *Second Spira* in 1719 cast light on the relationship between Dunton and Sault, containing in their titles, however, much of what Dunton related in his *Life and Errors:*

(1.) *A KEY to the Second Spira,* (never published in any former Edition of that Narrative) in which Mr. *Richard Sault* (a Member of the *Athenian Society,* and late *Mathematics Professor* in *Cambridge*) is proved to be the *Second Spira*— By a *Letter* written by his own Wife,—by *other Persons* of undoubted

Credit,—and—by the Secret History of his Atheistic and Debaucht Life. and

(3.) *Double Hell, or an Essay on Despair;* Occasion'd by Mr. *Richard Sault* (the *Second Spira*) crying out in Mr. Dunton's hearing, I am Damn'd! I am Damn'd!

Dunton was none too scrupulous toward his unfortunate colleague, as shown by his method of obtaining the "evidence" introduced in this edition:

> as to Mr. *Sault,* 'tis certain he had liv'd *a very debaucht Life several Years;* for going my self one day to visit him (whilst he lived with Mr. *Smith,* Master of the *Athenian Coffee-House* in *Stocks-Market*) Mr. *Sault* being gone abroad, I found in his Chamber a Letter writ to him by *one of his Whores,* reflecting upon him for giving her the Pox, and taking no manner of Care to get her cur'd: And 'twas thought also he gave the *foul Disease to his Wife,* (a Woman of distinguisht Wit and Sence) but has own'd (under her own hand) that her Husband once forc'd her to *Slander an innocent Person,* meerly to revenge the Discovery she had made of his Whoredom. (p.25)

Dunton then asserted that Sault

> attempted to debauch (i.e. *make a Whore*) of one of his Servant Maids, by offering to prove to her, that *Adultery was no Sin.* I had this Discovery from her own Mouth, (and the Person is still living who said it;) so that the World may depend upon it for a certain Truth, That Mr. *Sault* (the Real *Second Spira*) was the Lewdest as well as the Falsest Man that ever came into Being; and therefore, tho' his *Servant Maid* was too honest to accept of his Lewd Proposal, yet 'twas but reasonable to think that a Man that attempted to wound the Conscience of a *virtuous Maid,* and that had himself lived in a Course of the vilest *Debauchery* many Years, should one time or other fall into a *deep Despair:* Or (in plainer *English*) become a true Subject for a *Second Spira* himself.

In concluding his rather shaky quasi-legal case against Sault, Dunton presented what he felt to be both logical and affective reasons: "Mr. *Sault* said the *Second Spira* was Dead, that neither *my self* . . . nor *no other Person* might ever suspect that *Richard Sault* himself was the *Second Spira,*" and " 'tis *wholly* impossible that any Man should *Act Despair* so much to the Life, that did not REALLY feel it himself."

Dunton's nineteenth century editor, J. B. Nichols, saw fit to remove silently from the text of *Life and Errors* the author's assertion that slanderous remarks against him "were *invented* by S——t, *to revenge the Discovery* [Dunton] *made of* [Sault's] Wh—m, *and whisper'd about by a Reverend Brother. . . .*"[12] In the note on Sault by the Cambridge antiquary Charles Henry Cooper, the author's restraint in treating the *Second Spira* suggests that he did not consult the 1705 edition of *Life and Errors:*

> Dunton, although he appears to have acted as respects this book in perfect good faith, suffered greatly in his reputation when it was discovered that the public had been imposed upon. He asserts his belief that Sault had himself felt the terrors of conscience which he so powerfully depicted.[13]

If "the Methodizer" and *J. S.* would not vindicate themselves, Dunton concluded, he was "not obliged to bear them Company." He has, however, thought it proper to set the *Second Spira* in a true light, "for [he] can't run every where to answer Slanderers" (p.26).

The "KEY" contains an act of piety done with economy, a second serving of funeral baked meats, in the form of an elegy "lamenting Mr. *Sault*'s Death, in *Algebraick* Terms." Dunton explained that since Sault "was no ways Inferior to Dr. WALLIS in *Mathematick Learning,*" he had now, in 1719, built "his *Monumental Tomb*" with almost the same materials he had used to perpetuate the fame of the learned Oxford mathematician, John Wallis. Such a practice was not new for Dunton, as seen in his use of Swift's *Ode* to William III in the *Dublin Scuffle* (see Chap. 12, p.216).

To memorialize Sault, Dunton excised the first sixty-six lines and the last four lines of an elegy to Wallis which he had published about 1703, the date of Wallis's death, in effect removing a "vision" framework from the poem.[14] Since in the remainder there is no mention of Wallis's name, no further change was necessary except for the addition of an introductory couplet and an alteration in the title of the poem; in *THE MATHEMATICK FUNERAL; OR, A MONUMENT ERECTED TO THE MEMORY OF THE LATE PIOUS AND LEARNED DR. JOHN WALLIS, IN ALGEBRAICK TERMS*, there is substituted "Mr. Richard Sault, (The *SECOND SPIRA*)."

The poem would not have been out of place in the pages of the *Mercury;* a sample will show how little Dunton had changed over the years:

> Here *Second Spira* I'll lament thy Fall,
> And give thee (at my Charge) the following FUNERAL.
> I'll have the solemn Pomp, and stately Show,
>   In *Geometrical Progression* go:
>   Sage *Algebra,* with Eyes cast down
>   By *Cubes* and *Roots* encompass'd round
> Shall lead the VAN, . . . (p.27)

Dunton's misgivings about the *Second Spira* and its methodizer came long after he had reaped the profits of its many editions. One must conclude that in its time the hoax was a commercial success and that discovery of it or even suspicion of it did not cause any immediate break in the relationship between author and publisher. The *Athenian Mercury* continued to be published twice weekly for almost three more years with as many questions as ever about algebra, geometry, and physics, Sault's *forte,* as well as with advertisements of his tutoring services.[15] Furthermore, Dunton published his translation of Malebranche in 1694, and advertised it in the *Mercury* with a testimonial by John Norris.[16]

ii

The prominence of the *Second Spira,* however, created a challenging opportunity for a satirist. It is a great pity that the chance was seized only by a writer as limited as Elkanah Settle, whose *New Athenian Comedy* was published anonymously in 1693.[17] There is no record of any performance. The wordiness of the text and its lack of the kind of "spectacle" found in Settle's more successful works, such as the *Fairy Queen* (1693), an operatic version of *A Midsummer Night's Dream,* suggest that the author did not have performance in mind. Dunton's own prejudiced criticism of the attempt is for once tenable: "This Play was a poor Performance, writ however, on Purpose to expose us, but fail'd so far in the Design of it, that it promoted ours. . . . Mr. *Settle*'s *Genius* was quite run out toward the conclusion of the *Third Act,* and cou'd not carry it an Inch farther" (LE,pp.257–258).

Dunton belittled not only Settle but poets in general. The common fate of poets was not a happy one. When he saw a man decide to be a poet he gave him up "as one *prick'd down by Fate, for misery and misfortune.* 'Tis something unaccountable, but one wou'd incline to think there's some indispensable Law, whereby Poverty and Disappointment are entail'd upon Poets" (LE,p.243).

Settle was an easy victim for his patronizing reflections upon the poverty of poets—not that Dunton was unsympathetic towards them. But since he received poetical questions *gratis* and retained Wesley to answer them at a shilling a number, he did little to relieve their needs.

The *New Athenian Comedy* was more than a casual thrust at a successful periodical. The play was the culmination of a carefully laid plot, the first stage of which may be seen in the *Athenian Mercury* for Tuesday 9 May 1693 (X.13.1), about two months before publication of the play.[18] A large part of this number is devoted to a letter from one signing himself "Your Unknown Friend and Servant, W. T.," in purported defense of the Athenians' answer to a question that had appeared four weeks earlier. The "Unknown Friend" explains why he has come to the aid of the Athenians: "I was surpriz'd lately in a publick Place among a great deal of Company to hear your Society Arraign'd of Blasphemy. . . . I who am wholly a Stranger to your Persons, must with the rest of the World do you that Justice, as to clear you from so malicious and undeserv'd Imputation." He thinks the *Mercury* "extremely diverting both to City and Countrey," and "manag'd with . . . scrupulous Niceness, in relation to Good Manners and Morality. . . ." Although the Athenians "may safely despise the Impotent Efforts of this Mushrome Adversary," or manage him themselves, their correspondent begs to assist them.

Their answer to the question, "Whither the Wind goes after a Storm," has furnished the enemy with a pretence to charge them with blasphemy:

> Man knows not whence it comes, nor where it goes,
> If he that sends it knows, he only knows.

For this answer, says their adversary, "God is not much beholding to you in point of his Omniscience, since you Question his Knowledge of Natural Effect and Cause." But their defender is of the opinion "that a Man might safely propose several things Hypothetically, or by way of Supposition, the certain truth of which things he never so much as doubted of," as demonstrated in "a thousand Instances out of Ancient and Modern Authors," as for example in Cato's Distichs,

> *Si Deus est Animus, nobis ut carmina dicunt,*
> *Hic tibi precipuè sit purâ mente colendus.*

"No Christian . . . that has read his Bible, can be imagin'd to Question whether God is a Spirit: and that the Composer of this, and the rest of the Distichs in that Book was a Christian, is very plain; For tho to gain it the greater Authority, it is fathered upon *Cato,* who was a Pagan of strict Morals, . . ."

Actually, "it was writ by a Pious Christian *Videl,* a Benedictine Monk, about the twelfth Century, whose true Name was *Franciscus de Sanctâ Clarâ.*" The same reason that clears the monk of the charge of blasphemy will clear the Athenians. Another case "very pat to the business in hand," W. T. found in "a Learned Countrey-Man of ours, *Johannes Nubrigensis* by Name," a physician who flourished in the reign of Richard II, and who was quoted "by the

Learned Antiquary Mr. *Ashmole* in his Chymia Sacra, p.48."

Frigida si sit Hyems, cur Aqua fumant Hyemales?

Certainly no one would think that its author doubted whether the winter was cold or not from his manner of expression. But "he is justly to be Charg'd with this gross Contradiction to sence, as your Society is with Blasphemy."

For "a fresh Instance" W. T. cited a song "from last Summers Opera . . . which every Milkmaid had since sung about the streets: *If Love's a Sweet Passion, why does it torment,* &c." The helpful correspondent continued with a wager that

> *not one of these Milkmaids if consulted, will give in her Opinion, that the Author of these words ever dreamt that Love was not a* Sweet Passion: *so true it is . . . we may lawfully propose the most received Maxim in the World in a Hypothetical way, and yet the thinking part of Mankind will never question or deny the Truth of it.* Gentlemen, *If you think this Attempt of mine may be in the least serviceable to you, I'll leave it freely to your Disposal to do what you please with it, and am with the greatest Respect*
> Your Unknown Friend and Servant, *W. T.*

The song came from Settle's opera, the *Fairy Queen*, as "*Represented at the Queen's-Theatre By Their Majesties Servants*" in 1692.[19] He had found it necessary to shorten the dramatic text in order to add numerous songs, and to make room for dances by fauns, naiads, woodsmen, haymakers, "the four Seasons," Juno, some monkeys, and for the conclusion, "A Grand Dance of 24 Chineses."

The editors of the *Mercury* responded unsuspectingly to the learned defense of their answer with a grateful note, saying that some of "our Unknown Friends *Civilities*" were

> as *undeserv'd* as the *Occasion* of 'em, tho' in others We hope he has done us Justice, since we are pretty Confi-

dent in all the Volumes of our Mercury yet extant, there has been nothing inserted by the Consent or Knowledge of the Society at least, which has been contrary to *Good Manners* or *Religion,* and that is Reason enough to make those our *Enemies* who are such to them. (X.13.1)

In the *New Athenian Comedy,* an honest gentleman, Freeman, shows that the authorities in W. T.'s letters are fictitious. Obadiah Grub (Wesley) triumphantly beats down the charge by asserting that he alone wrote that number of the *Mercury,* "raptim, as it were," and that nothing done outside the solemn conclave of the Society was vulnerable. (There is no doubt as to Grub's identity; he is described as "a Country Parson, by birth a *Grubstreetonian,* in his Sacerdotal Capacity a *Lincolnshire Sermonian;* but at present strol'd and eloped from his Canonical drudgery, and translated to an *Athenian Heliconian;* in plain *English* the *Poetry* and *Divinity Professor* of the Society."[20])

Among the other characters, "Joachim Dash, *Mathematician,*" is Richard Sault; "Jack Stuff, *a subtle, ingenious, half Author, half Bookseller*" is Dunton; "Jerry Squirt, *Casuist and Physician in Ordinary*" may be a composite of John Norris and some one of the quack doctors, such as Kirleus, so many of whose advertisements the *Mercury* printed; "Poll, the *Coffee-man,*" is Smith, for the scene is "S—— Coffee-house, Stocks-market;" and "Darby Fetlock, *an Under Turnkey of* Newgate," and "Dorothy Tickleteat, *an* Islington *Milkmaid,*" represent types whom Settle considered the most avid readers of the *Mercury.*

Making fun of the suspension of the *Mercury* the year before, the playwright put into Stuff's mouth a rationalization of Dunton's payment for a lawyer's services: ". . . it cost me near thirty Guineas . . . d'ye see." But ". . . I got a kind of Patent by it, and set up our Society a compleat Corporation, with a full promise of suppressing all Interlopers, whether Lord or Lady Mercuries, &c. and so the Money was not ill laid out."

We also learn a little of the economics of publishing, as

Stuff goes on to observe ". . . I must desire you to consider seriously that a poor Impression of 35 single quires of Mercuries and above half of them Return'd, d'ye see, will be a long time a raising of that summ; and therefore you must not take it ill if I pinch Commons a little, and retrench superfluities til I retrieve that loss, d'ye see" (p.3). (The repeated "d'ye see" in Stuff's speeches was perhaps a realistic imitation of a nervous habit of the real John Dunton.) Settle uses other information that must have been common knowledge at the time. Asked by Grub about the success of the *Second Spira,* "that glorious Apocrypha," Stuff replies that he has sold "Only some few small Impressions summ total about 18 thousand" (p.12). In turn, Stuff asks Dash what muse he invoked "for that sublime inspiration." Dash replies: "I was illuminated by a *Grub-street Apollo,* whilst the great souls of *Garagantua, Lazarillo,* Captain *Jones,* St. *Jago* Pilgrims, &c. were transmigrating Fires that animated me for the bold Montelion of that Golden Oracle." Grub joins in to insist that the work is "all pure *Elixir Atheniense,* the very Spirit and Quintessence of [Dash's] Mercurial SALT. . . . But for our friend and patron *Jack:* what buffets has he stood in defending, and what toyl and fatigue has he undergone in vouching and legitimatizing that spurious brat? . . . how many Crape gown Visitants, those more learned and formidable Curioso's, has he had to satisfie in the undoubted veracity of that prodigious *Ens Metaphysicum.*"

Stuff modestly replies that he is "the best Bookseller for such an Authour," with "a particular Talent that way;" he cites his publication of some posthumous pieces of his "own dear Daddys writing and composing" under his own name. He has "rob'd the very dead for no other Feather than the Titular Author to grace the Booksellers Scutcheon. After so currant a Slur on the world for meer vanity sake, 'tis hard, if in so much great and weightier an Importance as the profit and interest of so selling a copy as *Spira,* I could not strain a little Extraordinary point of modesty for so potent a Consideration" (p.13). Stuff closes the subject with the downright remark that "Truth and Honesty, Religion or

Conscience are no Athenian Arguments, we write for the penny, and there's an Answer for all" (p.16).

Act III begins with an extremely scurrilous attack upon Stuff's alleged sterility, which he laments as "my want of an Heir to my Copys (*viz.* to my Fee simple in ten Volumes of Mercuries, and the twice ten more you'l write me). . . ." There is also Freeman's revelation to the Athenians that they are victims of the plot engineered by "W. T." by means of the letter actually sent to the *Mercury* and published on 9 May 1693:

> Why Sirs, if those Bodlean Head-pieces of Yours, your deep *Athenian Universality,* instead of your Boasted Antiquity-Wisdom, had had Learning enough to have read but the History of Yesterday, you might have learnt that the famous *Franciscus de Stâ. Clarâ,* instead of a 12*th. Century* man was a late *Somerset* house Brother, a modern *Babylonish* Controversy Scribler (posibly living to this day,) and answer'd by Dr. Stillingfleet . . . my kind Friend your generous Vindicator, knew the depth of your *Athenian* swallow and digestion, and therefore not suspecting any danger of a Discovery, he prepared his sham accordingly (p.22).

Grub saves the day for the Athenians by pointing out that he had written that number single-handed:

> Was not that Mercury a pure By-brat of mine? Was it compiled any otherwise than raptim as I may so say? Was it concerted or discuss'd in a full *Athenian* Consistory? No Sir, 'twas only a private slip of my own. And as such, the whole Society stand fair and unblemisht. For look you Sir we pretend not to Infallibility *Ex Cathedra.* As men or so, in our severall private Capacityes we may have our oversights and Faylings; but as the whole Body of *Athenians,* in full *Sanedrim,* in General Council assembled we defy the whole world to overreach us, or less then Divinity and Oracle to slip from us. (pp.23–24)

After Freeman's triumphant departure, the Athenians laugh off their discomfiture and turn to the problem of Dorothy Tickleteat, the Islington milkmaid, who is troubled with what Squirt calls euphemistically "an over *Affluence of Humi*dity" (p.26). Squirt prescribes a patent medicine remedy, remarking, "These by-Jobs are the best of our Game, I am sure the Society would hardly buy us porridge without it." Grub concurs:

> Nay my Brother *Squirt*'s in the right for that. Do you think I have answer'd so many Rhiming Love Questions in our Mercurys for the meer Letchery of Poetry, or the Lucre of the poor penny Mr. *Stuff* can afford me for 'em? No, faith I have a deeper reach in my *Athenian Politicks*. For let me tell you 'tis not less then twenty (and twenty to that) kind Couples that I have Exercised my Sacerdotall Function on, upon no other Recommendation then my being so true a Love Advocate, and so good a Friend to the Mathematicks, and got good Yellow Boys, and good Sack Possets into the Bargain. (p.27)

When Dash expresses admiration for Squirt "for tickling up dear Dorothy so sweetly, and hitting her humour so to a hair," Grub makes a revealing rejoinder:

> Oh that we must all do if we hope to thrive in this world. I would not give a Groat for him that can't tickle all fancies. For Instance when I Courted my *Non-Cons* Daughter, do you think I came to her in my terrible Tantivy Gown, with a pair of dreadfull Pudding Sleeves, and attacqu'd her in high flown Orthodox? Death! that had been enough to have frighted the whole family. No no Sir, I prudently and wisely came uncased, came in querpo, and woo'd and wedded her *de froquè*. (pp.27–28)

The play ends in a wild melee in which Freeman and his friends return to the coffee-house and kick the Athenians down stairs.

The *New Athenian Comedy* was published anonymously

with the imprint of a fictitious bookseller, *"Campanella Restio."* It shows an intimate knowledge of Dunton's affairs, suggesting that the play was a rear-guard action helped by Brown, unhappy at his failure to put the Athenians out of business the year before. The facetiousness of the dialogue of the play bears strong resemblance to that of the *London Mercury,* and other works of Tom Brown's. Although Dunton seems to have been sure Settle was the author, he may have been mistaken.

Stuff's assertion that he had secured a kind of patent through buying his way out of the suspension of the *Mercury* was for the time being quite true. No rival in the form taken by the *Lacedemonian Mercury* emerged again during the lifetime of the *Athenian Mercury;* if Dunton himself gave the real reason for the demise of his periodical three years later it was the increase in newspapers containing "real" news. No periodical wholly devoted to questions and answers became prominent again until 1707, when the *British Apollo* began publication, although Defoe's *Review,* five years after the *Mercury*'s demise, had a question department about which Dunton complained bitterly.[21]

How and why, then, was the *Athenian Mercury* able to continue until 1697? A part of the answer lies in the uniqueness of its contents. The editors adhered to a principle now so widespread that it goes almost unnoticed: there must be something for everyone.

CHAPTER 6

[1] *Ein erschröckliche Historia von einem, den die feinde . . . gezwungen haben,* 1549; *Exemplum memorabile desperationis. . . . cum præfatione J. Calvine.* Genevæ, 1550.
[2] Date uncertain.
[3] *Writings of John Greenwood* 1587–1590 (ed. Leland H. Carlson) London, George Allen and Unwin. 1962, p.6.
[4] Also attributed to Bacon is the *History of the Life and Actions of St. Athanasius,* together with the *RISE, GROWTH, and DOWN-FALL of the ARIAN HERESIE* (1664) has on its title page the curious inscription, "by N. B. P. C. Catholick." A Puritan attitude is shown in the "Preface," where the author points out that Athanasius never referred to the Pope with any higher degree than "the beloved Damascus Bishop of great Rome."
[5] "Printed by Henry Denham for William Norton."

⁶ *Grace Abounding* (ed. Roger Shurrock), Oxford, 1962, pp.49–50.
⁷ I have not been able to examine a "First Edition," Wing's S. T. C. lists four editions of the work, all dated 1693, one of them called "Fourth Edition" (S 733 B [Sault, Richard]), one called "Sixth Edition" (S 733 C), and one with a Boston, Mass., imprint; to these should be added the Huntington Library example, "Second Edition." Four editions were advertised in the *Mercury,* the latest on 4 February 1693 (IX.16).
⁸ Referred to by Dunton as "Mr. *Sanders.*" LE, p.219.
⁹ N. B., *Fearful Estate.* . . . , p.33.
¹⁰ "The register of St. Andrew the Great, in Cambridge, records the burial there of Richard Sault, on 17 May 1702." C. H. Cooper, "Some Account of Richard Sault," *Cambridge Antiquarian Communications,* Cambridge, 1879, III.37.
¹¹ Sault's wife Sarah, Dunton's half-sister, oldest of four children by the father's second wife, was at least seven years younger than Dunton. *Dunton's Remains,* pp.20–21; Hatfield *Secret History,* p.81.
¹² LE, p.229. Compare *Life and Errors* (1818), p.165: "I do not speak this out of prejudice to Mr. Wesley; for to forgive a *slight* is so easy to me, it is scarce a virtue."
¹³ Cooper, *Cambridge Antiquarian Communications,* III.43.
¹⁴ The elegy to Wallis is in *Life and Errors* (1818), pp.658–661.
¹⁵ X.27 (Tue 27 Jun 93): "THE MATHEMATICAL SCHOOL in *Adams Court* in *Broad-street,* near the *Royal Exchange,* London, is now Open'd; where *Algebra, Geometry,* and all the usual parts of the Mathematicks will be Taught. By *R. Sault,* Math. Profess. Those that desire, may be Instructed abroad. Youth boarded. The Undertaker Obliges himself to Teach by Letters in any place in England, with the same Expedition and Success as by a Personal Attendance, when once a Correspondence is settled."
¹⁶ XIV.2 (Sat 26 May 94): *"Whereas it was design'd at first to print the* English *Translation of* Malbranches [sic] Search after Truth, *in* Fol. *this is to give Notice, that the Undertakers,* John Dunton *and* Samuel Manship, *(that they may sooner gratifie the Expectation of the Learned World, and that so useful a Work may be every Bodies Money) design to print it in 2* Volumes, *(as 'tis in the* Original) *upon a very fair Letter and Extraordinary Paper, done out of* French *from the* Paris *4th* Edition, *by Mr.* Sault, Matth, *of whose Abilities in performing so Nice and Learned a Work,* John Norris, M. A. *very well satisfy'd, after some Converse with the said* Mr. Sault, *as he has express'd himself by Letter to some of his Acquaintance in* Town, *and therefore, as also for some other Reasons, has desired to be excus'd from his promise of the revisal. The first* Volume *will be Publish't in two Months, being now in the Press, and the 2d. with all possible Expedition, the Translator having began the Work above twelve Months since."*
¹⁷ *New Athenian Comedy; containing the Politicks, OEconomicks, Tacticks, Crypticks, Apocalypticks, Stypticks, Scepticks, Pneumaticks, Theologicks, Poeticks, Mathematicks, Sophisticks, Pragmaticks, Dogmaticks, of our most learned Society.* (The name of the bookseller,

"Campanella Restio," is apparently the author's whimsy.) Compare the following from the *Mercury*, X.8 (Sat 22 Apr 93): "Every Body's Mercury *Being resolv'd to try for once whether 'tis possible to please all our Customers in this dead time of* Trade, *We present 'em here with a Mercury, the result of all our* Studies *who are in or near the* Town. *consisting of* Divinity, Poetry, Metaphysicks, Physicks, Mathematicks, History, Love Politicks, Oeconomicks, *and to reach yet further,* Visions *and* Revelations; and if all this don't *please ye, We must e'ne despair of doing it.*" Nine questions are answered, the first, on divinity, being "What's Blasphemy?"

[18] MS. note on title page of Huntington Library copy, "6 July."

[19]
> If Love's a Sweet Passion, why does it torment?
> If a Bitter, oh tell me whence comes my content?
> Since I suffer with pleasure, why should I complain,
> Or grieve at my Fate, when I know 'tis in vain?
> Yet so pleasing the Pain is, so soft is the Dart,
> That at once it both wounds me, and tickles my Heart.
> I press her Hand gently, look Languishing down,
> And by Passionate Silence I make my love known.
> But oh! how I'm Blest when so kind she does prove,
> By some willing mistake to discover her Love.
> When in striving to hide, she reveals all her Flame,
> And our Eyes tell each other, what neither dares Name.

While a Symphony's Playing, the two Swans come Swimming on through the Arches to the bank of the River, as if they would land; they turn themselves into Fairies, and Dance; at the same time the Bridge vanishes, and the Trees that were Arch'd, raise themselves upright. Pp.29–30.

[20] *New Athenian Comedy*, p.2. In his Preface, Settle alluded to the engraving of the Society in the *Young Students Library*:

> *But there alas, they are pleased to wrap their Faces in* Mosaic Veils *very magisterially intimating that they are Persons that daily converse so near with* Divinity, *that their* shining Faces *are too dazling for humane View, and therefore no less kindly than modestly, thus like* Bays *his* Morning *pictur'd in a Cloud. I confess Mr. Engraver has made a pretty Jolly Company of 'em; but there indeed the Painter is a little too poetical; and our Athenians have a little strain'd a point; For when the true Muster Roll of that not over-numerous Society shall be examined, for supply of that defect, you must consider that the veil'd Faces are by way of Faggots to fill up the Troop . . . like Guns in a Fireship, a Tire of painted wooden Tools to make up the Show.*
>
> *However, no disparagement, the fewer the Hands, the harder the Labor, and consequently the greater the Honor, the Illustration of which Honor is subject of our present Entertainment.*

[21] This man has done me a sensible wrong, by interloping with my 'Question-Project' . . . I am 200*l.* the worse for De Foe's clogging

my 'Question-Project.' His answering Questions Weekly put a stop to my 'Monthly Oracle:' for, though his answers were false and impertinent, (and for that reason his interloping continued but a few weeks) yet, being published every Tuesday, they ruined my 'Monthly Oracle:' for most are seized with the Athenian Itch, and chuse rather to be scratched *Weekly,* than stay till the *Month* is out for a perfect cure. Such a dolt as I have laid the Plan of near Fifty Books (besides Sixty which I have written since my confinement). Then it is strange that such a first-rate Author as Daniel De Foe should be so barren of new Projects, that he must interlope with mine; but the mischief he endeavoured to do me will fall on his own head; for I have now set up a 'Whipping-Post,' and resolve to lash him (if he dare draw either pen or sword) until he has done me justice. And in the mean time I will take the satisfaction to tell the World, that whatever questions De Foe has answered shall be all answered again (with the best of his Thoughts, and my own Improvements); my resolution being to publish an entire Volume of the 'New Oracle' every year, till the 'Question-Project' is completed.

John Dunton, *Whipping Post* (1706), pp.423–24.

7

Dunton Invites the Muse

No other periodical of the century printed as much verse or made as much over it editorially as the *Athenian Mercury*. Beginning in January 1692, a "Poetical Mercury" was published about once a month, in which any question submitted in verse was answered in kind, usually in the same number of lines and the same verse form as the question. Forty-three numbers of the *Mercury* contain poetical questions or occasional poems.[1]

The editors did not begin publishing poems, however, without some preparation. There had been in early numbers some scattered questions about poets, as for example one inquiring the true reason for Ovid's banishment, and answered, most probably by Wesley, who had a kindness for Dryden: ". . . I am thus far of the same Mind with Mr. *Dryden,* that his [Ovid's] having seen something more than ordinary in *Augustus*'s Gardens, was partly the Reason thereof" (I.21.6). The desire of the age to know who was the best poet and what the best poem was satisfied in Volume II, Number 14:

> The best *Poem* that ever was *made* is the *Universe,* and he who *made* that, the first and best *Poet.* But for artificial Poems, not to meddle with the Scriptures, a great part whereof, as part of *Job,* several of the *Psalms,* the *Canticles, Isaiah, Lamentations,* &c. is undoubtedly the best and noblest Poetry in the World. It is *Virgils Æneids.* . . .[2]

Toward the end of 1691 there appeared a question signaling that poetry was to be given more importance in the *Mercury:"Is there ever a* Poet *among the Athenian Society, and suppose a* **Question** *shou'd be sent in* Verse, *shou'd it be answer'd in the same?"* The reply was also an invitation: " 'Twill be time enough to answer this when the Querist has made the Experiment" (V.1.1, Tue 1 Dec 91). In addition to the "planted" question and answer, there was in the same number what might be called moral preparation for the new project, in the question:

> *Whether Songs on Moral, Religious or Divine Subjects, composed by Persons of* Wit and Virtue *and set to both grave and pleasant Tunes, wou'd not by the Charms of Poetry, and sweetness of Musick, make good Impressions of Modesty and Sobriety on the Young and Noble, make them really in Love with Virtue and Goodness, and prepare their minds for the design'd* Reformation?

In their vigorous affirmative to the main question the editors pointed out that music was an intellectual as well as a "sensible" pleasure, and that vocal music was of all the most moving, "especially when good Sence, good Poetry, good Tunes, and a good Voice meet together;" virtue thus adorned, therefore, should be all the more amiable.

> But still the Question is, who shall be her *Tyre-woman?* For she may tarry a long time before our Poets will trouble themselves about it. And here naturally enough wou'd come in a Discourse of *Divine Poetry and Poets,* but we have too much Business already to *Digress,* or discourse on that Subject, unless our Question call'd us more immediately unto it.

In addition to arousing some Athenian poet, the inquirer wanted the *Mercury*'s opinion of a "late *Pastoral Poem,*" on King William at the Battle of the Boyne, a poem that did not appear in the *Mercury* but was obviously known to the Athenians.[3] A poetical reply apostrophizes the author of the pastoral as the "Dear unknown," asking *"What secret Nectar through thy Lines does flow? / What* Deathless beauties *in thy Garden grow?"* Not all is praise, however, says the Athenian poet:

> *I must accuse thee too,*
> *When thou hadst done so much, no more to do,*
> *When to the brink of* Boyne *thy* Hero *came*
> *There to break off* the chase of him and Fame,
> *Where had been Albion now, had he thus stood,*
> *But floating in another* Sea of Blood?

Gildon quoted the entire reply in the *History of the Athenian Society,* to illustrate the conformity of "the Poetical Member of this Society" to the rules of Horace in his avoidance of *"Obscurity, Trifling, Bombast, meaness* both of thought and Expression, and *affected copiousness,* which is a spining out a thought into various, and synonymous Expressions . . ." (p.25).

"What can be more *fine,* and sweet," asked Gildon, "than these Verses? What more Poetical? What more correct?" If not all the poetical answers came up to this standard, it was because some questions sent in verse should have been in prose, or because the "Poetical Member" chose to write in burlesque, "very witty, and pleasant," or in epigram. An illustration of this last appeared at the height of the Athenians' quarrel with Brown in response to a charge of plagiarism:

> Whatever *borrow'd Lines* our *Works* have shown,
> This we dare swear, that thine are all thy own.
>   (VII.5.5)

The "Dear unknown" was Elizabeth Singer (1679–1737), a young woman of eighteen, later Mrs. Rowe, who, like Swift, offered her first efforts to the Athenians. Although the poem on William III did not appear in the *Mercury,* many others of her composition did in the years to come, especially in 1694 and 1695; in 1696 a collection of her works was published by John Dunton, containing among others, the "late *Pastoral* Poem." In this poem Miss Singer had indeed balked at the thought of going on to describe the ensuing bloody battle and took refuge instead in a pretty picture of naiads thronging about the king as he strode into the water.

To a reader's guess that a "Mr. S——" had written the

lines praising Miss Singer's work, the *Mercury* replied with all politeness:

> Not to reflect on that Ingenious Person, we have no need of going out of our own *fixt Society,* which consists of *several Members* read in all Sciences, some of which have already appear'd publickly in this *kind of Study,* from whom the World shall soon have a further account. (V.10.7)

In January 1692 the first "Poetical Mercury" appeared. It contained not only contributions from the "fixt Society" but also, from Dunton's own wedding celebration in 1682, an "Epithalamium" of forty lines, in response to a request that the Athenians depict *"the Nuptial Joy"* of a happy man (V.11.7). Its author, as Dunton revealed in the *Life and Errors,* was "an *ingenious Gentleman,* (at that time a Student in the Reverend Mr. *VEAL*'s House)" (LE,p.97). There is implicit an offer to go on fulfilling such practical needs in the concluding remark of this number: "When we have received Questions enough for another *Poetical Mercury,* the World may expect such another Entertainment."

In the next month, just a few days after the *London Mercury* had opened fire, the *Mercury* published by request an elegy on the great chemist Robert Boyle, who had died on 30 December 1691. The querist charged the *Mercury* with raising the standard of poetry, for he asked the editors to prevent the subject of Boyle's death being "murder'd . . . *with some* Bellmans persecuting Ditty *equally nauseous for Folly and Nonsence*" (VI.2).

Introducing the elegy, the Athenian poet remarked that "We design'd according to our promise to have return'd an answer to this Question in the 12 Numbers that are now in the press, to compleat our *5th Volume,* but being earnestly importuned for a speedy Answer, we have thought fit here to insert An ELEGY, On the Death of the Honourable *ROBERT BOYLE,* Esq; Fellow of the Royal Society."

The poem, a fairly regular pindaric in eight stanzas, touches all the expected stops:

> Nor *Thames* alone, even hostile *Sein* does mourn . . . ;
> How much to Boyl the Learned World does owe
> The Learned World does only know.

The poet asked Galileo to lend his wondrous glass to "descry some new unwonted Star," Boyle's soul. Death, he wrote, found Boyle, like Archimedes,

> . . . intent
> On the Success of some Experiment,
> . . . .
> Stay hasty Death, one moment more he cry'd!
> *I have it now,* says he, *with Learned Pride,*
> Then big with the dear *Demonstration,* dy'd.

The *London Mercury* reacted at once. In answer to the question of whether "that ingenious person who writ the elegant Pindaric on Mr. Boyle, was not the very same Individuum Vagum, who some years ago composed the Pindaric upon the grunting of a hog," Brown replied that those who had read both "make no scruple to conclude, that they proceed from the same numerical fit" (LM I.4.5). It was no secret that Wesley was the poet of the Athenians at this time.

The occasional poems in the *Mercury* were the only ones to receive any critical notice. Besides the remark in the *London Mercury* there was a critical essay in the *Moderator* that summer on the Athenians' dull performances as occasional poets. The poetic staple of the *Mercury,* however, was the rimed answer to the rimed question, truly beneath notice in its quality but of interest because of the variety of subjects dealt with. A typical number devoted to such questions came out three weeks after the elegy on Boyle. Six poetical questions, all but the last answered rather briefly, ask how bodies are moved, what an idea is, why reason cannot guide one to heaven, why men take a chance in the lottery of marriage, and what is *"Natures* profound *and* secret Mysterie." The Athenians' definition of an idea may have been in reaction to Locke's interpretation of all sense impressions as ideas, for it appears to insist upon idea as memory:

> What e're *Impressions* outward Objects make,
> The ductile Fancy is prepar'd to take,

> Stampt on the Brain, the *Signature* receives,
> Which still behind its Airy Image leaves;
> To this the Mind adverts, by this we all
> That's absent see and this *Idea* call.
>
> (VI.8.2)

John Norris, the poet and philosopher who agreed to assist the Athenians incognito when they began their project, two years before this poetic answer, had attacked its concept in the first published criticism of the *Essay concerning Human Understanding*, as "Impression without Consciousness."[4] But the *Mercury*, which never praised Norris for his accomplishments as a philosopher, was almost always on Locke's side. *Supplement III* (pp.2-3) contains Le Clerc's criticism of Norris's *Cursory Reflections* upon Locke's *Essay*, in which Norris is chastised for "not having well comprehended his meaning whom he criticizes upon." The greater likelihood is that Dunton never understood the philosophical differences involved but was shrewd enough to see that praise of Locke was easier and safer than support of Norris, a comparatively obscure man.

ii

Up to Volume Eleven, when the "Pindarick Lady," as Miss Singer was styled by Dunton, came to the aid of the Athenians, the poetry of the *Mercury* was mainly the work of one man, Samuel Wesley, who could provide both occasional poems, such as the elegy on Boyle, and facetious rimed answers to mischievous questions.

Maggots had already demonstrated young Wesley's flair for the incongruous, a leaning toward undergraduate satire, and a juvenile enjoyment of pedantic humor. In the **"EPISTLE TO THE READER,"** he quoted a significant passage from Francis Osborn's *Advice to a Son:*

> The way to Elegance of Stile, is to employ the Pen upon every Errand, and the more trivial and dry it is, the more Brains must be allow'd for Sawce. Thus by checking all ordinary Invention, your Reason will attain to such an Habit, as not to dare present you but with what is excellent.

Wesley was sure that if he wrote "silly enough" his books would sell *"as well as any Christmas Tales and Wonderments;"* if his readers stuck upon something that looked like reason, *" 'tis but making a small leap, and they're safe and sound upon the* Terra Firma *of* Nonsense *agen."*

It would be better not to fill his book with explanation, Wesley concluded, but rather to leave puzzles for grammarians "a thousand years hence" to worry over. *"How would poor* Homer *bless himself, were he, like his own* Ulisses, *to return, and find how he is, since his Death too, improv'd into a* Statuary, *a Captain, a Moralist, a Politician, and would you think it? a Divine too. . . ."*

In *Maggots* may be seen Wesley's facetiousness and his practicality. The whole production fitted in with the practical jokes of the young Nonconformist seminarians and of Oxford undergraduates, and its publisher, Dunton, was not far removed from apprentices' tricks. Young Jonathan Swift and his friends at Trinity College, Dublin, found the book a good source for speeches to put in the mouth of *Terrae Filius* in a Tripos entertainment.[5] One of the dedicatory poems Dunton printed in *Life and Errors* as by "Samuel Warper, M. A. Late of Exeter College," was obviously by Wesley and shows by its many Homeric references and its thorough acquaintance with Dunton's "rambling humour" that author and bookseller were kindred spirits, as well as brothers-in-law.[6]

The Wesley who wrote for the *Mercury,* however, showed himself capable of greater seriousness. His matriculation at Oxford had marked the beginning of a change that was borne out further in his ordination as a priest of the Church of England in 1689, his service as a curate in London, and as a chaplain aboard the Fleet. On dry land again, he was a curate in Newington Butts, Surrey, beginning in 1690. He had married in the meantime and had to eke out his living, as he testified in a letter, by "correcting to a Press & scribling a little now and then."[7] His connection with the Annesley family and his financial need both led him to Dunton, but writing never became his chief source of income. In midsummer, 1691, he assumed the curacy of South

Ormsby in Lincolnshire, worth £50 a year, a considerable increase in income and sorely needed. Although frequently in London, he still depended on the post to deliver many of his contributions to the *Mercury*.

Wesley underwent some political as well as religious change. According to his son John he sided with King James for a period, not surprising in view of his move from the Dissenting academy to Oxford in 1683, when he was twenty-one years old. In 1688 he contributed a short poem in English to a collection of verse, mainly in Latin, in honor of the birth of the Prince of Wales.[8] Much later, however, in a sermon on the reformation of manners, published in 1698, he revealed that James's treatment of the Fellows of Magdalen had turned him against the King.[9] His political attitude during the early years of the *Mercury* is shown in a letter he wrote from South Ormsby in August 1692, explaining his refusal to oppose the Test Act on the grounds that his business was "not . . . Politicks but Obedience."[10]

Wesley's serious poetical compositions were, by 1692, in harmony with his ecclesiastical role. In *Maggots* he had written: *"were I in my Sober Sences, writing Reasonable prose, I should not be so sawcy. . . . But 'twill here I hope be taken only for a little Spice* of Furor Poeticus" (pp.47–48). Nothing could be further from this expressed attitude than his solemn undertaking, begun as early as 1689, of a poetic *Life of Christ,* in ten books and over ten thousand lines, designed to repair Milton's omissions from *Paradise Regained* and advance the story to its terrestrial end. Published in 1693, it had a second printing the next year, and a second edition in 1697. It is delightfully ironical that Charles Harper, its publisher, secured for it sixty copper plates, including an engraved title page allegedly by William Faithorne, for the author had boasted in *Maggots:* "*here wants a hundred and fifty Copper-plates . . . as inseparable a mark of an* omnium gatherum *as the Cloven foot is of* Mephistopheles" (A5).

The suspension of the *Mercury* about a year before publication of the *Life of Christ* provided Wesley the needed respite from hack work to finish his scholarly poem. He observed near the end of his preface that he would have mended much that he found amiss had he lived in an age "where a man might afford to be Nine or Ten Years about a Poem." He seems actually to have completed the work in about three years, sharing most of that time with other demands, not the least of which was writing for the *Mercury*.

The *Life of Christ* was dedicated to Queen Mary, and within the poem Wesley combined a tribute to her with one to the Virgin Mary.[11] The Epworth living, which he received in 1696 but did not occupy until the next year, was in the Royal gift and may have been his reward for the dedication and a consolation for not having received the Irish bishopric Lord Normanby had sought for him.[12] In his old age Wesley lamented not being able to dedicate his Latin commentary on the Book of Job to Queen Caroline as the third dedication to a queen,[13] for between the commentary and the *Life of Christ* he had dedicated to Queen Anne the *History of the Old and New Testament Attempted in Verse* (1704).

The contemporary success of the *Life of Christ* was due in part to the editions of Milton being issued by Jacob Tonson, especially the subscription folio in 1688 with Dryden's lines under the Vertue portrait of the author as engraved by Faithorne. Wesley's poem, with copious notes, and his prefatory essay on heroic poetry, show his admiration for Milton.[14] The notes freely acknowledge borrowings from *Paradise Lost,* and the preface displays a breadth of knowledge and a depth of reasoning that Milton would not have found comtemptible.

Like Milton, Wesley would not give his entire allegiance to neo-classical rules governing the heroic poem. He argued that Homer used mythology because that was the predominant form of ancient learning. A real hero, he suggested, would be *"Truth it self,"* capable of stronger persuasion upon the reader than a mythical one (p.iii). History itself could be both diverting and admirable, its introduction saving the poet the trouble of invention. Wesley hoped to prove, in fact, "that Fiction is not necessary to the principal Action of our Heroic Poem"—not because it mattered to him what his own poem should be called, but in defense of Cowley's *Davideis,* which some had denied was an epic "because the Subject thereof is a true History" (p.iv).

Again like Milton, he approved of the use of mythology in a Christian poem, though he agreed with the French critics "that *Christianity* and *Heathenism* ought not to be *confounded,* nor the *Pagan Gods* mention'd but *as such.* . . ." (One is reminded of "Hesperian Fables, if true, true here only.") With great spirit Wesley attacked Boileau's disapproval of using the heathen poets' names for their gods and heroes. Why not transplant into modern verse what was found in ancient Hebrew poetry? An advantage for poets of his own generation was that they knew more history and could use it in poetical composition. In answering Boileau's question as to what pleasure can come from hearing the howlings of repining Lucifer, Wesley wrote:

> I think 'tis easier to *answer* than to find out what shew of *Reason* he had for asking it, or why *Lucifer* mayn't *howl* as pleasantly, as either *Cerberus,* or *Enceladus.* And let any one read but his speech, in *Milton's Paradice almost equall'd* in Mr. *Dryden's State of Innocence,* and I'm mistaken if he's not of the *same Mind;* or if he be not, and it gives him no *pleasure,* I dare affirm 'tis for want of a true taste of what's really *admirable.* (p.ii)

In the *Life of Christ,* Wesley showed his admiration for Milton by borrowing a passage entire from *Paradise Regained* with a handsome acknowledgment in a note:

> I believe I need not tell the Reader, I here begin to make bold with Mr. *Milton,* about twenty of whose lines I've wrought into my Storm, for a very good reason, because they're extremely *fine,* and I could not get near so good of my own. However, I've own'd and mark'd every one of 'em, nay even each half Verse for which I have beholden to him.[15]

Those who wrote commendatory verses for the volume were less humble than Wesley toward the great Puritan poet. Nahum Tate wrote:

> Our leading *Moses* did this Task pursue,
> And liv'd to have the *Holy Land* in view;
> With vig'rous *Youth* to finish the *Success,*
> Like *Joshua* you Succeed, and all *Possess.*
>
> . . . .
>
> Here, *pious Souls,* what they did long desire,
> Possess their dear Redeemer's Life intire:
> Here, with whole *Paradise regain'd* they meet,
> And *Milton*'s noble Work is now compleat.

Thomas Taylor, in his poem to his "Ingenious Friend Mr. Samuel Wesley," made a triple comparison, first between Milton and Dryden, who

> . . . swoll'n with a nobler Pride,
> Out of the common road once step'd aside;
> Bravely went on where *Milton* broke the Ice,
> And sweetly mourn'd the *loss of Paradise;*
>
> . . . .
>
> What *Mortal* cou'd have been with him compar'd,
> As he *began,* had he but *persever'd!*

Cowley too, wrote Taylor, might have succeeded, had he chosen *"the blessed Jesus"* rather than *"David,* that mighty man." But Cowley was cut off before he had finished, and drew his subject "but to the waist."

Henry Cutts fetched his comparisons from the New World. Addressing Wesley he cried:

> You (with *Columbus,*) not alone descrie,
> But conquer (*Cortez*-like,) new Worlds in *Poetry.*

Peter Motteux, the well-known journalist and translator, published his own dedicatory poem in the *Gentleman's Journal* also (July 1693, pp.233–235). He may be suspected of irony in his comparison of the plight of the London journalists, "The Town our Cage, where we must *starve* or *sing*," with that of "Much happier Wesley" who left the hurry of the town "for more peaceful Climes." (South Ormsby was scarcely idyllic as described by Wesley in the poem.)[16]

Wesley identified himself in the *Mercury* by answering

the very first poetical question in the periodical with praise of Milton, whose *Paradise Lost* "and some other poems of his will never be *equal'd*" (II.14.3). Furthermore, in October 1693, four months after the *Life of Christ* was published, Milton's works were recommended in the *Mercury* as suitable for the young poetry enthusiast, this in answer to a question submitted by "the Poetical Lady," Elizabeth Singer. That answer was a clear reflection of Wesley's preferences as expressed also in the Preface to the *Life of Christ* and throughout the poem itself. A modest disclaimer of excellence for his own poem also identifies the writer as Wesley:

> Quest. *What Books of Poetry wou'd you Advise one that's Young, and extreamly delights in it, to read, both Divine and other?*
>
> For Divine, *David*'s Psalms, *Sandys*'s and *Woodford*'s Versions; *Lloyd*'s Canticles; *Cowley*'s Davideis; Sir *J. Davis*'s *Nosce Teipsum, Herbert*'s and *Crashaw*'s Poems; *Milton*'s Paradices; and (if you have Patience) *Wesley*'s Life of Christ. For others, Old Merry *Chaucer, Gawen Douglas*'s Æneads (if you can get it) the best Version that ever was, or We believe ever will be, of that incomparable Poem; *Spencer*'s Fairy Queen &c; *Tasso*'s Godfrey of Bulloign, *Shakespear, Beaumont* and *Fletcher, Ben. Johnson, Randal, Cleaveland*, Dr. *Donne, Gondibert, WALLER,* all *DRYDEN, Tate, Oldham, Flatman, The Plain Dealer*—and when you have done of these, We'll promise to provide you more. (XII.1.4)

This reading list for the young is an excellent example of those poetic tastes and traditions viable in the 1690's. Aside from his personal preference for Douglas's *Aeneid,* Wesley's liking for Donne on the one hand and his own contemporaries Dryden, Flatman, and Wycherley on the other is indicative of a period that looked both ways.

A reader wrote in a few weeks later to defend Wesley: "*In a Paper of yours some Weeks since, wherein you direct your Quaerent in his Choice of Books of Poetry, I find you*

Advise Mr. Wesley's *Life of Christ to be read, but with the Words (if you have Patience) scurvily interpos'd"* (XII.18.1). The reader, having read the poem himself, held the work and its author in the highest esteem and knew of others as well who were *"pleas'd frequently to recommend it to the reading of all Lovers of Religion and Ingenuity."* What material objections could the editors make to justify their *"slurring Parenthesis?"* The Athenians responded nobly, first protesting that some would suspect them of being too great friends rather than enemies of the poet, and would think therefore that they had made this question themselves. Rather than a slur upon the poet, their parenthesis was a recognition of the shortcomings of the readers, for

> the Genius of the Age is generally too impatient to go through any thing that requires both Perseverance and Thinking. Now by that Judgment we had form'd on the reading Mr. *Westley*'s Poem, which perhaps We have done with some Application, We found that 'twoud be a Disadvantage to it if any shou'd take it by snatches, picking a Piece here and there, since without they read the whole, they wou'd miss that Oeconomy and Order of the Design which you so much commend.

Wesley quoted from his own poem, in XIV.29.5, in answer to a question whether Christ was visible to the people when he was set on the pinnacle of the temple.

> *Flee* [misprint for *Thee*] *from yon Court, the Vested*
>   *Priests perceive,*
> *Their Morning-Sacrifice unfinish'd leave.*
>   (III, 146–147)

and again:

> *Plunge hence, in sight of all th'admiring Town,*
> *And in the Altars Flames waft softly down:*
> *So shall the wondring World due Honour bring,*
> *At once adore the God, and hail the King.*
>   (III, 1017–1020)

He also combined business with pleasure in repaying a friend for past favors with such a complimentary poem as

To Mr. Tate on His New Poem of the late Promotions, &c., in which he drew close the bonds of the poetic fraternity:

> Shame on the *Blatent Beast* which lewdly says
> We of th'inspired, *Barter,* or *Sell* our *Praise:*
> 'Tis a *just Debt,* to *shining Vertue* due,
> From you to your great *Theme,* from *us* to *you.*
> . . . .
> Thy easy *Numbers, soft* as *Love,* present
> *Chains,* not of *Slavery,* but of *Ornament:*
> The *willing Words* in *decent Order* flow,
> Of each we say it *cou'd not but be so.*
> With such a *pow'rful,* yet a *gentle sway*
> High *Heav'n* commands, and all the *World* obey.
> (XIV.3)

iii

The tone of the *Mercury*'s verse was not always lofty. There was plenty of doggerel and some playful, clever acrostics too. On one occasion the Athenians, with no apology to Dryden or Shadwell, urged themselves to write duller doggerel than anyone else:

> Rouze *Athens!* Rouze! or thou art excell'd.
> And for ever and ever out-*Doggerell'd.*
> *Flecknoe*'s an Ass, and *Jordan,* all men know it,
> And *S---le*'s no better; here's your true *City-Poet!*
> *Hexameter, Pentameter,* all together,
> *Pindaric* or *Saphic,* chuse you whether!
> . . . .
> You are inspir'd, there's no doubt of ye
> With *Beef-Broth* strong, and potent *Coffee!*
> For Natural Dullness, Line for Line,
> Could never reach a pitch like thine.
> (XV.25.5)

In similar vein an acrostic query describing "SOBERNESS" was answered with one on "DULLNESS" that incidentally puffed the Athenians' original meeting place:

> D ull, dull Acrostick! wherefore art thou come?
> U ndoubtedly thy Author's drunk with Mum.
> L ate did he sit, and plenteously carouse
> L ikeliest of any at *Smith's Coffee-house.*
> (VI.13.6)

Nothing of Dunton's or Sault's indicates any talent for verse. In the *Life and Errors,* Dunton proved he could write doggerel and acrostics, although he was not above claiming as his own a good poem by Carew and a bad one by Swift.[17] Sault produced 350 lines of rimed couplets in *A New Poem on the Late Illustrious Congress at the Hague* (1691), dedicated to Lord Lansdowne and characterized by such gems as "*Health* to the *Royal Pair,* and may we see/ Their *Portraitures* in a long *Progeny.*" The many slurs against Wesley's writing in the *Life and Errors* reflect Dunton's later jealousy of his brother-in-law, but there is no evidence of a break between the two men before 1697. In the *Gentleman's Journal* for April 1694 (pp.75–77), Peter Motteux published "An Ode on St. Cecilia's Day" by Samuel Wesley, with a headnote that explains why there was little of Wesley's verse in the *Mercury* after 1693:

> I have here an Ode written sometime since by Mr. Wesley, which has not been seen in Town, and so cannot well be said to want the charms of Novelty. I am sure it has all the others that can be expected in a piece of that nature, and we might be apt to censure its ingenious Author's resolution not to *versifie* any more, if any thing could be attempted in a poetic style, after the *Life of Christ,* with which Mr. *Wesley* has taken his leave of the Muses.

Fortunately for Dunton, at the time when his poetical brother-in-law ceased to "versifie," a new star arose, a young woman of Dissenting background who nevertheless had her thoughts transformed to verse by merely repeating the name of Dryden.

iv

The *Mercury,* trying to serve as a means for popular education, had almost from the outset encouraged correspondence from women upon cultural subjects. Dunton had even tried to set up an adjunct publication, the *Ladies Mercury,* which appeared on four successive Mondays, 28 February to 17 March 1693; before that, in the first volume of the *Mercury,* he had provided much space for questions from women.

The most important question was that which first appeared in May 1691, *"Whether it be proper for Women to be Learned?"* (I.18.6). The answer to it states clearly the Athenians' approval of education for women. Some, they observed, are happy enough if women "can distinguish between their **Husbands Breaches** and another *mans.*" Still others think it pardonable if women can read but would not trust them with writing. *"A Degree yet higher,* are those who would have 'em read **Plays, Novels,** and **Romances,** with perhaps a little History, but by all means are for terminating their Studies there, and not letting 'em meddle with the **Edge-tools of Philosophy,** for these wise Reasons, . . . it takes 'em off from their Domestick Affairs, . . . fills 'em too *full of themselves,* and makes 'em apt to despise others." The Athenians listed these objections for the purpose of rejecting them, for their conclusion was that women had as noble souls as men, "a finer Genius, and generally quicker Apprehensions," and should therefore be allowed to become as learned as they were able.

Most of the answers to women's questions in the *Athenian Mercury* were given in the spirit shown at this early date. The *Ladies Mercury* may have failed precisely because it apologized for its presumption in emulating the Athenians. Its first number promised no encroachment upon the Athenians' province of examining "Learning, Nature, Arts, Science, *and indeed the whole World."* Rather, the newcomers were *"contented to bound our narrow* Speculation, *to only that little Sublunary,* Woman. *Whilst* Religion *and* Heaven, *and other Sublime Points, are your* Gamaliel Studies; *We are for sitting down with* Martha's *humbler part, a little homely* Cookery, *the dishing up of a small Treat of* Love, &c." In the second number the writers asked that they might not be troubled with "Questions relating to *Learning, Religion* &c. we resolving . . . not to infringe on the Athenians."

Dunton found a new way of pleasing the ladies, however, within the same year that the *Ladies Mercury* failed. On 21 October 1693 (XI.30), the *Mercury* printed two poems, introduced with the following note:

> *We receiv'd the following Verses from a Woman, which tho' they contain no Question, and are somewhat uncorrect, yet for the Honour of her Sex, and that uncommon Genius that shines in 'em, we think not improper to insert in our* Mercury.

The poems were sent by Miss Elizabeth Singer, of Frome in Somersetshire. Within the next two years she was to contribute many poems and become known to the readers of the *Mercury* only as "the Pindarick Lady." Three days after printing her first poems, the *Mercury* devoted an entire number to eight questions *"from the* Poetical Lady," including the request for a reading list, cited earlier in this chapter. The questions range from a serious one, *"Whether it's not a Crime to be True to one that's False to his Honour, his King and his Countrey?"* to a playful one, *"Who was—but stay, you can't Conjure, and therefore I was as good e'ne let that Query alone"* (XII.1). The Athenians replied: "And least We shou'd be taken for Conjurers, We'll for the self-same Reason let alone the answering it."

The Athenians' high regard for educated women was again emphasized soon after this. In answer to the question whether women could make any considerable progress in learning, they replied that women had superior powers of memory, due to the moist constitution of their brain, and that their sedentary and solitary life was further favorable to study. As for other sciences, if women joined together with men in the discovery of them, there was no doubt but that their curiosity would sharpen men's wits.

Since knowledge was dependent upon the purity and simplicity of the individual, the safest course women could take to preserve their purity and chastity was to make provision of learning and knowledge. "For 'tis a thing unheard of, that a Woman was learn'd, and not Chast and Continent; which the Ancients design'd to represent by *Minerva* the Goddess of Sciences, and the Nine Muses, all Virgins." In their praise of Elizabeth Singer's first poem in the *Mercury*, a paraphrase of Habbakkuk 3, the Athenians made plain that its author was the epitome of their womanly ideal. To

Miss Singer's forty-eight lines, they responded with eighty-four of their own, beginning:

> We yield! we yield! the *Palm,* bright Maid! be *thine!*
> How *vast* a *Genius sparkles* in each *Line!*
> How *Noble* all! how *Loyal!* how *Divine!*
> (XI.30)

From this poem we learn that Miss Singer was the author of the "late Pastoral Poem," praised earlier by Gildon in the *History of the Athenian Society* (p.25). The Athenians wrote:

> Great *William* claims thy Lyre, and claims thy *Voice,*
> All *like himself* the *Hero* shew,
> Which *none* but thou canst *do.*
> At *Landen* paint him, *Spears* and *Trophies* round,
> And *twenty thousand Deaths* upon the slippery ground:
> . . . .
>
> Thus sing, *Bright Maid!* thus and yet *louder* sing,
> Thy *God* and *King!* . . .

This encomium to Elizabeth Singer, ridiculous though it is, indicates the Williamite fervor of the time. The Athenians may indeed have been making certain that their political stance would prevent another suspension, but their made-to-order verse also indicates a change in the character of the periodical, toward a more personal journalism. Their compliments and exhortations elicited from Elizabeth Singer many more contributions, all introduced with additional admiring commentary. In a little over two years, two dozen of her poems were printed, the last in December 1695 (XIX.18). *Poems on Several Occasions,* published by Dunton in 1696, included all these in its sixty-seven pages, along with some replies penned by the Athenians and twenty more of her poems which had not appeared in the *Mercury.* The *Miscellaneous Works in Prose and Verse of Mrs. Elizabeth Rowe,* posthumously edited and published in 1739, contains none of the poems from her maiden work. Her reputation in the eighteenth century was not as the Pindarick Lady, in fact, but as Mrs. Rowe. Widowed in 1715 after a marriage of only five years, and until her death in 1737 devoted to pious works and devotional poetry, she became a protegée of Isaac Watts, who warned Dunton to stop referring to her.[18] Her verse was imitated by Pope in *Eloisa to Abelard*,[19] Matthew Prior conceived a hopeless passion for her,[20] and Dr. Johnson, though he felt that all human eulogies were vain for one applauded by angels, yet expressed admiration of "her brightness of imagery, her purity of sentiments."[21] Her volume of imaginary conversations in the hereafter, *Friendship in Death* (1728), enjoyed a vogue and earned from the German Romantics Klopstock and Wieland the appellation "die göttliche Rowe."[22]

For the Athenians, Elizabeth Singer was a kind of female poet laureate, dedicated to defending King William in verse against all his enemies. *Poems on Several Occasions* has a prefatory poem extolling her modesty—"Prepare then for that Fame which you despise!"—and praying:

> Let Heaven and Heaven's Viceregent always share
> Your noblest Thoughts, and your most Dutious care.
> WILLIAM's a Name, you're Fated to Record,
> No Pen but yours can match the Heroes Sword.
> . . . .
> Let harden'd Traitors know what 'tis to abuse
> The Patience of a King and of a Muse
> Let 'em no more a Monarch's Justice dare,
> Draw off his side, at once, and END THE WAR!

Philomela herself expressed veneration toward Dryden in *A Pindarick, to the Athenian Society,* as

> *Dryden!* A name, I ne're could yet rehearse,
> But straight my thoughts *were all transform'd to verse.*

So inspired, she went on to praise the Athenians for the example they had set: "So much the *heavenly form* did win:/ Which to my eyes *you'd painted vertue in.*" She closed on a note of humility not unlike that expressed in the earlier pindaric by Swift:

> Oh, could my verse;
> With *equal flights,* to after times rehearse,
> Your *fame:* It should as bright and Death-less be;
> As that immortal flame you've rais'd in me.
> A flame which time:

> And Death it self, wants power to controul,
> Not more sublime,
> Is the *divine composure of my Soul;*
> A friendship so exalted and immense,
> A *female breast* did ne're before commence.
>
> (XVII.29)

These lines answer to Steele's description in the *Spectator* of "Numbers . . . as loose and unequal, as those in which the *British* ladies sport their *Pindariques.*"[23] The significance of such writing as hers was better demonstrated in *Poems on Several Occasions,* where in an admiring preface Elizabeth Johnson makes an impassioned defense of women's intellectual powers, and numbers Miss Singer among the *"Bunduca's* and *Zenobia's,* . . . *Sappho's,* and *Behn's* and *Schurman's,* and *Orinda's,* who have humbled the most haughty of our Antagonists, and made 'em do Homage to our *Wit,* as well as our *Beauty."* We may smile at the names in this roll call and at its extravagant assertion of complete triumph, but both features were symptomatic of the increasingly liberal attitude toward the female intellectual. The Athenians with their cries of "We yield!" may appear overindulgent of the literary faults of their female poet, but they were not patronizing. Their consistently respectful attitude toward the Pindarick Lady was more than reaction to a precocious talent. She provided a focus for their feminist sympathies. Dunton, as always somewhat mischievous, once teased his wife by starting a "Platonic" correspondence with Miss Singer. The younger woman, "being fully satisfy'd there was nothing but Innocence (or *a Platonick Courtship*) design'd," enclosed in a letter to Dunton one to his wife in the expectation that Mrs. Dunton would have *"a FEMININE ITCH"* to open the envelope. Iris replied to Philomela that she was not wrong in her expectation; such eavesdropping was *"a Freedom we Women take, that are bless'd with such* obliging Husbands *as I have."* She was able to divert herself *"with the Thoughts of that Pure and Vertuous Friendship, which was begun between* Philomela *and* Philaret." She *"ever esteemed* Platonick-Love *to be the most Noble, and thought it might be allowed by all"* (LE,pp.265–266).

Wesley and Dunton were married to women of extraordinary background and capabilities. Elizabeth Dunton managed her husband's bookshop. Susannah Wesley influenced the careers of her most illustrious sons as much or more than Samuel did. Mrs. Dunton tolerated her husband's whims and appreciated his good qualities, and his best acts in support of greater liberty and respect for women were accomplished while she was at his side.

Elizabeth Singer enjoyed her small share of an increasingly liberal attitude toward the female intellectual. At first men expressed their wonder not that a woman could write well but that she could write at all; but starting early in the Augustan age a steadily increasing number of women, many of them encouraged by the poets, wits, and philosophers of the age, published poetry under their own names with considerable success. Elizabeth Singer's frequent contributions were on subjects that had been established by Cowley and exploited by his admirers in quantity during the last forty years of the century: scriptural heroes, divine or seraphic love, and the soul. No innovator in verse, she wrote pindarics, which were fashionable and free enough of metrical restrictions to permit a modest talent to flourish. The *Mercury*, as the most copious publisher of poems during that time, had a steady and highly respectable source of supply in Elizabeth Singer.

The *Athenian Mercury*'s muse was a Christian one, at first Orthodox, but not rigidly so, then Dissenting, but gently and thoughtfully so. Samuel Wesley and Elizabeth Singer together contributed to the personal quality of the *Mercury* in ways not possible in prose answers to questions. When they wrote for Dunton both were young and enthusiastic, delighted to appear in print, and not yet made grave and introspective by the trials of life. Both were caught up in the reforming spirit of the last decade of the century. Their verse breathes confidence in the triumph of virtue, the power of human and divine love, and the overthrow of evil. To Dunton belongs the credit for the shaping idea of the *Mercury,* but "the Poetical Member" of the Athenian Society and "the Pindarical Lady" gave to the periodical another of its unique qualities for its time.

CHAPTER 7

[1] V.11 (Tue 5 Jan 92); other poetical numbers are: VI.2 (Sat 6 Feb 92); VI.8 (Sat 27 Feb 92); VI.13 (Tue 8 Mar 92); VI.15 (Tue 15 Mar 92); VII.5 (Tue 12 Apr 92);VII.15 (Tue 17 May 92);VIII.6 (Sat 17 Sep 92) [1st no. after suspension]; VIII.10 (Sat 1 Oct 92) ["A Challenge to Vice and Atheism"]; VIII.14 (Sat 15 Oct 92); VIII.21 (Tue 8 Nov 92); IX.7 (Tue 3 June 93); IX.22 (Sat 25 Feb 93); X.3 (Tue 4 Apr 93); X.11 (Tue 2 May 93); X.22 (Sat 10 June 93) [The *Doggerel Merc.*]; X.27 (Tue 27 Jul 93); X.29 (Tue 4 Jul 93); XI.13 (Tue 22 Aug 93); XI.22 (Sat 23 Sep 93) [*Dogg.*]; XI.30 (Sat 21 Oct 93); XII.14 (Sat 9 Dec 93); XII.22 (Sat 6 Jan 94); XII.27 (Tue 23 Jan 94) "To the most Illustrious Prince LEWIS of *Baden,* On his Happy Arrival in *England*" and "The *Jacobite* Verses To the Invincible *French* LEWIS"; XIII.3 (Tue 13 Feb 94) "A PARAPHRASE *Of* David's *Elegy* on Saul *and* Jonathan, 2 *Sam.* 1"; XIII.30 (Sat 19 May 94); XIV.3 (Tue 29 May 94) *"To Mr.* TATE, ON *His New Poem of the late Promotions,* &c."; Questions 1 and 2 "From the Pindarical Lady"; XIV.5 (Tue 5 June 94) 1. "From a Woman"; 2. ". . . from the Pindarical Lady"; XV.4.1,2 (Sat 15 Sep 94); XV.13.1,2 (Tue 16 Oct 94); XV.21 (Tue 13 Nov 94); "*Mr.* Mason's *Poem upon Death";* XV.25.1–5 (Tue 27 Nov 94); XVII.8 (Sat 27 Apr 95) *"Doggrel Mercury";* XVII.22 (Sat 15 Jun 95); XVII.23 (Tue 18 Jun 96) "all written by the ingenious Pindarick Lady"; XVII.29 (Tue 9 Jul 95) *"A Pindarick,* to the Athenian Society" by the Pindarick Lady; XVIII.4 (Sat 27 Jul 95) *"To* Codrus," *"A Pastoral Elegy"* by the Pindarick Lady; XVIII.11 (Tue 20 Aug 95) "*By Dispair,"* "To Orestes"; XVIII.16 (Sat 7 Sep 95) four poems by the Pindarick Lady; XVIII.22 (Sat 28 Sep 95) *"To Celinda,"* "Thoughts on Death" by the Pindarick Lady; XVIII.28 (Sat 19 Oct 95) "AN Hymn to Learning, Written upon occasion of Ladies Dispising it in Womankind, &c. DEDICATED TO THE Athenian Society, *By a Young Lady";* XIX.17 (Tue 24 Dec 95) four poems by the Pindarick Lady; XIX.18 (Sat 28 Dec 95) a poem by the Pindarick Lady; XIX.19 (Tue 31 Dec 95) Poetical Mercury; XIX.21 (Tue 7 Jan 96) 3 poems by the Pindarick Lady; XIX.26 (Sat 25 Jan 96) "Morecraft the Usurer Over a *heap* of *bad Mony.*"

[2] In XII.1.4 (Tue 24 Oct 93), Gawen Douglas's translation, which Wesley favored, is recommended as the best.

[3] V.1.5 asks for their thoughts upon *"the Late Pastoral Poem,* &c."

[4] Norris, *Cursory Reflection upon a Book call'd, An Essay concerning Human Understanding* (ed. Gilbert D. McEwen), Los Angeles, Augustan Reprint Society, 1961, p.8.

[5] See Chapter 1, pp.6–7 and n.15.

[6] LE, A8–b2. Also in the *Voyage Round the World.* Dunton noted

(LE, b *verso*): "*This POEM was sent to me in a Letter, whilst I was on my Travels in the Year* 1686; *and was answered in a Letter, Dated from* Cologne, *which coming to my* Reverend Friend *Six Days sooner than he expected he could not forbear to think it a* MIRACLE."

[7] H. A. Beecham, "Samuel Wesley, Senior: New Biographical Evidence," *Renaissance and Modern Studies*, Univ. of Nottingham, 1963. VII, 88–89; 106–107.

[8] *Strenæ Natalitæ Sereniss. Principis Walliæ*, 1688, Sig. U.

[9] *A Sermon concerning Reformation of Manners*, London, Charles Harper.

[10] Beecham, "Samuel Wesley, Senior," p.106. John Wesley (b.1703), published a number of anecdotes concerning his father. One of these, in the *Methodist Magazine* (1784), p.606, was that Samuel left his wife when she refused to say "Amen" to his prayer for King William, telling her that if they needs must have two kings they must then have two beds. A letter of Mrs. Wesley's written in 1709, in which she called William a usurper, lends some credence to the anecdote. See Tyerman, *Life of Samuel Wesley*, p.252.

[11] Wesley's note to the phrase (*"Hail* Mary!") was apologetic: "I hope there's nothing *superstitious* in this *Poetical Address* to the *Blessed Virgin*, as I'm sure there's no *Flattery* in that which follows it, nor will either therefore offend any *judicious Reader*, any more than *Hail, bright* Cecilia, &c." *Life of Christ* (1693), p.68.

[12] "To Her most Sacred Majesty MARY, By the Grace of GOD. QUEEN of *Great Britain, France* and *Ireland*, &c. This POEM Is most humbly Dedicated BY *Her Majesties most Loyal, Most Obedient, And most Dutiful Subject and Servant*, S. Wesley" [following title page].

Tillotson wrote to the Bishop of Salisbury, 31 August 1694: "My Lord Marquis of Normanby having made Mr. Waseley [sic] his chaplain, sent Colonel Fitz gerald to propose him for a bishopric in Ireland, wherewith I acquainted her Majesty; who, according to her true judgment did by no means think fit. Their Majesties have made Dr Foley Bishop of Down, and Dean Pulleyn Bishop of Cloyne." Tyerman, *Life*, p.194. (Had Wesley been made Bishop of Down he would have been Swift's first bishop.)

[13] Ltr., Samuel Wesley to Samuel Wesley, Jr. dtd. Epworth, 17 Dec 1730. Tyerman, *Life.*, pp.409–410. (John Wesley was at the time stigmatized as "Father of the Holy Club" at Oxford, and Samuel the Younger had offended Walpole with his satire on the Cabinet.)

[14] For an introductory treatment of this essay, along with its text and that of the *Epistle to a Friend concerning Poetry* (1700), see Edward N. Hooker, *Series Two: Essays on Poetry, No. 2*, (1947), Los Angeles, Augustan Reprint Society.

[15] "Notes on the Third Book," *Life of Christ*, p. 108. Beginning with *Paradise Regained* IV.411, "From many a horrid rift abortive pour'd. . . ." Wesley used forty of Milton's lines, altering them to maintain rimed couplets and interpolating many of his own composition, in III.639–776.

[16]   . . . from the Face of *Men* remov'd away,
     In a mean Cot compos'd of *Reeds* and *Clay*,

> Wafting in Sighs th'*uncomfortable Day:*
> Near where th'*unhospitable Humber* roars
> *Devouring* by degrees the neighb'ring *Shores:*
> *Life of Christ* I.749–753 (p.20)

[17] See Chap. 12, p.216.

[18] See LE(1818), p.xxix. A letter written in 1717 and signed "J. W." warns Dunton to stop using Mrs. Rowe's name in print. Hatfield, p.345, guesses the writer to have been Watts.

[19] Compare *Eloisa to Abelard,* II.99–100: "Alas how chang'd! What sudden horrors rise! / A naked Lover bound and bleeding lies!" with "Upon the Death of her Husband" *Miscellaneous Works* (1739), I.113–114: "The smiling vision takes its hasty flight, / And scenes of horror swim before my sight. / Grief, despair, in all their terrors rise, / A dying lover pale and gasping lies."

[20] See "To the Author of Love and Friendship: A Pastoral," *Literary Works of Matthew Prior* (ed. Wright and Spears), Oxford, 1959. I.199–200.

[21] James Boswell, *Life* (ed. Hill) Oxford, 1887. I.312–313.

[22] Theodor Vetter, *Die göttliche Rowe,* Zürich, Friedrich Schultheis, 1894, p.4. For a recent appreciation of her prose work, see John J. Richetti, "Mrs. Elizabeth Rowe: The Novel as Polemic," PMLA, Vol. 82, No. 7 (Dec 1967), pp.522–529.

[23] Richard Steele in the *Spectator* (ed. Donald F. Bond), Oxford, Clarendon Press, 1965. No. 366. III.376.

8

Science for Everyman

The Athenian Society has an undeserved reputation for charlatanism in science. The discovery that the "Great Unknown" wrote for money and were controlled by a bookseller has led to the assumption that their answers to scientific questions, and even the questions themselves, were not to be trusted. Since the Athenian Society was a commercial venture its members did not display the dignity and the disinterested love of learning shown by some of the contemporary Fellows of the Royal Society. The absence of a purpose as lofty as that of the Royal Society, however, should not be taken as proof that the Athenians were exploiters of ignorance. The questions about science in the *Mercury* reveal, in fact, a strong interest in scientific principles, and the frequency of explicit and informed answers shows that the Athenians were conversant with recent works in English on scientific subjects. The amount they wrote about science was second in quantity only to the *Philosophical Transactions* during the same period, and covered the entire spectrum of scientific subjects. The reports in the *Philosophical Transactions,* however, were meant to be read by scientists, while the *Mercury* purveyed rudimentary information to those who knew relatively little about science.

The word *science* in the 1690's did not have the same meaning as it does today. "Natural philosophy," as it was called by most writers, meant the study of the phenomena of the physical world and the establishment of generalizations about them, but it still had, with a few notable exceptions, a somewhat limited concept of objective observation of phenomena. There was ready acceptance of the experimental findings of such men as Newton, Hooke, Gilbert, Boyle, and

Harvey, but the general public was not really aware of the basis of scientific findings in careful observation. In the *Mercury* there are examples of the acceptance of incomplete observations upon scanty authority, and of failure to distinguish among the products of exact observation, mere speculation, and fanciful notions with no foundation in fact. Such occasional indiscriminate acceptance of half-truth, however, should not be allowed to overshadow what is also present —recognition of the work of the leading scientists of the time, and frequent, competent popularization of their ideas.

The large number of questions about science in a literary periodical is significant in itself. Their number in individual volumes of the *Mercury* varied erratically, from a low of seven in the twelfth volume and nine each in the first and nineteenth to a high of one hundred twenty-four in the second.[1] The average is about thirty-nine questions per volume, and the total of seven hundred sixty amounts to about twenty percent of all questions in the twenty volumes of the *Mercury*.[2]

The quantitative distribution of questions tells something of the history of the *Mercury*. Volume One was experimental, rushing off in all directions, mentioning over two hundred literary, historical, philosophical, and scientific sources, in support of answers on over five hundred topics. At a point about midway in the eighteen dated numbers of the first volume the agreement was drawn up naming Wesley and Sault as Dunton's writers for the project, and Dunton alleged that John Norris, too, agreed to advise them *gratis* (LE, p.256). The small number of science questions in Volume One as a whole and their nearly complete absence from the undated numbers, nineteen through thirty, show an early lack of plan. Not until the Athenians had agreed upon the scope of their work and effected a division of labor based on their respective talents did scientific questions assume their due share of space. Even then the writers were somewhat handicapped by the lack of reliable up-to-date information. Indexed scientific works were still scarce.

The large number of science questions in Volume Two, however, suggests that some self-criticism was soon at work.

After the deluge of facetious and trivial questions of the first volume, mere novelties became much less prominent and were replaced by solid facts about the physical world. Both Sault and Wesley were at their neediest during the period of the early volumes. Wesley, first as a chaplain, and then as an obscure country parson, wrote as much as he could. Richard Sault, prior to his success as a tutor and author of a textbook on algebra, found that general science brought him a shilling a page.

Only three numbers of the second volume lacked science questions. In this volume for the first time appeared questions that were to become familiar in later volumes because the editors, tired of pointing out that a question had already been discussed, answered anew without reference to earlier pronouncements. Some of the most common concerned the ebb and flow of the sea, the existence of a perfect vacuum, earthquakes, the spots on the moon, the element of fire, and the relationship between man and the other animals as representing divine order.[3] In Volume Two all conceivable variations were played on these themes, and a new feature, medical advice of a very simple nature, was added.[4]

There were, surprisingly, sixty questions on science in the ten numbers of Volume Twenty, the last volume of the Athenian project. Only a few of these had appeared previously: one on the nature of light, a great favorite throughout the six years of publication, another perennial about the spots on the moon, and one on the difference in the floating position of a drowned man and a drowned woman, in the answer to which the editors contradicted an earlier opinion.[5] Since voluntary suspension of the *Mercury* had been announced in the Preface to Volume Eighteen, and had actually been in effect for fifteen months between the nineteenth and twentieth volumes, it would have been no surprise had the final ten numbers of the periodical consisted altogether of warmed-over questions. Volume Twenty may be simply another example of Dunton's undaunted optimism over his projects, although it is noteworthy that in his subsequent attempts to revive Athenianism he paid little attention to science.

Mere numbers admittedly prove nothing about the scope and reliability of scientific information in the *Mercury,* except that a large number of questions provides more opportunity for error. In *Jonathan Swift's Relations to Science,* Mrs. W. C. DeVane condemns the Athenians as "usurpers of science," "lacking in scientific discrimination" (p.86); they "had not the slightest pretence to being considered of vital importance to the world of science. Not one of the four men concerned in [the Society] was directly connected with the scientific movement. Not one of them could be fairly considered of profound or even notable mental ability except John Norris, and his connection with the Society while decidedly valuable to them was neither definite nor permanent" (pp.84–85).

What we see today as a lack of discrimination appears in the *Mercury* in an occasional acceptance of conclusions based upon insufficient or dubious observation, and in their giving monsters and maggots equal importance with valid scientific data. For example, the first question in Volume Two, Number 1, about the image in a mirror, is answered briefly and accurately; the first question in the next number is about a cow *"which on the* 25th *of* March, 1691, *calv'd a monstrous sort of a Calf, about eight Miles from* Bath *in* Somerset-shire, *with an Excrescence of Flesh like a* Commode." Some crude joking in the answer about the power of the imagination in conception suggests that the writer did not take the question very seriously. The writer also cites the answer to an earlier question on prenatal influences, in which he had declared that he did "indeed very much doubt the *Truth* of some prodigious *Instances* which are brought on this *Head,* and still must take leave to do so, 'til we have some more unquestionable *Authority* for't than Sir *K. D.*'s [Kenelm Digby], who being a *Traveller* as well as the famous Sir *H. B.* [Henry Blount] has been thought by some to take as great a *Liberty* in *Physicks* as the other in *History"* (I.15.2). Blount wrote *A Voyage into the Levant . . . with particular observations concerning the moderne condition of the Turks* (1636).

Although Newton has been pictured as a lonely explorer

of uncharted regions, his scientific contemporaries were more characteristically desirous of sharing their knowledge by putting it into easily understandable terms. Robert Boyle, the patron saint of the *Mercury,* was outstanding in his charitable concern for the dissemination of knowledge about natural philosophy among those unable to educate themselves. This was the attitude that influenced the Athenians, and although they could not think as well as Boyle, they could write better. They made no claims of infallibility or omniscience in scientific matters, although their most positive answers are those about algebra and geometry. In these Sault demonstrated an understanding of the latest developments then arising from the work of Descartes, Leibnitz, and Newton and already popularized to some degree by John Wallis.

Like many of the virtuosi, who were after all seeking knowledge even though sometimes in ridiculous ways, the Athenians sometimes made wrong conclusions based upon incomplete investigation, influenced, as the entire age was, by the open conflict between orthodox religious belief and the emerging concepts of natural philosophy leading to natural religion. In this they made the common mistake of fearing that science could and would replace religion.

Volume Eight, which took five and one-half months to publish because of the suspension from July to September 1692, was third highest in the number of science questions, second highest having been Volume Three; and no subsequent volumes except Twenty came near its total.[6] The resolution taken in the Preface to Volume Seven, written at the completion of that volume, accounts in part for the large number of science questions in Volume Eight: "having a great many *abstruse* and *ingenious* Mathematical Questions upon the *Board,* in order to dispatch 'em with all convenient *speed,* we are resolv'd to insert *one* or *more* in every *Mercury,* 'till they are quite clear'd. . . ."

Then too, after the suspension science could have held an appeal for Dunton as a "safe" subject to pursue until he had learned how he stood with the new Licenser. One recalls that the discussion of politics and religion was forbidden in the by-laws of the Royal Society, and it was publication of a political opinion, even though obliquely phrased, that had closed down the *Mercury*.

The smallest number of science questions in any single volume of the *Mercury,* just seven, appeared in Volume Twelve. The small number there and the low average in the seven succeeding volumes coincide with that period in Sault's life when he wrote the *Second Spira* as well as an algebra textbook and a two-volume translation of *La Recherche de la verité* of Nicholas Malebranche.[7] The falling off of questions about science was a negative demonstration of Sault's importance to the Athenian project. It leads one to take more seriously the praise heaped upon him in the *History of the Athenian Society,* in which Gildon wrote:

> All that I have to inform the World of the Mathematician, is, that he is the Person that first put the design in execution, . . . and I shall only add here, that his Learning is as universal, as his Sence of things is *fine,* and *curious.* So that this *Society* seems to be composed by something more than human Judgment, in selecting able men, since each of them is sufficient to perform this mighty task alone. (p.14)

On the last page of the *History,* Gildon printed a letter from the mathematician, disowning the name of mathematician and modestly disclaiming the praise already showered upon him, for he looked upon *"the Applause and Scandal of the Age to be* Synonimous words *amongst such as are really wise, and the reverse of 'em much more eligible to* Sir, your humble Servant, *R. S."* (p.36).

As a mathematician Sault was fortunate at this time in his association with William Leybourne, who had published for many years on the subjects represented in *Pleasure with Profit,* "Consisting of RECREATIONS OF Divers Kinds, viz. Numerical, Geometrical, Mechanical, Statical, Astronomical, Horometrical, Cryptographical, Magnetical, Authomatical, Chymical, and Historical." To this *omnium gatherum* in folio, Sault's *Treatise on Algebra,* separately paginated, was appended. Bearing the imprint of both Dunton and Richard Baldwin, the title page announced a design "to Recreate Ingenious Spirits; and to induce them to make farther scrutiny into these . . . Sublime Sciences. AND To divert them from following such Vices, to which Youth (in this Age) are so much Inclin'd."

The separate title page of Sault's work announces that the work was done "According to the late Improvements, applied to Numerical Questions and Geometry; with a New Series for the speedy Extraction of Roots; as also a Converging Series for all manner of adsected Equations."

Sault was identified on the title page as Master of "The MATHEMATICK SCHOOL in *Adam's Court,* in *Broad-street,* near the *Royal Exchange,*" and so he advertised himself in the *Mercury* for the first time in June 1693 (X.27).

Leybourne was a man given to mouth-filling, Urquhartian titles for his works: *Panorganon, Astroscopium, Panarithmologia.* Like Sault, he supported himself by teaching mathematics, advertising that he boarded young gentlemen students, and giving as references a globemaker, a mathematical instrument maker, and a hydrographer. Both he and Sault were aligned with the technicians of science, so essential to the Royal Society and so much respected by all experimentalists. As early as 1674 Leybourne had been engaged to make a survey of the property of the Stationers Company,[8] and Dunton praised him in later years as having done "as much Honour to the Mathematicks, as most Persons you can Name—*There's something masterly in all he writes*—As to his *Cursus Mathematicus,* and his *Panarithmologia,* they will never be equal'd" (LE,p.327).

Sault showed in the preface to his book his alertness to the new relationship discovered between algebra and geometry:

> Algebra depends upon the same Definitions and Axioms that a considerable part of Euclid's Elements do, and may therefore very justly be call'd a New Geometry, tho it has no small Advantage above that which is commonly called by that Name; since the Substance of

whole Sciences at once are sometimes comprehended in one single Algebraic Theorem.

He was not reluctant to advertise his own book and belittle a rival's in the *Mercury,* in the course of answering a request to solve an algebraic equation:

> . . . to avoid an affected Equation in this and most other Questions, and by consequence to avoid the Trouble that Mr. *Kersey* and his Followers are always put to, let the same Question he proposed, let b (as before) $= 4225$. . . . Which in much more simple Terms than the Common Methods will give for speedy and short Methods of resolving Numeral Questions, whether by one or more Positions, whether determin'd or undetermin'd, see the NEW TREATISE OF ALGEBRA, lately writ by Mr. *Sault,* Mathem. in *Adam's-Court* in *Broad-street.* . . .[9]

Sault's contemporary reputation is shown by his participation in a remarkable scheme to set up a kind of tutoring school to be financed by a lottery. Forty thousand tickets were offered at twenty shillings each by a group of London booksellers, including Dunton, all of them respectable members of the trade. An advertisement of "The ROYAL ACADEMIES" appeared on Friday 22 February 1695 in *A Collection for Improvement of Husbandry and Trade* (VI.134), occupying half a folio page in the weekly journal published by John Houghton, an apothecary and Fellow of the Royal Society.

The list of teachers and subjects is impressive. The great Henry Purcell was to be one of the four teachers of organ and harpsichord. The lute, viol, violin, and flute were to be taught, as well as singing, dancing, and fencing. There were to be six language teachers, of Latin, Greek, Hebrew, French, Spanish, and Italian; and two teachers of *"Writing,"* which was to include "Arithmetick, *Vulgar* and *Decimal,"* and "Merchants Accompts."

Richard Sault and Abraham Demoivre were to be responsible for a staggering array of subjects: algebra, geometry, trigonometry (plain and spherical), gauging, use of the globes, projection of the spheres, geography, dialing i.e. surveying, astronomy, navigation, fortification, gunnery, optics, perspective, "Dioptricks, Catoptricks, Mechanicks," architecture, converging series, conic sections, and "Arithmetic of Infin."—all these offered in Latin, French, or English.

The lucky winners of the lottery tickets were to attend either of "two great *Academies*," near the Royal Exchange or in Covent Garden,

> where all that have Prizes shall be admitted, having Power to Chuse any one Language, Art, or Science, for each Prize, and to alter that Choice as often as they please by Transferring their Tickets for some other Accomplishment, paying only five Shillings for each Transfer, thus may they continue, learning as many things as their Several Capacities can acquire in the time of four years.

The advertisement was repeated throughout March in Houghton's *Collection* and the *Mercury* advertised the project in April and in July, asserting success and support for the academies. In April the lottery was about to be staged:

> *The Undertakers of the* Royal Academies, *having met with great Incouragement from his Majesty, as also by the Advancement of a considerable sum of money upon it, have resolved to draw the 25th of this Instant* April; *and those that come not in by that time, will lose considerable advantages.* (XVII.5)

In July, however, the lottery was forgotten. New proposals, on a folio half-sheet, described the Academy as self-supporting.[10] It was to have five hundred extramural and one hundred internal or boarding students, the former at six pounds a year, the latter at thirty pounds, or fifty pounds for a student and his servant. Each student was to take one "science" at a time. Five persons were to be chosen from among the parents or guardians of the students to serve as trustees. The undertakers were to hand over three thousand pounds for the trustees to deposit as security for carrying out the project. Low tuition rates were possible

> because his Majesty has been graciously pleas'd to promise, that so soon as it shall please God to bless us with a peace, he will very considerably encourage the Design, and in the mean time has given us £1000 towards the building of a very *large and noble Academy*. . . .

Richard Sault was one of those ready and able to serve in the cause of popular education. He was well prepared for such a venture by his experience of writing for the *Mercury* and his association with Wesley and Dunton. It is a pity that circumstances did not favor the Royal Academy. Although the subscription books were advertised as open and waiting, the absence of any further public notice after July 1695 must be taken as mute evidence of a still birth.

Sault himself was last seen in print in an article in Latin published in Volume Twenty of the *Philosophical Transactions* in 1698.[11] Its subject, the notation of mathematical fluxions, demonstrates the writer's acquaintance with Newton's theory of vanishing quantities. Leibnitz's work is mentioned also. The *Mercury* gives good evidence of how much Sault knew about science. If we had Dunton's account book perhaps we could tell who was responsible for the more sophisticated information and who put in the kind of answer that was more "curiosity" than fact or valid hypothesis. We do know, however, that Sault most probably and Wesley certainly had instruction in the sciences in Dissenting academies, which prepared them to answer many questions on the physical and biological sciences. (There is no evidence that Sault attended a university, and his professional and family relationships with Dunton suggest that he was a Dissenter.)

Although there were great scientists at the Universities, their influence upon undergraduate instruction was negligible in comparison to the sort of instruction provided in the academies of the Dissenters. For these schools, often harassed, forced to move from place to place, and even closed by the sheriff's men, yet showed a greater awareness of scientific progress and made a far more enlightened attempt than the universities to transmit new concepts to the students. Some, such as Isaac Watts, the hymn writer, attended the academies in preference to the universities, and found in scientific instruction a way of reconciling the realities of the physical world with the realities of their religious faith.

The best known of the academies was conducted by Charles Morton at Newington Green and attended by Samuel Wesley and Daniel Defoe.[12] Wesley spoke well of Morton's instruction, but objected to the fanaticism of his fellow students and chose to continue his education at Oxford.[13] For Defoe, the immense practicality of Morton's scientific instruction had great appeal and exercised upon him a strong formative influence.[14]

A look at Morton's *Compendium Physicæ,* the work which Wesley and Defoe studied at the academy, shows us how the seventeenth-century Dissenter, outside the universities, could learn about natural science. The work is made up of thirty-one chapters, each one an essay on a particular discipline or body of knowledge, as in Chapter 1, "Of Physicks or Naturall Phylosophy in Generall;" or an element, as in Chapters 7–10, concerning fire, air, water, and earth; on heavenly bodies, as meteors and comets in Chapters 12–16; on processes, as in Chapter 20, "Of the Growing Faculty;" on human faculties, such as seeing, hearing, smelling, and "Interior Senses," in Chapters 23–26; and finally, in Chapter 31, "Of the World." The modern printed text was taken from a copy dated 1687. It was "modern" for its time, for Morton rejected Cartesianism and frequently quoted Boyle, both actions consistent with the Athenians' anti-Cartesianism and their reverence for the "Christian Virtuoso."[15]

The Athenians belonged to neither of the two most important categories in the scientific community—the university-educated experimentalists and the technologists or instrument makers, whose services made possible increasingly sophisticated enquiries into the secrets of nature.

Wesley was closest to the first sort in that he had some scientific education as well as a university degree earned in classical languages, philosophy, and divinity. Sault was closest to the technologists, as shown by the list of his credentials in the "Royal Academy" proposals.

In a sort of journalistic trinity, Wesley could stand for learning for its own sake, somewhat touched with pedantry; Sault was the "new" scientific man, using the language of mathematics with ease, answering what was asked in the most concise terms, and providing a practical demonstration wherever possible; and Dunton was the holy ghost who made it possible for these polymaths to be heard from, week after week, in a penny sheet.

Perhaps their undertaking was damaged when by 1693 it became apparent that they were neither gentlemen nor virtuosi, and were in fact paid by the number for their services. That Dunton's identification as a bookseller cancelled all respect for the Society, however, is questionable. Swift pilloried him in *A Tale of a Tub*, but as the publisher of editions of bogus gallows confessions, not as the projector of the *Mercury*. The continuation of the *Mercury* up to the time in 1696 when newspapers could flourish in large numbers shows that the periodical continued to be bought and read long after the fictitiousness of the Athenian Society became general knowledge. If we consider that Swift, alert for every new intellectual development early in the decade, did not satisfy himself about the respectability of the *Mercury* in 1691–92 until he had visited Oxford and Moor Park, we can imagine that less aggressive intellects would have accepted the Athenians much more passively and approvingly.

Concealment of questioner and answerer was essential for the *Mercury* as a profitable venture, but the practice of secrecy did not create intellectual irresponsibility, or misguided efforts to torture desired meaning from authorities. Like Bishop John Wilkins, the Athenians did not "think it a good Course to confirm Philosophical Secrets from the Letter of the Scripture, or by abusing some obscure Text in it."[16]

Were the Athenians actually closer to the virtuosi than to the "sincere" inquirers into nature? Bishop Sprat had complained of the virtuosi in his *History of the Royal Society* (1679), that "the chief progress that has hitherto been made, has been rather for the *Collection* of *Curiosities* to adorn *Cabinets* and *Gardens,* than for the Solidity of *Philosophical Discoveries*" (p.386). Yet those whose history he wrote were still predominantly amateurs.

Dunton as a bookseller was certainly devoted to the collection of wonders, rarities, and curiosities. Questions are numerous in the *Mercury* about monstrous births, and poltergeists, apparitions, disembodied voices, mermaids, iron flies, and all sorts of marvelous inventions. Descartes described the wonder-mongers as those "who seek out things that are rare solely to wonder at them, and not for the purpose of really knowing them."[17] But still the common tendency was to marvel at oddities in nature, not to doubt them.

The wonders in the *Mercury,* however, could exist side by side with eminently realistic interpretations of such natural phenomena as eclipses. Asked whether the sun could be totally eclipsed, the Athenian writer pointed out that he could eclipse the sun himself by putting his hand between his eyes and the sun, but the eclipse during the Passion of Christ he thought to be "design'd, tho natural, as Comets, for tokens of Gods displeasure" (V.4.6). A few years later, Bishop Berkeley in his *New Theory of Vision* (1709) conjectured that a person with newly acquired vision might judge ". . . his hand, the interposition whereof might conceal the firmament from his view, equal to the firmament" (sec. LXXIX).

On the humming of the bee, the Athenians reported that "A very Learned Inquirer into Nature has made Experiments, and asserts, That without either Head or Wing they will make such a Noise." They cite Aristotle's explanation that the sound is caused by an inward spirit,

> upon a *Pellicle or little Membrane,* about the Precinct or Pectoral Division of their Body. . . . And

so if the Head or other parts of the Trunk be touched with Oyl, the Sound will be much impaired, if not destroyed; for those being also dry and *Membranous* Parts, by Attrition of the *Spirit,* do help to advance the Noise, and therefore also the Sound is strongest in dry Weather, and very weak in a rainy Season, and towards Winter, for then the Air is moist, and the inward Spirit growing weak makes a more languid and faint Allision upon the Parts. (IV.2.12)

As so often in this time, the construction of mechanical curiosities was thought to prove the high quality of "Learning, Judgment, and Invention" of their time:

Ælian and *Pliny* mention one *Myrmecides,* that wrought out of Ivory a Chariot with four Wheels, and as many Horses, in so little room, that a little Fly might cover them all with her Wings;—As also a Ship with all the Tackling to it, no bigger than that a small Bee might cover it with her Wings. Tho these were great Curiosities, and probably of one Mans Invention, we need not seek beyond the Limits of our Island for its parallel. In the 20*th.* Year of Q. *Elizabeth,* one *Mark Scaliot* made a Lock, consisting of eleven pieces of Iron, Steel, and Brass, all which, together with a pipe Key to it, weighed but one *Grain of Gold;* he made also a Chain consisting of forty three links, whereunto having fastened the Lock and Key before mentioned, he put the Chain about a *Fleas Neck, which drew them all with ease.* See the Inventions and Experiments of the Royal Society, which will abundantly convince the Querist, that our Age has as active and busie Spirits for Invention as any former Age in the World. (II.11.2)

Here journalistic values triumph over those of intellectual significance. The tiny lock and key made by Mark Scaliot, and the chain with which a flea could pull them were presented in the *Mercury* with as much importance as an *ad oculum* demonstration of the circulation of the blood. The appeal to the example of the Royal Society as "active and busie Spirits for Invention" is an attempt to raise the trivial to importance.

Curiosity-mongering was a hindrance to the appreciation of scientific method. So also was a definition of credible evidence far too wide to permit testing. For example, a question about the existence of centaurs, *"or other discoursing Creatures produced between the race of Men and Brutes,"* brought a reply in which Plato and Plutarch were the authorities for an affirmative answer. The Athenians allowed that a great many false things were imposed upon the world, but that it would be wrong to label as false all that we hear,

> We believe there have been Centaurs, Satyrs, &c., we will give you our reasons, and leave your own Faith at liberty. We find that *Plato* in *Convivio Sapientium* relates, That a Shepherd presented to *Periander* a Foal born of a Mare, that had the Neck, Head and Hands of a Man, the rest like a Horse, yet the Voice of a Child. *Diocles* affirm'd it ominous, and presag'd Divisions, but *Thales* affirm'd 'twas Natural, and said Horsekeepers ought to be married. *Plutarch* in *Sylla*'s Life mentions a Satyr, with the Circumstances of taking it, and letting it go again. . . . We read of one that was shown in *Alexandria,* under the times of *Constantine, Pausanias* makes mention of 'em in an Island where he was driven by a Storm. We cou'd tell you more out of *Pliny,* if his Authority wou'd pass, as well as many other Authors, which our narrow limits won't suffer. (V.7.7)

The editors' disparagement of Pliny, whose authority was by this time universally doubted, suggests that all the evidence for the existence of centaurs was to some degree suspect in their own eyes. Such questions about oddities are overshadowed by ones in which some concrete evidence figures, and by answers that include demonstration and refer to contemporary scientific theory. Questions on optics, a newly advanced subject in the 1690's, are outstanding in the sensible replies made to them, as in this about reflection: *"What's the Reason that when we view our selves . . . in a Glass, the Image appears as far behind the surface of the Glass as the Object represented is distant from it?"* (II.1.1).

The author of the query is urged first to consider the nature of vision and next, *"the Doctrine of Reflection, wherein he who has but just lookt into Opticks* knows that the Angles of Insidence and Reflexion are equal—from the due comparing of which Principles will arise the natural and genuine solution of this Problem." A clearly drawn cut with an explanation accompanies the answer.

The answer to a question about the heat of the sun is more speculative, the editor consenting "to talk for once like a thorough-paced Aristotelian" in explaining that fire, being of greater activity than any other element, whirls round with the sun more easily even than the earth's atmosphere does with it (V.5.1).

Frequent questions about the sun reveal the common reader's great curiosity about the subject. A long question requesting clarification on four matters illustrates the general state of knowledge.[18] (The querist had found two or three of his questions "in part answered" in other *Mercuries*, all of which he owned.)

> Quest. 1. *Is the Sun the same Elementary Fire supplied and fed with cumbustible* [sic] *matter, as a Torch, Candle, &c?*
> Quest. 2. *If so, whence hath it the vast supplies of matter needful for the continual supplies of so large a Luminary, being——times bigger than this Globe of Earth?*
> Quest. 3. *Where, or how doth it purge it self of that incombustible matter, Rust, Ashes &c. or do those earthly parts frame New Worlds, as some hold?*
> Quest. 4. *If Light be a Body, as you hold, how doth its Rays so safely and speedily penetrate the close pores of Glass, that no other Spirit, or any thing else in nature, that I know of, can penetrate, or at least so speedily.*

The Athenians qualified their first answer, saying "We must not determine too positively of things at such a great distance, especially since we know so very little of those things that we dayly converse with, which continually fall under the Cognizance of our senses." The answer is twofold, on the hypotheses of the sun as liquid fire, or else as "extream subtle fine matter put in a mighty motion." In either circumstance, motion causes heat and heat causes motion, and matter "is never Red till the particles of which 'tis composed are altered, and as it were, made a New Body, but allowing either *Hypothesis*."

To the second question they replied that there was no necessity for such supplies of fuel as used on earth, for the sun, being "the Central part of our Vortex, all the Planets tend to him as their Center, much more his own parts, which fly not away from him but continually move with him or which is the same thing, burn."

To the third they reply: "We know nothing at all of the matter of purging; those earthly parts or *Maculæ,* after some little time, being also put into a brisk motion, lose their Colour, and look like the rest: those that believe they make new worlds, have better Intelligence, or at least stronger fancies than we have."

The corpuscular theory of light is firmly upheld in the final answer, bolstered with recent authority:

> Light is the finest matter in Nature, more subtle and Quick than any thing in the whole universe, as is evident from its coming from the *Satellites* of *Jupiter* in so very little time; how much suttler and quicker it is than the motion of the Air, or what we call sound, is evident from the firing of a piece, whose sound (if a great way off) comes not to us in a considerable time. 'Twas one of *Des Cartes's Errors* who would have it made in a Instant through the universe, at least in right lines, or where nothing intercepted, tho it's sufficiently prov'd by *Hugens* and others, that it moves gradually, as other bodies do.

The Athenians' awareness of contemporary theory is shown also in their answer to one of the first questions about the sun to appear in the *Mercury: "What Matter is the Sun made of, and Whether or no is it a Flame?"*

Answ. Take the newest and best Account those Modern Astronomers give us, who have for many Years considered this glorious Star by the help of the Telescope: And they tell us, That 'tis a Body of Fire, unequal in it's Surface, and composed of several parts of a different Nature, some fluid, other solid; that it appears, his Disque is a Sea of Fire, wherein is perceiv'd a perpetual agitation of waves of Flame: That in some parts may be seen as it were burnings, in others spots like thick Smoak, neither without the Sun, but seeming to proceed from his *Disque,* appearing and disappearing, encreasing and decreasing, the Fire showing it self casually among those black Smoaks, which are the Spots we perceive in this great Luminary. Father *Kircher* thinks they are the Foams, or Froth of the *Fire,* which the Sun exhales and evaporates out of it's Body; but Mr. *Azout* and Mr. *Hugens* rather think that they are only appearances occasioned by the Undulation, or waving of the Air. (II.18.3)[19]

The Athenians observed, as an afterthought, that sun spots appeared dimmer at crucial times, *"as for a whole Year when* Caesar *was murthered. . . ."*

They were a little more gullible in regard to wonderful biological phenomena, some no more physically verifiable than the existence of centaurs. They accepted as a possibility, for example, that a corpse touched by its murderer would bleed, but possible only within the bounds of providence and dependent purely upon God's will (II.1.24).

Their first remark suggests that the editors accepted the superstition wholly: "We meet with many Instances of this Nature, as the *Waters* of *Jealousie* amongst the *Jews* for the Tryal of Adultery." But they cite medical opinion: "Physicians tell us that Blood Congeals in the Veins presently after Death, and afterwards in two or three days becomes *liquid* again, as its tendency to Corruption." Some attribute this to "the sense wherewith all things are endu'd," remaining in these dead bodies,

> so that having a sense of their Murderers, and perceiving them near at hand, they suffer two very different Motions, *Trembling* and *Anger,* which cause such a Commotion of Blood, that it flows forth from the Wound: And several other Opinions we have about it, *but all of 'em inconsistent with Reason* [italics mine] . . . for either there is a *Natural Cause* of this, or there is not; if there's none, the Dispute is at an end, and we must referr it to a *particular Providence* of God Almighty, in discovering Murderers by this way.

The reasoning here is not unlike Locke's in accounting for phenomena having no apparent immediate cause. The editors' conclusion carries the reasoning very nicely to its logical absurdities:

> but if it be by a *Natural Cause,* it must be either *Sympathetick* or *Antipathetick;* if by Sympathy, it follows from their way of arguing, that one kill'd by a Bullet at a distance (the Murder'd not knowing who it was) can have no emotion of the Spirits when the Murderer is by, and the *Animal Spirits* cannot be more *sensible* and knowing when the Man is *dead* than when he is *alive;* as also, if the Person *murder'd* were kill'd in his *Wifes Arms,* and his *Relations* defending him, here his *Relations* should bleed (not he) at the sight of the *Murderer.* If it be supposed to be effected by Antipathy, then it would concenter all the dead Persons Blood, and make it retire to the Heart instead of bleeding; so that we conclude such *Instances* are meerly *providential,* and the immediate Effects of *Gods Justice,* when they really happen.

Yet the Athenians had a sound knowledge of the circulation of the blood. In the same volume of the *Mercury* their answer to a question on amputation gave full credit to Harvey's demonstration and showed a good grasp of its significance. Asked *"how the Veins and Arteries of an Arm or Leg*

Amputated, can be Reunited to continue the Circulation of the Blood," they replied:

> When the *Inquisitive Doctor* Harvey first asserted the Circulation, this was one of the Objections raised against it by them, who could not presently admit it then. . . . the Controversie is in *Waleus* his second Letter to *Bartholin*. . . . if a Hand or Foot be Amputated, then the Arteries do not carry the Blood so far, and consequently the Veins cannot fetch back any Blood from thence; . . . there is no need of Re-union or Anastomases, which this Question supposes. (II.19.2)

Their information compares favorably with that in William Wotton's chapter on the circulation in his *Reflections upon Ancient and Modern Learning,* published in 1694. Wotton chided Sir William Temple, his general adversary, because Temple seemed "unwilling to believe the *Circulation of the Blood,* because he could not see it" (p. 218).

The *Mercury* received some questions about chyle or lymph fluid: what is it? how is it made? and how is it turned into blood? (X.20.7–8). The answers given are striking in their substantive resemblance to the pages on "chile" in *Compendium Physicæ*. The answers in the *Mercury* are more compressed and latinate, and lack Morton's modern authorities, analogies, and invented mnemonic couplets of the sort found throughout his books such as:

> Chew, tast, and Swallow food, and in a while
> The Stomach heat, and ferment make it chile
> (p.128)

The Athenians describe the manufacture of chyle in one long sentence:

> The Stomach by the help of its Fibres embraceth closely the Meat thus chewed and swallowed, and mixeth therewith specifick fermantaceous Juices, bred in its inner Coat, and impregnated with the Saliva, then by a convenient Heat there is made a Mixture and Eliquation of all, for the fermentaceous Particles entring into the Pores of the Meat, do pass through, agitate and eliquate

its Particles, separating the purer from the Crass, and making them more fluid, so that they make another form of Mixture, and unite among themselves into the resemblance of a Milky Cream, after which together with the thicker Mass with which they are yet involved, by the Constriction of the Stomach they pass down to the Guts, where by the Mixture of the bile and pancreatick Juice they are by another manner of fermentation quite separated from the thicker Mass, and so are received by the Lacteal Vessels, as the thicker is ejected by Stool.

Morton gave deliberate consideration to the source of the "dissolving menstruum," the belief of the ancients that it came from veins near the kidneys, or that it was leftover chyle like the culture of sour milk in "an Irish bonny Clauber pot," or, as Dr. Charleston had it in his *Natural History of Nutrician,* an acid phlegm separated from the blood through the coeliac artery (p. 178).

These differences are what one might expect between Morton, the teacher and spectator, working with students, and the Athenians, explaining to readers who have no opportunity to test the source. The advertisements in the number of the *Mercury* dealing with digestion point up the failure of the age to apply scientific observation in verifying some phenomena which people wished to accept on faith. One announces "Mr. Increase and Mr. Cotton Mather's New Discourse conserning the New-England WITCHES and WITCHCRAFTS . . . to which will be added the Observations of a Person who was upon the place 6 or 7 days, when the suspected WITCHES were first taken into Examination: As also an *APPENDIX,* giving an Account of the late Dispossession of a Person in *England* by Fasting and Prayer. . . ." (Charles Morton approved of the New England trials, but there was little opposition to them altogether.)

Another recommends: "Elixir Stomachicum . . . *Not Purging, but Cordial only,*" a remedy advertised in this number and in many other numbers of the *Mercury.* The Elixir was *"to be drank at any time . . . in any Liquor, as Ale,*

*Tea, Mum, Canary, White-Wine, A Dram of Brandy, &c.
. . . it procures a good Appetite, helps Digestion, expels all
Wind, Strengthens the Stomach, purifies the Blood, and destroys the Scurvy, . . . these six things (especially) it does
beyond belief, without you experience it."*

When experiments are referred to in the *Mercury* there is either the implication that they were performed by the Athenians themselves, or the explicit statement that they have been recorded in the *Philosophical Transactions of the Royal Society*. In answer to a question about a wind-broken *horse*, the editors cite an experiment performed on a dog by "The late great Physician and Virtuoso Dr. *Lower*," in which he cut the nerves leading to the diaphragm, "on which it immediately fell a breathing like a *wind-broken* Horse. Whence we may inferr, that when a *Horse* is affected with that *Disease,* those *Nerves* are accidentally broken by hard *straining,* as they were separated on *purpose* in the *Dog* when the Doctor made the *Experiment*" (IV.17.2).

Some answers to scientific questions state that the writer conducted an experiment himself. Even though the experimenter might have sent both the question and its answer to Dunton, the implication allowed is that it was done by one of the Athenians or all in concert. To the question of where swallows go in the wintertime (I.8.4), the answer is that, first, swallows "follow the heat, and visit the Southern Countries," but that those unable to make the long flight stay behind and take refuge in buildings or caves, "where Cold makes 'em senseless and void of all appearance of Life, *as I have try'd by pricking and dismembring 'em without any sense of Pain*" [italics mine]. Unlike Dr. Samuel Johnson,[20] the writer doubted the story, widely circulated, that swallows wintered in a cluster in a pond of water, "joyned together, holding one another by the Legs, Wings, and bills . . . ; it looks improbable how they should find one another under water, or be all in a mind to fall together; [he would] rather suppose that they crept into some hollow bank near the Water, which broke and fell in with 'em."

As to whether they could revive again, although he disbelieved Pliny's assertion that in Egypt the sun formed creatures out of the very mud, yet he could believe "that the Sun meeting with Organs already capacitated for Animation, together with some other natural Cause, may revive Swallows." Here again the writer asserted that he had made an experiment, in this instance bringing back to life flies that had been drowned two or three days, by the heat of the sun or the application of warm ashes.

There was a widespread notion at this time that swallows hibernated rather than migrated. Charles Morton discussed the problem in *An Enquiry into the Physical and Literal Sense of Jeremiah viii.7*.[21] He disbelieved stories "of Swallows lying in clay Lumps in the Bottom of Rivers; . . . because the Water and Earth are too cold Quarters, in the Winter, for such Summer Birds." If the birds did not breathe "while they lie in their Sweeven, or Wintersleep . . . in the Spring morning, when they should awake, it is scarce conceivable, how their Feathers should be in a Trim to lift them out of the Water." He had heard of "Heaps of Swallows lying in the Clefts of the Rocks near the Sea; but . . . never yet could speak with any one that ever saw them so," though he himself had lived many years near the sea. He found it "very strange, that no curious Persons, inquisitive into the Nature of Things, should procure any of those sleeping Swallows, to observe the Progress of Nature concerning them" (p. 561). Morton's conclusion, based upon calculation that a bird could fly at one hundred twenty-five miles an hour for sixty days, was that migratory birds spent the winter in the moon (pp. 565–566).

The answers to important science questions in the *Mercury* are relevant to the Athenians' position on reason and religion. They show a preoccupation with the great intellectual issue of the time, described by Richard S. Westfall as "the degree to which supernatural knowledge supplements and corrects reason."[22] Reason stood for the method of natural science, in which the evidence of the senses or of mathematical propositions brought absolute certainty. But that certainty was limited to the concerns of natural science; in religion a different kind of certainty, called by Bishop Wilkins "indubitable certainty," depended upon faith. Like

Boyle, the Athenians believed that human reason was imperfect, but that in its ever-expanding search for truth in natural philosophy, it would reduce the seeming contradictions with the truth of revelation.

The crux of the issue was demonstration. Boyle argued, in the *Discourse of Things Above Reason* (1681), that both in natural philosophy and in religion we accept things beyond our understanding, things that cannot be fully demonstrated. Yet we try, we push as far as we can with reason, recognizing all the while that apparent contradictions between reason and revelation arise because of the limitations of the human intellect. The Athenians' answer to a carping question about the Boyle lectures, not long after their establishment in accordance with Boyle's will, reveals the Society's great admiration for Boyle:

> *Whether in the* Monthly Lecture, *founded by Mr.* Boyle, *more can be said than* Socrates, Plato, Tully, Plutarch, *or Bp.* Wilkins, *and Mr.* Ray, *have already published, and whether the 50* l. *per An. might not have bin as well spent in distributing those Books* gratis, *as establishing those Anti-Atheistical Lectures?*
>
> *Answ.* We meet with no Body (but a *Lacedemonian* Atheist) that cou'd have the Confidence to censure so good, so great, so pious an Act, of perhaps one of the wisest Testators since *Solomon,* wiser much by far than their great Patron *Hobbs,* whose greatest Attainments at his Death could neither satisfie nor resolve *that leap in the dark.* This was neither like a *Philosopher* nor a Christian, we mean not like Mr. *Boyle,* who underwent the *Change* as familiarly as a Natural Experiment: No doubt but this great Mans Friends will be able to find out such Persons as can manage the Subject of Atheism to its disinterest, and what has bin already perform'd has not bin so mean as to be baffled by a *look to't,* or a *Judas's* censure, *it had bin better to have bin given to the Poor,* . . . but 'tis the hard fate of such Fools, to take a censure or banter for argument, and when they are most serious, and wou'd prove in earnest, they can

bring nothing but what (with a little alteration) is as conclusive against the existence of their own Soul, as of the Christian Religion. (VII.12.13)

The Athenians' concern with the threat of atheism here is a clue to their relative conservatism. They were not yet ready to go as far as Locke in asserting that no articles of belief should be accepted that contradicted the testimony of the senses. To their mind, Boyle had been a philosopher *and* a Christian, sure of the existence of the soul into eternity because of, rather than in spite of, what he knew about the physical world. Theirs was an emotional response. Except in the answers to mathematical questions, an emotional commitment to orthodox religious belief is not far away from the center of the answer to any science question in the *Mercury*. The Athenians' definition of a miracle illustrates their commitment (they believed miracles to be ceased, according to prophecy, since biblical times, and reason told them "that the *Divine Power* will not interpose where there is no need on't"):

The summ is, By a *Miracle,* we mean any *strange thing* wrought by the *Power of God,* either mediate or immediate, for the *Confirmation* of his *Truth,* or setting forth his *Glory*. And the way to discern such *Miracles* from the Illusions of wicked *Daemons,* or *Men,* is by their *Confirmation* of *Truth,* or *Superiority* of *Power*. (II.9.7)

Like the virtuosi, the Athenians revealed a faith in the harmony of science and religion, and like most seventeenth-century scientists, believed that the ultimate test of findings in natural philosophy should be their confirmation of divine truth. If they saw the danger to the doctrine of particular providence in the mechanical conception of nature, they did not take it seriously. It is significant that the last question to appear in the *Athenian Mercury* concerned the divinity of Christ, and that the affirmative answer was made complacently.

Only a few scientists wrote anything comprehensible to

the common reader. Boyle's little book of one hundred inexpensive recipes for treating common diseases was exceptional in its simplicity,[23] but for the most part the scientists wrote for each other, not for the public. The Athenians were among the first to translate scientific knowledge into understandable language for the casual reader. Outlets for scientific knowledge were few because not many booksellers would take the financial risk of publishing scientific books, and hence the contribution of the *Mercury* was more valuable than it would have been in an age when primary sources were more easily available. The "science writer" is a product of the late nineteenth century and today we have superbly understandable writing about science in newspapers and periodicals. But for purveying popular science in the seventeenth century, the *Mercury* stood almost alone.

CHAPTER 8

[1] The following categories are represented: astronomy, chemistry, education (in science and application of science to education), ethnography, geography, geology, mathematics, medicine (including specific claims for patent medicines but excluding magical cures), meteorology, mineralogy, natural history (mammals, birds, fish, insects, plants, reptiles), navigation, the occult when plainly related to natural causes, oceanography, physics, physiology, psychology. Only the widely inclusive term of natural philosophy was used by the writers themselves.
[2] In these computations each of three entire numbers on Burnet's *Theory of the Earth* (VIII.28–30), two on the "brutal mechanism" (IX.18–19), one on the lodestone (X.16), and one on the barometer or "weatherglass" (X.19), is counted as a single question.
[3] These most frequently asked date back to Vol. I: 3.2; 4.8; 10.5; 1.7; 7.1; 10.4; 25.10.

Volume Two was one of those read by Swift in 1691 and from which it is probable he exploited several scientific concepts, a sound one expressed in the question on the rainbow (II.20.1), in stanza II of his *Ode to Sancroft* (1692), and a whimsical one (*"Is it true, that a Lyon won't prey on a pure Virgin?"* II.8.5) used satirically in *Tatler* No. 5. See Mabel Phillips' (Mrs. William C. DeVane) unpublished dissertation (Yale 1925), *Jonathan Swift's Relation to Science,* pp.122ff; pp.142–146. [Issued by University Microfilm, 1968.]
[4] The identity of the medical writer has not been ascertained. He was satirized in the *New Athenian Comedy,* and Dunton advertised his addition to the staff, but beyond this there is no information about him.
[5] XX.3.2; 8.6; 7.4 (cp. II.24.12, in which it was alleged that there would be no difference).
[6] Totals for the volumes were: I, 9; II, 124; III, 68; IV, 46; V, 32;

VI, 38; VII, 41; VIII, 67; IX, 11; X, 55; XI, 35; XII, 7; XIII, 22; XIV, 31; XV, 31; XVI, 16; XVII, 28; XVIII, 29; XIX, 9; XX, 60. The relative importance of these figures may be seen by comparing the number for each volume to an average figure of three hundred questions per volume.

[7] *A search after truth* . . . 7th May 1694, *Stat. Reg.* III, 440. Vol. I printed for Dunton and S. Manship (the latter Norris's publisher), 1694; Vol. II for Dunton alone, 1695. The running title is: *A Treatise of the Nature of the Humane Mind, and its Management for Avoiding Error in the Sciences.*

Dunton set such store by Sault's translation and was so eager to publish it before Thomas Bennet brought out a rival one by Thomas Taylor (entered 22 May 1694, *Stat. Reg.* III, 441), that he persuaded John Norris, then the chief proponent of Malebranche in England, to look over some of the manuscript and allow his approval to be cited in the *Mercury.* Dunton advertised, XIII.29 (Tue 15 May 94): "This is to give further Notice, that the Translation of *Malbranch's Search after Truth,* is going on with all possible Expedition, that so good a Piece will admit. This Work will be Published without Subscriptions in a few Weeks, Printed on an extraordinary fine Paper and Character in Folio; and done into *English* from the *Paris* 4th Edition, by Mr. *Sault.* Part of the Translation has been seen by John Norris, M. A. upon whose Approbation and Revisal, the whole will be Publisht."

[8] Cyprian Blagden, *The Stationers Company: a History, 1403–1959,* London, G. Allen & Unwin, 1960, p.301.

[9] XIV.2.5 [misnumbered 3]. The term *affected,* also encountered in Sault's book as the specialized variant *adsected,* means a compounded equation, i.e. containing different powers of an unknown quantity. The term was just coming into use at this time.

[10] In both bound collections of the *Mercury* at the Huntington Library, this sheet follows XVII.30 (Sat 13 Jul 95) and precedes the title page of XVIII.

[11] "Curvæ Celerrimi Descensus *investigatio Analytica excerpta ex literis R. Sault. Math. D°. . . .*" *Philosophical Transactions,* XX.425–426.

[12] Morton matriculated at Cambridge in 1646, when he was twenty, came to New Inn Hall, Oxford, two years later and, in 1649, was admitted as a scholar at Wadham College where John Wilkins was the "intruded" warden. He was admitted to the Bachelor of Arts degree in 1649, M. A. in 1652, and in 1653 was incorporated *ad eundem* in Cambridge, as Wesley was to be forty years later. At Wadham, Morton was in the company of a dozen or more of the scientific lights of the time, the men who were soon to become founders and charter members of the Royal Society of London, and whose thinking and experimenting would then be given to the world by means of the *Philosophical Transactions.* Morton's subsequent history demonstrated that he was a natural teacher who but for the harassments by the government would have remained in England to train generations of scientists. His *Compendium Physicæ,* a scientific syllabus of which his students made their own manuscript copies, is a superb illustration of the state of scientific knowledge

at the time, particularly of the physical sciences, and of its author's pedagogical methods.

[13] *A Letter from a Country Divine to his Friend in London,* London, R. Clavel, 1703, pp. 6,13.

[14] Lew Girdler, "Defoe's Education at Newington Green," *Studies in Philosophy,* Vol. 50 (1953), pp.573–591. Defoe's association with the *Mercury,* although somewhat obscure, may have included some scientific contributions. Parts of his *Essay on Projects* (1696) bear striking resemblance to some of the scientific essays in the periodical.

[15] VI.27.11: *"Descartes* wou'd have Beasts to be nothing else, but *Machines* insensible of either Pain or Pleasure, and wrote a particular Treatise to this effect, but by his leave, we are so far from believing Animals to be meer *Machines,* that we dare to undertake to prove that Trees, Herbs, *&c.* are in their principal parts sensible of most exquisite Pain, . . ."

[16] "Discovery of a New World" in *Mathematical and Philosophical Works,* London, 1707, p.66.

[17] "The Passions of the Soul," in *Philosophical Works* (transl. Haldane and Ross) Cambridge University Press, 1931, I.365–366.

[18] XV.19.4. A question that reveals downright ignorance or facetiousness gets a short answer, as that for *"What place doth the Sun set in, and where doth it rise? Answ.* All the World over." III.1.4.

[19] Athanasius Kircher (1602–1680), a German Jesuit, was best known for a compendious work on magnetism. Adrien Auzout (d.1691) was one of the first astronomers at the Paris Observatory.

[20] James Sutherland, *Defoe,* London, Methuen and Co., 1937, p.23.

[21] *Harleian Miscellany* (1744) II.558–567. The *Enquiry* was "written by an eminent Professor for the Use of his Scholars, and . . . published at the earnest Desire of some of them."

[22] Richard Westfall, *Science and Religion in Seventeenth-Century England,* New Haven, Yale University Press, 1958, p.163.

[23] *Medicinal Experiments,* London, S. Smith, 1692.

9

Money and Matrimony

The *Athenian Mercury* still comes alive today because of its sincere interest in people. In writing about personal problems the editors were sometimes flippant, vulgar, or facetious, but never casual. They offered for their time the closest thing to personal journalism, and their advice on the conduct of personal affairs was in steady demand throughout. No extravagant claim should be made for the service rendered by men who were, after all, primarily concerned with getting a penny; one can only point out that week after week they answered questions, and answered them interestingly.

The Athenians reflected prevalent, fairly orthodox attitudes toward social behavior, expressing themselves both in social criticism and in their solutions of particular and detailed problems submitted to them. John Dunton's later deterioration is not apparent in the social attitudes of the *Mercury*. The sympathetic response to the problems of apprentices was his, and the strictness of Samuel Wesley shows in the severe answers to those who would remarry in haste.

The customary quick movement from question to question does not allow the personalities of the writers to emerge as strongly as those of the great essay journalists of the eighteenth century. In numbers devoted to a single question or in an occasional long essay answer, Wesley or Dunton may seem to be speaking, but even then there is little of the pervading air of the gentleman's club found in the *Spectator,* or the measured wisdom of Johnson in the *Rambler*. The social questions in the *Mercury* generally are more worthy of examination as characteristic of their time than as stylistic accomplishments.

Because of the difficulty of identifying the actual authors of most items, the answers quoted from the *Mercury* will be ascribed to "the editors." The reader will therefore have to imagine a composite figure as handing down the answers, and the image in his mind's eye will more appropriately be that of the Wesley who sat for his portrait as Job than of Dunton briskly managing the whole project from the Raven in the Poultry.

The answers to questions here classified as "social" were generally filled with the spirit of reform, especially those delivered during the period when the movement for "Reformation of Manners" was at its height, sponsored especially by London clergymen and inspired by Queen Mary. Wesley is said to have made himself unpopular with his Lincolnshire parishioners by attempting reform single-handed in both South Ormsby and Epworth,[1] and he was the one singled out by Tom Brown for satire as a prude.[2] Yet the earnestness of the answers is frequently relieved by humor, and made less stuffy by an apparent desire to be truly helpful rather than censorious as the *Spectator* tended to be.

The Athenians obviously considered themselves the best channel for the transmission of suggestions and information from the public to Parliament to help the legislators fashion an act of reformation. In August 1691 the *Mercury* issued a call for *"remarkable* Occurrences *or scruples relating to the* New Reformation" (III.3). Special full-page advertisements were published extolling William's virtues and explaining that the king would take personal charge of the reformation once his preoccupation with military operations came to an end. In the meantime such loyal and concerned individuals as the Athenians would do their utmost to stamp out vice and encourage religion. The request for relations of illustrative personal experiences was a familiar device of Dunton's.

The Athenians went so far as to offer services beyond a published answer. Like Samuel Richardson in his later tea table counselling of maidservants and shopgirls, they were willing to become involved beyond the printed answer. To the apprentice who had cheated his master the Athenians offered two alternatives according to the circumstances—if the master was a good man, confess and pay up as soon as possible; if he was "an ill man," save up money to repay him secretly. They asked the apprentice to let them know his decision and concluded: *"You shan't want our further Counsel upon further Application to us"* (III.12.3).

The reforming zeal of the Athenians showed in their advice to a woman whose husband was selling all his goods to set up as his mistress a widowed sister-in-law. They suggested that the wife get friends to intercede, but if that failed, "send but the Name of the Parties with such attestations as we have no reason to doubt the truth thereof . . . and we'll endeavour to get 'em both (if both deserve it) into the Honourable Preferment of the *Black Roll* in the next Edition" (XIII.20.7).

To a woman who asked where to get a husband, the editors replied that had they her name they would insert an advertisement at the end of the paper, but lacking that, suggested she go where women were fewest, to the Plantations (II.13.5). To another who would not marry a man disappointed in his first love till the Athenian Society resolved the question of whether it was possible to love twice, they quickly replied that the majority believed it possible (II.6.3).

Either as their own practical joke or as a facetious answer to some female reader's facetious question, they printed the following exchange:

Whether your stock of Sagacity is exhausted, or you grow wanton, and luxurious, by your Profits? If not, pray what's the matter wi'ye? For I'm sure our Sex once took ye for their Champions, *whereas now you leave us here, and take no manner care of us?*

Bedlam, Octob. 16.1694.

Answ. Alas, poor Lady! We ne're pretended to that heighth of *Knight-Errantry* as to *Storm Enchanted Castles* for the sake of your fair Sex neither. However, as soon as e're we have dispatch'd all the business that lies before us, and Answer'd all the Questions that are or shall be Propos'd, we promise to trip over to your new Airy Apartment, and if we can't relieve your misfortunes, at least share 'em with you. (XV.26.4)

The Athenians, in the Preface to Volume Eighteen, expressed their irritation with "trifling and impertinent love questions," and hoped that sometimes they had talked "as gravely and usefully" as they could on subjects of a higher nature. In spite of this pious wish, the great bulk of questions in the *Mercury* are social rather than philosophical. If the last decade of the century was indeed the inception of the age of "prudent mediocrity," as A. O. Lovejoy has called it, the Athenians helped at its birth, for except in facetious passages, they counselled prudence above all.

The editors believed the fall of man the original cause for the corruption of their times. The human body, from Adam's fall subject to the diseases brought on by the enforced change of climate and diet, "now groans for a Renovation" (III.17.5). They felt, however, that the English race in particular had deteriorated. In response to a confession of perjury the Athenians asked:

> Where's the ancient *Honour* and *Honesty* of the English? . . . We are grown almost a *Nation* of *Cheats*, and which is worst of all, Men won't *Cheat* upon the *Square;* one engrosses more knavery than his *Neighbour*, for if it went round equally, there would be nothing lost. (XIV.24.2)

Informers against vice they found more nearly tolerable than those against Dissenters, for the offenses of the vicious were wicked in their consequences and not just violations of the letter of the law (III.7.4). The Athenians wished that the penalties of the laws could be talked of less and executed more (III.14.2). Their opposition to dueling, however, was founded less on its illegality than upon Christian scruples:

> he cannot be my Friend that would engage me in Dueling, contrary to my Reason, Law, and Religion,—'Tis a base little Spirit that loves *Revenge* and *Error*, but he that *begs pardon for his mistakes is generous, because*

*it is a **Debt**,* and what is due ought not to be withheld—read *Seneca.* (III.2.1)

It was the Athenians' opinion that allowing polygamy would not make for "a more temperate Age. . . . All *Intemperance* the more 'tis indulg'd the higher it grows." As an example they cited Turkey, where, the law allowing two wives, some would have two hundred, or "as many as they cou'd get" (III.4.4). Still, the editors did not think that everyone would indulge himself even beyond what the law allowed, for they advised a man who had scruples about resuming courtship of a lady whom he admitted courting while his wife was still living, "just to gain her acquaintance," that he and the lady might "proceed honorably enough to the highest Bond of Friendship: For things are, as they are in their own Nature, and not what prejudices of Custom, and the groundless Opinions of the Age represent 'em" (IV. 23.3).

Prostitution, or "night-walking" as Dunton called it, was singled out for special treatment, suggesting that Dunton or his informant followed a practice still useful to muckrakers. A notice in the *Mercury* for 28 July 1691 set the stage for a complete revelation of the habits of London prostitutes:

> We have received a Letter from a Gentleman, wherein he desires to know whether it be convenient to insert in our answer to it *an Account of his late six Nights Rambles,* with the Confessions he has got from those Creatures about their first Engagements, their struggles *with Conscience,* and the Methods of their stiffling [sic] it by their *Habits in Lewdness:* Wherefore we advise the Gentleman, if he pleases, to send 'em speedily, and they shall be inserted in our next *Tuesdays Mercury.*[3]

The following Saturday it was reported that the gentleman had promptly complied by sending confessions obtained from several lewd women, some of them "of no mean Rank," and that the whole would be published the next Tuesday as a warning to "Vicious Persons." These revelations would displace the questions on love and marriage, originally planned for that number (III.3). In the next number appeared the story of the *"six Nights Rambles"* together with an explanation of the best methods *"to detect the vile haunts and practices of those lewd women called* Night Walkers."

The *first Night* I travers'd the *Pall-Mall,* and read the Face of every unmask'd Lady I met; and if mask'd, I started some Question that still gave me an Indication of their Temper, endeavouring to light upon as *refin'd,* yet *modest piece of Wickedness* as I could; at last having made . . . the *best of the Market,* away we walk'd to drink upon the *Bargain.* So after several Glasses, and some little insignificant Prittle-prattle, I fix'd my Eyes upon her, and said,—*Madam, methinks I read some Lines and Characters of Goodness in your Face which are not yet absolutely defac'd: Your Education, I'm confident has not been unhappy: Pray be free, and tell me, Are you yet Proof against the Lashes of your Conscience?* (III.3).

The interviewer reported a partial success in his efforts to make her consult her conscience, for the woman at last said to him, "I hope the *Novelty of this Enterprize* may have new Effects upon me, and keep me from doing such Actions as must be repented of, or I am undone."

The next night it was "a City Madam" who made proof of the interviewer's virtue, for he related that, "After having drank a Glass or two, she began to draw a little too near me. . . ." He escaped this threat by the Duntonian shift of pretending to be a spirit.[4] The third subject was "A Savoy Bird" whom he felt "nothing can reclaim but Afflictions." Number four was with an old friend who was caressing her near the Maypole; when he asked the friend the time, "the Lady scowrd off." Number five was tenderly educated but had a spendthrift brother. The story of number six was so much like "that of Paphnutius converting a Harlot" that he could not forbear telling the whole story of how Paphnutius took the woman to the most secret room in the house, where she could be seen by only God or the Devil, and asked her "if she would do it under God's eyes." The poor woman was so shamed that she put herself on bread and water and lived afraid to use the name of God. So she continued for three years, when she died.

Only quite inexperienced female readers of the *Mercury* can have imagined wholesale reformation of whores to be possible by this method. Male readers would have considered the undertaking, however wholesome its aim, as essentially unrealistic. Allusion to male responsibility for prostitution is conspicuously absent from the *"six Nights Rambles."*

The sensational journalist's choice of topics and manner of appealing to the reader do not change very much. The *Mercury* shows no advance beyond the practices of such writers as Robert Greene and Thomas Nashe a century before. The confidence game, the marriage market, the temptations of the theater, smoking, swearing, quarrels over cards, women, and drink, and, pervasively, the problems arising from the inevitable flaws in human character, are treated again and again in the *Mercury*. It is not surprising that the editors, when they betray their sympathies, favor the petty malefactor against the grand cheat, the ignorant transgressor against the Machiavellian manipulator.

Answers to questions about the forgiveness of debts reveal how far ahead of their time the Athenians were in condemning imprisonment for debt as both impractical and un-Christian. They were asked:

> *Whether the keeping so many hundreds as are kept in Prisons (begging of Bread) for Accidents and Contingencies in Trades, when those that keep them there know they are not in a Capacity to pay 'em, be not a crying Evil, and contrary to all Christian Presidents* [sic], *Practice and Custom of Forreign Nations? and whether it ought not to be redress'd in Parliament?*
>
> *Answ.* We are no *Dictators* to the Parliament, but are well assur'd, that tho' 'tis a common Practice, yet 'tis so far from a Christian Temper, as certainly *excludes the Practitioners out of Heaven, without Repentance;* for there are none there that cannot forgive impossible

Debts, none but what are merciful, pitiful, and in short Imitators of the blessed *Jesus*. (IV.1.2)

The editors' scorn for the false bankrupt was fully as strong as for the unforgiving creditor, and shows again their feeling that Parliament should revise the laws that permitted such an unfair division of justice.

Their contrast of the petty criminal's treatment with that of the "great" man anticipates Swift and Fielding, especially such characters as Jonathan Wilde. For example, a querist complained that his brother, who owed a great deal of money, had deposited enough with him to pay the debts but refused to allow him to do so, and the Athenians responded:

> indeed it seems a *Hardship* in our Laws, that a poor Shoplift shou'd be Hang'd for breaking in and pilfering a few Goods, not perhaps 5*l*. nay, not perhaps twenty Shillings value, and yet one that takes one hundred, two hundred, or a thousand Pounds worth, after having rioted away one part of it, shou'd with impunity carry off the other into the *Mint* or *Fryers,* and send it going after the same rate, or else deposit it in a second or third Hand, who if he keeps it from the Creditors, is just as honest as the *Pick-pockets receiver,* who *hands away the Prey* which his *Brother Rogue* has *angled* for. (III.16.3)

On the other hand, the Athenians insisted upon the restitution of stolen money as always necessary where at all possible, although the offender was "not obliged to expose his fault personally, since Custom and the prejudice of the Age will meet the greatest sincerity with an uncharitable Treatment" (IV.1.2). Dunton's account of his own narrow escapes from arrest in 1685 and 1687 because of having given surety for the debts of a sister-in-law suggests that he voiced the *Mercury's* sympathetic attitude toward those who had innocently blundered into difficulties with the law and society over money.

Of all subjects dealt with, the largest was marriage, and

here the editors made frequent reference to the law, hardly ever suggesting secret and private action which might circumvent legal requirements concerning divorce and remarriage. Here too the personal experience of the editors should be kept in mind. For almost the entire period of the *Mercury* its three editors were bound together not only by their journalistic pursuit but also by their close family ties. Dunton was to enter the disastrous years of his life upon the death of Iris in May 1697, a few weeks after he had resumed the *Mercury* with Volume Twenty. The breaking up of Sault's marriage is difficult to date but it probably occurred not long before he moved to Cambridge, after the final suspension of the *Mercury*. As for Samuel Wesley, although according to his son John he differed with Susannah on several occasions, his history was one of steady agreement throughout forty-eight years of marriage.[5]

Advice on marriage was both serious and humorous. The conventional ironies of marriage supplied the basis for humor on the subject: Why marry? How to get a husband or wife? How to get along with a contentious wife or an abusive husband? To a single woman who wanted a husband, the editors offered space for an advertisement if she would just send in her name (II.13.5). For another they provided a prayer guaranteed effective but not blasphemous (II.15.1). Their advice to a woman whose suitor would neither marry her nor release her was: " 'Tis but justice to publish his fame . . . (send his Earmarks and we may perhaps give him a small lift)" (XIII.21.1). A woman who wished to reclaim a bad husband was also offered some free advertising:

> Show him this *Mercury,* and tell him if he don't amend, his *Name* shall be printed in't at length the first *Tuesday* of the next Month. But to be graver . . . be as patient as possible, unless the Husband's such a *Brute,* that this manner of behaviour will but make him more *insulting.* (III.4.2)

Men were advised what kind of woman to marry. One asked whether a woman of good temper and no religion was preferable to an ill-tempered but religious one. The editors chose the former, for there were some hopes for her. Of women in general it was their opinion that "if they *bridle* not their *Tongue,* all their *Religion* is *vain*" (IV.13.9).

To what seemed the saddest story of all about an abused husband the editors gave the lightest treatment. A man who had married "a pretended widow" who kept a public house, complained that she scolded him, chased him with a poker, the spit, or whatever came to hand, scratched his face, gave him no money, cuckolded him, and hid the profits of the business from him. The editors replied skeptically:

> *Alas poor Darby!* If one half of this be but true, thou'rt e'ne in a very woful Pickle, and requirest the *Charitable Assistance* of all *well-dispos'd Husbands*—as ever they hope for Pity if they shou'd come into the same *deplorable Condition.* . . . (**XIII**.1.9)

Such a wife they were sure it was impossible to mend. They advised her husband to get the help of three or four stout fellows to "mew her up in some Garret," sell house and furnishings, and retire to the country out of danger, serene in the assurance that such a woman could take care of herself.

Less violent methods were suggested for the subduing of another headstrong and unruly wife. The husband was advised to give her rope enough, "for she's not to be made Civil by any thing but the *worms.*" If the unfortunate husband wished to try working miracles, however, the last desperate remedy was to *"Watch her Tame* . . . a way to tame even Lyons, and it may be Tygers too." He was to beat a drum till the woman was struck deaf and dumb with the noise; to let her blood under the tongue and in both arms to prevent scolding and fighting; to draw her teeth and cut her nails. But to end on a note of moderation, the husband was told that "the surest way of all is, being a *good Husband yourself,* for 'tis bad Husbands are very often the Cause that the wives are no better than they shou'd be" (III.13.1).

The "note of moderation," which comes as a relief from the rest of this answer, indicates another attitude not characteristic of the time. In this place and several others the Athenians urged a single standard of married morality. Husband and wife needed to recognize and respond to each other's needs and to share responsibility for keeping their marriage a happy one.

Even the man with a handsome wife could be happy; if the wife had virtue as well as beauty, "there's no fear but one will be sufficient guard to the other" (III.4.12).

The Athenians' version of the Puritan ethic was revealed in their answer to a young woman trying to choose between taking music lessons and keeping the money she had:

> . . . it's plain, the Lady would be capable of doing more good, relieving more poor, &c. as well as living comfortably her self, if she were worth a Thousand Pound, than if she sung like a Cherubim, whereby she'd get no more than a *Poet,* or a *Ballad-singer.* Nor is there any reason why she mayn't still improve her skill both in Vocal and Instrumental Musick, as far as she has an Opportunity, notwithstanding her wise Choice, if left at her liberty; For 'tis certain that Ten Hundred Pound Bags, clinking in ones Chamber, would make most Excellent Music. (XIV.30.4)

The Athenians were not the ones to discourage men from marrying. They provided a succinct, one-word answer to the following query:

> Quest. *I've wrote before on the following subject, but cou'd receive no answer. I've been too often prevail'd upon by the allurements, &c. what's your advice in this matter?*
> *Answ.* Marry! (XVI.24.2)

The *Mercury* was as much the target of practical jokers as any organ committed to giving free advice on social matters, but the editors were equal to most humorous sallies, as the following exchange illustrates. A man who asserted that he had sinned, then reformed and confessed his sins to his wife, asked the Athenians if he should still have *"a godly Minister . . . search him throughly, and help him discover the plague of his Heart?"* He was, he continued,

> *never drunk but in the best drunken Company; never Swear nor Curse but in a great Passion; never much sought opportunity of Whoring, but only when the Whore and opportunity met; never loved them, but always cast them basely off. . . .*

"This is a very sad Account," wrote the Athenians, "and deliver'd a little too merrily (if true) for in our Opinion, 'tis impossible but that an abhorrence of such Impieties cou'd have found more resenting expressions of their Nature" (IV.16.2).

Responses to questions put more seriously dealt most often with financial or legal matters relevant to marriage; philosophical or merely superstitious expressions in regard to the power of divine influence, predestination, or dreams in marriage; and the ethics of making vows, keeping letters, or courting a woman already spoken for.

A husband and a wife made separate inquiries of what to do when financial problems prevented a happy marriage. The husband asked approval of a trial separation until his position improved, to which the Athenians gave grudging consent: "but as the Apostle immediately adds, it must be, *so as to fasting and Prayer, and then come together again, that Satan tempt 'em not to Incontinence*" (IV.2.7).

A man whose inheritance was balked by relatives after he had married, asked if it would be a sin for him to abstain from intercourse until his fortunes had revived. Abstention for more than a short time, wrote the editors, would lead to a great many sins. They counselled adjustment to straitened circumstances, for *"Industry is bless'd always with a Competency . . ."* (IV.8.3).

Another wife, on the other hand, confessed to putting aside money without her husband's knowledge but with no intention of doing anything with it of which her husband would not approve. She was told that neither partner should dispose of a farthing without the other's concurrence (V.9.2). This reply was consistent with that given to the question of love or convenience as the better basis for marriage:

> Love without the necessary conveniences of Life, will soon wear *thread-bare,* and Conveniences without Love,

is no better than being chain'd to a Post for the sake of a little meat, drink, and clothing. But if we compare the small degrees of each together, much Love and moderate Conveniency is far better than the most plentiful Estate with little or no Love. (V.3.3)

A realistic view of marrying for money was often expressed in the *Mercury,* as exemplified in the answer to the question of whether a poor man might marry the relative of a rich friend without the friend's knowledge. The Athenians approved, if the lady had enough money for both of them and if the rich friend opposed the match *merely* because the man was poor (III.15.4). Of the three editors, Dunton was apparently the only one who ever married for money, and that in his second marriage soon after the death of his first wife. His hopes of a dowry to pay off his debts were dashed so violently, however, that he published a number of angry pamphlets against his mother-in-law and became estranged from his wife.

Presumably out of deference to the patent medicine advertisers, there was little medical advice in the *Mercury,* but the legal profession earned no such consideration. Questions about the legal status of the principals in a marriage, and about the ownership of property as affected by marriage, are frequent. Some of the questions had to be answered out of a knowledge of ecclesiastical law rather than civil law; for example, a woman whose fiancé had revealed that he was a Catholic wished therefore to break the marriage contract. The Athenians answered that no contract was valid that could not be kept without sin and advised the woman to "consult our Bishops" (V.9.8).

Again, the question of a marriage between the brother and daughter of the same woman sent the editors to "the Canon it self, which says, 'That none shall marry within the Degrees prohibited by the Laws of God and expressed in a Table set forth by Authority, *An.D.* 1553. (in the Reign of Blessed Qu. *Elizabeth* [!])" (V.13.3).

A question as to whether a marriage performed while the groom was drunk was a marriage according to the law of God brought a vehement "No!" from the editors. They thought the act "a sacreligious Rape committed upon the Soul," and "all Persons concern'd in such actions . . . a sort of *Spiritual Pimps*" (III.5.2).

The rigidity of divorce law is pointed up by the frequency of questions about the circumstances which would permit husband or wife to leave a partner without due legal process. A woman asks whether it is a sin for her to leave a man who abuses her, is a debauchee, and "as she thinks" is therefore not married to her "by the Laws of God and Nature." The reply to this question is one often repeated in the *Mercury*. The woman has sufficient cause for divorce from bed and board, "but the Law allows no second Marriages whilst either party lives" (III.25.6).

Such complaints came not only from wives. A tavern keeper whose wife drank wine with the patrons of the establishment and then conferred favors upon them, asked how he could reform his wife without losing trade. He was advised to do nothing if content with cuckoldry but if not, to get witnesses in order to divorce the woman (XI.6.3).

Desertion, especially by husbands gone to the plantations, was another frequent cause for inquiries concerning divorce and remarriage. A woman whose husband had left for Virginia eight years before and who wished to remarry was advised that the law which had formerly required seven years' absence to establish desertion as grounds for divorce had now been reduced because navigation and commerce were so well settled that a man had less excuse not to make his way back. The law of God, however, the editors felt made no exception. They told the woman "to secure the *Quiet of her Conscience,* and advise with the *Ecclesiastick Authority,* since the other gives her the Liberty she wants" (IV.7.3).

The observance of vows relative to marriage, although not required by common law, the editors considered to be morally necessary, but their grounds for this position could on occasion appear to be nothing more than superstitious fear of violent retribution. Their answer to the question of whether a marriage contract could be violated by accident or in error illustrates the *Mercury*'s position. No marriage contract could be cancelled even with the consent of both parties without peril of damnation for the vow breaker, "altho' our Common Law takes no notice of it, for Marriage is like a Deed of Gift, there's no recalling it when once done [and] . . . publick solemnizations are only to the satisfaction of the World, to avoid Scandals and make proper Objects for the Law to work on, in matter of Issue, Debts, Mortgages, and to give other Persons notice from intruding into such a Right or Propriety." There follows the instance of a young man who, having wished he might break his neck if he broke his vow, got a maid with child, scorned her, sought other women, and then while lopping a branch off a tree, fell and broke his neck—"And thus the *Vow-breaker* met his wish'd for fate; *And 'tis well if all his punishment was cancell'd by such a Judgment"* (III.6.8).

Two weeks later the parents of a young lady asked whether they could, without breaking the law of God, break the contract of marriage into which their daughter had been cunningly trapped by a bully. After citing their earlier answer, the editors observed that parents have "greater Propriety over their Children than the Age is generally aware of." They were not in favor of marriage against the consent of the child, but the child could not dispose of himself without the consent of the parents. The instance next given of parental power suggests that the answer was written by Wesley, for it is of Job's slaughter of his children when God permitted the Devil to have power over him. Since parental power is founded upon "the rights of Nature," the parents are obliged to vacate the contract, and especially if the woman herself desires it. If they don't, she can't do it herself, but if they do break it, she can't hinder them (III. 10.3). The entire answer is an interesting foreshadowing of *Clarissa Harlowe*.

Another clarification of contract was offered in response to the question of the validity of a marriage in which the principals had been privately married "but not bedded." They were declared to be not married "before an *Actual knowledge of each other."* A public marriage meant no more than a private one except that it rendered the principals subject to law, but contracts were "a matter of greater

Moment than is commonly believ'd, and ought to be as warily effected (if at all) as publick Marriage" (V.2.4).

The dominant attitude throughout the questions on marriage and courtship is a kind of matter-of-factness, an attitude found even in questions about the emotions of one in love. The querist who asks why love cools after marriage is informed that custom is the cause and that it cannot always prevail over the charm of variety; but virtuous love will prevent satiety "and *Wit* has always something entertaining and new, that's the *Salt* and *Spirit* which keeps the sweets of Matrimony from growing vapid, dull, and disagreeable" (II.13.3). But the Athenians blame the King of France for attempting to enslave the English with the notion that to love one's own wife is evidence of a low spirit, an assurance to the reader that emotion is not entirely disregarded.

The question of whether all marriages are made in heaven is interpreted to mean basically, *"Whether every Man and Woman who marry together were predestinate to the same"* (III.5.5). If predestination means such a necessary determination of actions as to make them cease to be human, free, and rational, the editors can see in the concept only an excuse for imprudence and folly, to be made use of by evil persons as well as weak ones:

> but the Providence of God does really interpose and preside over all humane actions, *suo modo,* or in such a way as is agreeable to it's [sic] own Justice and Wisdom, and the Nature of Man, and if in other actions, certainly in this, which is of the highest concern as to the *happiness of Life,* so as to permit the *evil,* and dispose to the *good;* but this . . . inferrs no manner of necessity upon us, nor in the least takes away the freedom of our actions, which we feel we have in whatever we do: thô Reason tells us there's one above us, and thô it may perhaps fall short in its Enquiry how these things can be well reconciled with one another. (III.5.5)

The forces which make a marriage work were certainly in part divine. Anyone planning marriage needed the assistance of heaven, and the union of souls in true marriage was like the music of the spheres, "too exquisite for our dull senses" (II.18.1); yet in considering whether to marry or not, one needed to recognize that marriage was what the principals made of it (II.15.3).

Platonic love was acceptable as a subject for verse, but the editors cautioned against any action in the guise of Platonic love that would interfere with a legal and established marriage. Thus their advice to a young man, unmarried himself, in love with a married woman, but willing to wait until her husband died, was that he must not in the meantime covet the woman or commit adultery. He was urged further to read Bishop Sanderson's *Cases of Conscience*.[6]

In the anti-Aristotelian vein of the times, the editors asserted that Aristotle was responsible through his jealousy of Plato for calling all abstract notions Platonic, "thô in truth *Aristotle* was the fool in that, and *Plato* the *wise man*, as may be seen by comparing their Morals together. The word *Platonick* yet keeps its abused Sence, and Custom gives us a ridiculous Notion of it" (VII.13.4).

The rule of prudence is almost always present. Should a married woman keep the letters sent her by an old lover? It is quite all right unless she has a jealous husband, or if at marriage she loved the other more than her husband, or if the old lover might speak "unhandsomely" of her for keeping his letters (III.4.14).

Is a vow never to marry lawful? If it is a vow not to marry one, why doesn't it apply to all? If it is lawful, ought it to be broken? The diminishing force of the personal vow is reflected in the answer to these questions, an answer grounded upon a mechanistic philosophy. The body changes, so that man may not continue to have power over himself, "the Body being perfectly mechanical, and in some Cases refusing to obey the *Mind*." A "late Noted Man" is cited as having made a vow every morning not to marry till night in order to keep his body under control of his mind. An unlawful vow, however, or one impossible to keep ought to be repented of, that it was "so wickedly or rashly made" (III.8.4).

The *Mercury* abounds with instances of those "who have

wisht heavy Imprecations which happen'd to 'em," that is some such oath as "God Rot his Soul and Body, he would not" do thus and so. On such instances their opinion is expressed at length:

> That our Modern Atheists, who attribute all things to a *Regular Mechanism of Nature,* may plainly see the *Finger of God* in such Instances, since the ordinary Course of Nature is thus inverted, and that at such *Critical moments* when the Sin calls for immediate Vengeance; and by the by, we may observe, that *Disobedience to Parents,* and false Imprecations bear the greatest share of such immediate Judgments of God Almighty (V.6.1).

This opinion seems to depart from the highly practical tenor of most of their advice on personal problems. But those who had lived through the turmoil of the Glorious Revolution and who knew about the terrible physical suffering of Charles II during his last days could very well feel that God would not be mocked and that punishment really was delivered through an inversion of the ordinary course of nature. Knowledge of the laws, divine and human, and of potential punishment for the law breaker were therefore thought to be sufficient to regulate behavior.

The *Mercury* grappled with the subject of sin, the first extended treatment of it appearing in June 1691 as a reasoned response in the negative to one who believed in its philosophical necessity.

No, wrote the Athenians, God permitted sin "because the Nature of a Man requir'd this Permission or Liberty, who without this cou'd never have been a *free Agent,* nor therefore a subject capable of *Punishments* or *Rewards.*" The querist, they asserted, and Mr. Hobbes, "and we doubt most of the Necessity-men" knew too well the unallowable consequences of accepting their argument—that there could be no eternal punishment for sin if sin were truly necessary. The fall of Adam, they continued in the next question, was ordered but not ordained (II.10.1).

From abstract considerations of the nature of sin, the

editors could move to the more practical problem of how a husband should react toward an adulterous wife with whom he expects to go on living, since the law affords so little satisfaction and demands such difficult proof. In answer, the editors mentioned the Roman law, which sanctioned the husband's killing of both offenders, and observed that modern Italians were seldom more merciful even without such a law.

To forgive, however,

> there needs the very heighth of Christianity or depth of Stoicism . . . especially when neither the Civil, Common, nor Statute-Law have taken much Care of it. But still the more difficulty . . . the more still is the glory. And indeed if we shou'd examine the Case by the Principles only of Gallantry and Reason, it seems absurd for a Gentleman to hazard his Life for so lost a thing as one who has parted with her Honour; . . . The noblest Revenge therefore, wou'd be in our Judgments, to slight and scorn a Person who had been guilty of such an Action . . . and to trust their Punishment to t'other World.

Once again the editors supported a single standard of behavior: "Nor holds this only in *Women*, but in *Men* as well as they, since after we have abstracted from Custom and Opinion, (both very ill Judges) the Crime is much the same in one as the other" (II.3.2).

Although the editors treated most questioners as if their sense of *curious* and *ingenious* was *inquiring* and *learned*, they received and printed a more than sufficient quota of questions obviously made up to try editorial ingenuity and patience. Such a one concerned the marriage of a widower to the daughter of a widow, and that of his son to the widow herself. If each wife has a son, how are the offspring related to each other? This knotty problem, however, was dealt with seriously and at length, and a diagram provided, for, as the editors observed mildly, "We meet not with many such Instances in *Tables of Affinity*. . . ."

> The *Law of God and Nature* must certainly subject the Child to its Parent, notwithstanding any *superinduc'd Civil Law, or Law of Marriage.* . . . [The women] must according to the Civil Law reckon their Preheminence from the Stocks into which they are ingrafted; but the Daughter . . . must take place of her Mother, or her Husband loses his place—But we mention not this to encourage *Undutifulness,* which the *Law of God* will not dispense with, altho' even in such an Inversion it will dispense with the aforesaid unnatural Order in *Civil Preheminence,* which without a due discretion, may be an unhappy Novel of Temptation. (II.8.2)

An equally ingenious querist poses the question of the legitimacy of twin boys, vigorously begotten on a wife by her husband in what he thought was a liaison with a housemaid. The editors point out that the children are partly the husband's, partly the wife's, and that therefore "so far as the man was concern'd in their Generation, so far only they were *Bastards, wholly as to his intentionality,* and partly as to his Potentiality of an Act" (II.15.7).

In the category of comparative sinfulness is the question of whether it is *"the greatest Sin to be a Night-walker or to rebell against ones Parents?"* Either of them, replied the editors, was big enough for damnation, but for a direct answer, "we refer you to the order of their setting down in the ten Commandments, where Duty to *Parents* is press'd, before Adultery is forbid" (III.5.7).

The Athenians in their answers to social questions provide in the greater part an early example of journalists' customary adherence to conventional attitudes. Their wit was most often at the expense of those who would depart from convention, their guide lines were those of established religious doctrine and civil law, and their advice even to the most despairing of correspondents was to accept life as it was ordained to be. They were not cold to human suffering, however, as they showed especially in their expressed wish for fair treatment of delinquent debtors and bankrupts, and on this subject they departed most radically from conventional views. Their recommendation of a single standard of morality in marriage was also unconventional. But they wished more for the reformation of people than of laws and institutions. The effect, therefore, of their advice, on the whole so much more rational than sensitive, was more educational than consolatory.

CHAPTER 9

[1] Luke Tyerman, *Life of Samuel Wesley*, pp.412–415. He was frustrated in several attempts to bring parishioners to prosecution for adultery.
[2] See Chapter 3, pp.37–38.
[3] III.1. In September 1696, during the interim between Volumes Nineteen and Twenty of the *Mercury*, Dunton published eight issues of a monthly magazine, *Night Walker* or *Evening Rambles in Search after Lewd Women with Conferences Held with them etc. To be published Monthly till a Discovery be made of all the Chief Prostitutes in England from the Pensionary Miss, down to the Common Strumpet*. It contains the material previously published in the *Mercury* and more. For further description, see Chapter 12, pp.213–215.
[4] The pretense of being a spirit was the main device Dunton used in the *Post Angel* (1701). See Chapter 12, pp.220–222.
[5] Samuel was said to have been slower than Susannah in recognizing William as rightful king, and to have objected to Susannah's entertaining the mistress of a nobleman in the parsonage at South Ormsby. Neither allegation has been substantiated.
[6] XI.25.5. Robert Sanderson, who became Bishop of Lincoln in 1660, and whose Aristotelian *Logic* was read by Oxford undergraduates, had preached before Charles I often enough in 1636 and 1637 to cause that monarch to say, "I carry my ears to hear other preachers, but I carry my conscience to hear Dr. Sanderson" (DNB). Numerous English editions of parts of Sanderson's *Casus Conscientiæ* were published after the author's death in 1663.

10

Faith for Everyman

The identity of the Athenians was still veiled in mystery when they first announced their religious position:

> 'Twould be a satisfaction to the World to know of what Religion you are?
> *To which we answer, We are less admirers of* Names than Things, *but if* Appellations *will be satisfactory to the World, we are not ashamed to own our selves* CHRISTIANS, *and particularly, of the Protestant Church, as now Reform'd; and what ever Suggestions have been made to the contrary, we must fix it upon the Readers* misunderstanding of things, *and shall endeavour, as much as in us lies, to avoid either* Practices or Disputes *which may tend to widen the Breaches betwixt those who agree in the* Fundamentals of the Christian Religion; *and as an undeniable proof of this, we shall shew in answer to a certain Question we have receiv'd, that 'tis a Maxim of the* Jesuits, *to start differences about* Circumstantials, *and that 'twas them only, that by their Disguises and false Pretences, were the first promoters of the* many unhappy Differences *that are now amongst us, both in* Church and State. (Pref.,Vol.II)

Their careful avoidance of Protestant denominational labels, their appeal to "those who agree in the Fundamentals of the Christian Religion," and their promise of an attack on the tactics of the Jesuits, all indicate the path which the Athenians sought to follow through the prevailing maze of religious differences. They did not wish to offend moderate Nonconformists, such as Samuel Annesley, who differed from the orthodox on only a few of the Articles of Faith. They hoped as well to please all the orthodox except the High Flyers, whom scarcely anyone could please, by attacking the Jesuits, Quakers, and Anabaptists.

The suspension of the *Mercury* in 1692 because of pressure from the High Flyers taught the editors what would happen if they made any criticism too apparent to Jacobites. They found out to their sorrow that there was still strength enough there to stop the presses. But their attacks upon irreconcilable denominations of Dissenters during the whole term of the *Mercury*'s existence were safe from official displeasure if not from rebuttals by their victims, and such outraged responses produced opportunity to publish controversy.

Attacks upon Dissenters, particularly Quakers and Anabaptists, appeared in set pieces and often continued as a series, sometimes covering whole numbers. These represent Dunton's kind of sensational journalism, aimed at selling many copies. Questions seeking information about the Scriptures, biblical history, and formal aspects of religion appealed to Wesley, the clergyman, more than to Dunton, the journalist; they were a challenge to Wesley's learning, and the controversies raised were largely academic.

There is a recognizable kinship between the answers to requests for religious information and Wesley's major literary work, the *Life of Christ* (1693), where the poet's great learning outshines his poetic gifts. The works referred to there are recognizable to anyone who reads the religious questions in the *Mercury*. Some of Wesley's references were common to the age, to be sure, but certain of them he repeatedly referred to with admiration and respect.[1]

Every production of Wesley's, not excluding *Maggots*, shows its author's polymath tendency and his fascination with the minutiae of learning. His studies at the Dissenting academies and the University prepared him to write exhaustively upon almost any subject. His mind was stuffed with information, and his religious position was not extreme. He was moderate, not fanatical, and tolerant to some degree —although not disposed to change the laws to make things any easier for those whom the laws did not accommodate. For the *Athenian Mercury* his credentials were perfect.

When Wesley was a student in the Dissenting academies he was told what a wicked place Oxford was, and yet he was urged, as were his classmates, to enter his name there as a student in order to be ready when the righteous came once more into power to take his degree without having to subscribe to the abhorred Articles then standing as an obstacle. Instead of waiting for that day, Wesley went down to Oxford on impulse, was entered as a servitor at Exeter, earned his own way, and took orders almost immediately thereafter.[2] He served for over forty years as an Anglican clergyman of unquestioned loyalty. Yet he brought with him and kept for all his life some attitudes that were fostered by his upbringing in a Dissenting household and his early training in Dissenting academies.

One of these attitudes concerned the Second Coming. Millenarianism, or chiliasm as it was then more formally called, has had a long history, for its promise of a reward to the persecuted is most alluring. In its most literal form, as set forth in Revelation 1–5, a reign of a thousand years under Christ after His Second Coming is promised, but only to those who suffered the tribulations of the last days before Christ's return. The description in this passage holds forth no sensual attractions but suggests rather a kind of military government to get things established before final and unalterable judgments are made.

The ancient Jewish apocalyptic books were the chief foundation used by early Christian writers to support their beliefs in the millenium, but some later ecclesiastics rejected the ideas as "Jewish." The Greek church, in fact, excluded Revelation from the biblical canon, contending that it was a "Jewish" book passing for apocalyptic literature. Dionysius healed the breach somewhat in the second century by urging an allegorical interpretation of all such works, and Augustine largely succeeded in putting down the literal interpreters by teaching that the millenium had begun with the appearance of Christ on earth and that the Catholic Church in apostolic form was the true kingdom of Christ—in other words, that the millenium was already an accomplished fact, or at least well under way toward being so.

The later history of millenarianism is one of underground operations, so to speak, its proponents making common cause with the enemies of the secularized or political church. It appeared from time to time in the Middle Ages, and again at the Reformation, when it lent a strong tinge to Lutheranism. The Dissenters in seventeenth-century England, all favoring a more or less democratic church, saw in millenarianism a denial of the vested interests to which they were opposed.

There were millenialists among the orthodox, of course. Samuel Wesley was one of them. His biographers have been unanimous in commenting upon his lifelong interest in the subject, but the most convincing evidence appears in an early number of the *Mercury,* entirely devoted to answering the question: *"What think you of the* Millenium? *and whether do you believe 'tis yet to come, or already past?"* (IV.6.1).

Wesley thought well of the millenium, expecting it to come in the way described in Revelation. The "Anti-chiliasts" rejected it *because* it was Jewish, that is, described in ancient Jewish works, but Wesley pointed out that many passages in the Apocrypha, in the Psalms, in Isaiah, and in the Epiphanius of Methodius, Bishop of Tyre, also gave support to his position. Not only did Wesley find scriptural support for, "To come to Fathers: Our Enemies as good as give us all the *first,* and most of the *second* Century," but he also provided a long list of the Fathers, interspersed with brief comments upon the particular circumstances of their approval of the millenial idea. All in all, Wesley provided a spirited defense of his convictions.[3]

Wesley's answer to the question on the millenium aroused some objections, for in the Preface to the Third Volume he was moved to write:

If there be any who shall happen to be offended at our Notions concerning the Millenium, *for which we have much more to say than we had room to insert in a single*

> Mercury, *we desire 'em to send their* Objections *against it, and suspend their* Definitive Judgments *till they hear what we have to add further, which we promise fairly to examine, and if they convince us,* publickly to retract *our Opinion, as we have engaged in* the body of that Discourse.

Four years later the matter was still of interest to readers, one of whom asked the Athenians *"How many years, according to the exactest Computation of Time must it be, before the fall of* Antichrist *and his Kingdom"* (XVII.6.3, Sat 20 Apr 95). But patience had worn somewhat thin through the years; the editors replied that if the querist thought this a fair question he must give them leave

> to profess our selves not Prophets enough to answer it, being warn'd by the Fate of many persons of no contemptible Learning, who have all split upon this Rock, and expos'd themselves by fixing the Times and the Seasons, which 'tis not for them to know, and which the Father has put in his own power. . . . We . . . have observ'd the prudence of the Church of *Rome* in this matter, who shou'd know as much of *Antichrist* as other folks. And their Writers generally fix his very coming but three years and a half before the end of the world; That men may be sure not to look for him sooner.

According to Dunton's testimony, Wesley first took part in the Athenian project with the fourth number, Saturday 4 April 1691 (LE,p.256). In it a question on divorce was answered with the quotation of Matthew 5:32; *"Whosoever shall Marry her that is Divorced, committeth Adultery."* One on the lawfulness of polygamy among the ancient Jews was answered with historical fact and personal opinion.

Polygamy was customary among the Jews but not specifically permitted by law. It was disagreeable to the laws of nature and fraught with "the most fatal Inconveniences and unnatural Disturbances in Families and even Empires. . . ." The conclusion bears a Wesleyan stamp:

"*There's no earthly Happiness like mutual Love,* the more intense the one, the greater the other; but love divided into various Channels or Beds, is like a River serv'd at the same rate, *always lessen'd, sometimes lost."*

The sixth number of the *Mercury,* a week later, has three-fourths of its space devoted to the question of man's eternal soul. This number illustrates the short lapse of time between writing and publication, at least in the first numbers published. An advertisement at the end of Number 5 announced that "next Saturday Morning shall be discuss'd (at large) that Grand Disputable Question, *Whether brute Creatures have any sort of knowledge like to ours,* and *whether or no a Raven can speak?* Occasion'd by an Account of ONE that utter'd several Expressions; the Truth whereof is confirmed by the present Minister of *Wigmore,* and attested under the *Licensers* own hand."[4]

On the Saturday following, however, the immortality of the soul was determined affirmatively, the writer being unable to conceive its ceasing to be, and arguing that where there were no parts there could be no dissolution. A concluding note promised the discussion of brute knowledge for the next Tuesday—"But this is now dispatcht being of great moment, and taking up more time than was design'd. . . ."

First evidence of concern over denominational differences appeared in Volume One, Number 19: *"What is the meaning of the present Union between the* Presbyterians *and* Independents? *And whether a* Universal Accommodation *amongst Protestants may ever be expected?"* The Athenians had sanguine expectations, based upon *"the word of a king* on our side, the *suffrages* of an Archbishop, and several other Prelates, and this also confirm'd by the concurrent Notes of a *Lord Chief Justice,* and divers eminent Divines."

Published at the same time was their opinion that passive obedience and non-resistance, if not absurd, were at least injurious to society if carried to an extreme. They had little sympathy for clergymen suspended for refusing the oaths to William and Mary. Such ones, they thought, did not have as hard treatment as the Fellows of Magdalen College who were turned out "by the worst of Men" in 1687 to let in popery; for those now refusing the oaths could still preach (I.20.1). Both Wesley and Norris were still at Oxford when the Fellows were turned out, and remembered the event.

Three of the undated numbers of Volume One are filled with religious questions. The essay treatment of several of the questions reflects the greater leisure the writer had to prepare these numbers for the press. The opinion on the authenticity of Moses' authorship of the Pentateuch is a mixture of Old Testament historical data and warnings against Hobbes, Spinoza, and others who sought to weaken the authority of the books dictated by God to Moses (I.24). The story of Saul and the Witch of Endor occupies over half an entire number (I.27). Still other numbers are miscellanies of the sort of questions that appeared time and time again throughout the life of the *Mercury*—what was the sin of Onan? How may a man know when he is in the Covenant? In what estate shall we appear at the Resurrection? Where did the bodies of the saints go who arose with our Saviour?

Although the Athenians announced several times in Volume One that they would ignore questions they considered unfit for their pages, they devoted a full number in Volume Two to the question of atheism, on the ground that revealed religion was endangered by the prevalence of such misconceptions as represented in the questions received. They proposed, therefore, to *"ruin the very* Foundations *of* Atheism, [so that] *all the little* Superstructures *must of necessity fall to the Ground"* (II.25). Among the "superstructures" were the notions that Christianity had been invented at the fall of Jerusalem, that the book of Revelation was an invention, that martyrs were fools, and that all religious people, in fact, were fools. The first of the five questions dealt with in this number was:

Whether the Irish Massacre, *and the* Massacre *of* Paris, *together with the* growth *and progress of* Mahometanism, *be not greater Arguments that the* Machine *of the* World *follows the* dead Chain of Causes, *than any can be produced, that can rationally convince us of* God's Providence, *or his care of* Christianity?

The answer to this question is given here at length as a fair sample of the Athenians' method of attack:

> We must not, for every *little difficulty* in *Providence,* immediately *unhinge* the *Universe,* and deny any such thing as a *Supreme Being,* ordering Humane Affairs, *both because* we can, at least, *Morally demonstrate,* that there *is* such a *Being,* and that he *made* the *World,* and consequently, *all perfection* being included in his *Essence,* must and does *dispose* of, and *govern* it according to *fixed* and *equitable* Rules; any Objection against his *Providence,* being therefore only like a *Protestatio contra factum.* . . . And . . . we cannot only oftentimes *account* for these *difficulties* by the *fixed rules* of *Providence* and *Justice,* but also use those *very things* as *Arguments* for their *Existence,* since many of 'em were so clearly *foretold* by the *Spirit of God* so many *hundred years* before they happened. Besides, they may be both *natural Consequents* and *just Punishments* of *Sin:* For example, the *Apostacy* of the *Eastern Churches* to *Mahometanism,* and *Western* to *Popery,* were both the *effects* of that Vice, Laziness, Debauchery, *Irreligion, Discord,* and Ignorance which had over-run the *World,* and also, *just punishments* for 'em, and *both* clearly *foretold* before they came to pass. . . .

There is a continuity and identity of opinion within the undated numbers of Volume One that indicates a single hand. The comparative lack of pressure on the writer preparing the more discursive answers for the undated numbers permitted a greater expression of opinion as well as an ampler ground upon which to spread his authorities. The answers to persistent questioning of the authenticity of Scripture suggest most strongly the work of a single author.

> *Whence comes it that there's so great a* difference *between the* holy Scriptures *and* profane History; *in the* Names *of the* Kings *of* Egypt, Babel, *and other* Countries; *which seems the stranger, because some of those* Names *are the same in both* Histories, *as* Darius, Cyprus *and* Artaxerxes? (II.30.7)

"For the sacred *Histories,*" replied Wesley, "we are *sure* they are *true,* and consequently, if there shou'd be any *irreconcileable difference* between *them* and *others,* the latter must be mistaken."

The differences among languages, the inability of profane historians to agree among themselves, and their uncertainty, should occasion wonder that there are so many names alike rather than that there are some differences, although he conceded that the practice of giving the same names to a whole succession, as with the Pharaohs, caused confusion.

An inquiry about Bishop Burnet's doubts of the authenticity of *"a part of the Hebrew Josephus still extant in the Vatican at* Rome," brought admiring concurrence from the editors:

> That Ingenious Great Man having doubted of the Report, we shan't pretend to give our Opinion after him, unless in the *same Words;* for every one knows *the great Learning he has, the Inquisitiveness of his Nature,* and the Opportunities he had to be satisfied of the reasonableness or unreasonableness of the Relation, render'd him as capable a Judge of it as any *Person living.* (III.14.8)

Not only the authenticity of "original" manuscripts of Josephus, but also the historical authenticity of the work itself, were subjects for animated and often heated discussion at the time, part of a continuing readjustment of values in accordance with the usefulness to protestant theology of any particular work. The *Mercury* was no pace setter in this activity, but its compliment to Bishop Burnet shows its awareness of the trend.

The Athenians disparaged Rome's acceptance of Josephus, as indicated by the housing of his works in the Vatican library, yet Josephus was sometimes used in the *Mercury* as an authority even more reliable than Scripture. For example, in reply to a question of whether the Tree of Life and the Tree of Knowledge were different, Josephus is cited in the affirmative as representing the general view of antiquity, followed, however, by: "So the Scripture seems also not obscurely to assert" (III.17.4).

Among more recent authorities one of the most frequently cited is "The Learned and indefatigable Bochart,"[5] whose dissertation concerning the camel in his *Hierozoicon* yielded the knowledge that *Gamal* meant both *camel* and *cable*, and therefore gave a literal interpretation of the camel's passing through the eye of a needle. The interpretation of "the eye of the needle" as the narrow aperture of Needle Gate in Jerusalem, however, yielded "a *very beautiful and apposite Simile*" (III.17.8).

Scriptural authority posed no doubts for the Athenians. They asserted that the Bible was more historical than any other history, and could therefore be used to prove a point without reference to any other work. They admitted their inability to prove scriptural authority to an atheist, though not to an antiscripturalist or anyone who believed in God, even the deist, "who must believe the *Word of Reason to be the Word of God*" (III.18.2).

Human error, however, might creep into scriptural text, as shown in answering the question of how, in Psalm 133, the dew of Hermon could descend also on the mountain of Sion, some hundred miles distant:

> Our Opinion in this Case, with all due respect and deference for greater Men of a different Judgment, is, That by the *Mountains of Sion* here, are meant the *Mountains of Gilead*, which were part of the *Kingdom of Sibon*, King of the *Amorites*, and which are just under *Hermon*, and that the Word *Sion* here *crept* in by the mistake of the Transcriber instead of *Sibon*, their sound being the same, or very near, tho' there are some Letters differing in the Writing. (III.18.6)

Science and faith join hands to settle a quibble over Genesis 1:

> *That on the first day God ordained the day and the night, &c. and on the fourth day he made two great Lights, the Sun and Moon, &c. Pray what was that Light or Day, before the Sun was made, since we generally suppose the Day to proceed from the Sun, &c.*

Answ. There's an Innate Light in the Heavens; thus rotten Wood, Glow-worms, and many other things give light without the help of Reflexions. The Learn'd believe it was a Circumrotation of their own Light. (V.2.7)

Frequent questions about the soul were dealt with swiftly and positively. The editors saw no essential difference between a man's soul and a woman's, only an accidental one which would be eliminated at the Resurrection, when there would be "nothing of Sex, any more than in the Angels, in those who neither marry, nor are given in Marriage, therefore we believe that what superiority there is shall not be *eternal,* but shall cease as soon as this Life is ended" (V.3.2).

With perfect solemnity, the *Mercury* explained how Baalam, although a Moabite, could understand the ass speaking to him in Hebrew. In the first place, a Moabite would have understood Hebrew, since he would have learned it from his father, who learned it from his father, Lot. But Baalam was not a Moabite but an Aramite, who also would have spoken Hebrew (V.5.3).

One who doubted the existence of angels was given to understand that an angel was "a real immaterial Substance, in a distinct rank or order of Beings from that of men." Anyone who believed the Scriptures could not disbelieve this, for there the existence of angels, "their agency, duty and operations [are] often describ'd; . . . at least in 200 places of the Bible, in such manner, as distinct immaterial Substances must thereby be unavoidably intended" (V.10.2).

Miracles or miraculous signs seem often to have been rejected because of their acceptance by the Catholics. The answer to the question of the reason for *"the* Strake *on every* Mules *back representing a* Crucifix" illustrates such a bias: "The Reason on't is, because an *Ass* was his Father —If it be asked why an Ass has such an one, the Papists will tell you, its because our Saviour rode upon one, and therefore all the kind have been thus mark'd ever since; but there's as much reason that all Figtrees are curs'd because one was so. Had they bin but so civil to have confin'd the Miracle to all the *Strain* of that very Ass, the story had then had some Face with it . . ." (V.10.3).

John Dunton, "our Bookseller," sometimes used answers to religious questions to advertise books. In the same number that carried Sir William Temple's question on talismans is an inquiry as to the best text of the Old Testament, *"the vulgar, Hebrew, or the Septuagint?"* The reply is pure opportunism: "A full and satisfactory answer to this is to be had in Dr. *Lightfoot's* and Bishop *Usher's* Works, which make up part of our Young Students Library, which will shortly be put to the Press" (V.7.3). To another question in the same issue about the origin of the Apostles' Creed, Dunton replied that the forthcoming work would also contain a collection of ten forms of creeds mentioned in the hundred years after Christ (V.7.10).

As for a particular creed, orthodoxy claims a triumph in the answer to the following ecumenical question:

> *Suppose a Jew, a Mahometan, a Ch. of Englandman, an Anabaptist, a Quaker, and a Muggletonian, all living together in one House peaceable, and according to their own Principles—May they not all expect Happiness after this Life?* (III.23.4)

The Articles of Faith have answered the question for most of the orthodox, "pronouncing an Anathema on all those who affirm 'tis possible to be sav'd in any Religion, if Men live up to't."

There can be only one right but many wrongs. The Jew blasphemes the Savior and hates all Christians, "so he's gone." The Mohammedan's religion is "a Nonsensical piece of Imposture, and . . . he so mortally hates the Christians, that Dogs are the best Names he'll afford 'em, and expects his Paradise, such a one as 'tis, as the Reward of Murdering 'em." The Muggletonian hates the Bible and is full of blasphemy and nonsense. The Quakers "have held very dangerous and destestable Opinions." They have turned the Bible into "an odd sort of a jejune Allegory." They deny the Trinity and "embrace the other Socinian Dream of the Souls sleeping till the Resurrection."

Only the Anabaptist found much charity in the writer's heart. Although the Anabaptist had been fierce and dangerous in Germany, the writer hoped that English soil had "a little mended his Crabstock—For we must own according to their present Writings, there are not many Articles of Common Christianity, if any, which our English Anabaptists disown, besides that of Infant Baptism, wherein some Great Men in the Ch. of God have *err'd* together with 'em."

The fourth volume of the *Mercury* begins with a request for historical proof from other than scriptural sources, of the existence of Christ and the performance of his miracles. *"It may be of great Use to the settling in some young* Hobbists *a Perswasion of the reality of the Christian Religion"* (IV.1.1). The *Mercury* responded at length, beginning with "the Death of *Pan* in *Plutarch,* at our Saviours Nativity." Others cited are Origen, Tacitus, Simon Magus, Aristobulus, Justin Martyr, and Macrobius. "We might add a Cloud more of Witnesses, *viz. Pliny, Suetonius, Dion, Tranquillus, Cornelius, Tacitus, Ælius, Lampridius, Saturninus, &c.* . . . but 'tis hoped here is already more than is required for the Credibility of an *Alexander, Julius Caesar,* or any other Persons or their Acts, which our Doubters of Christ's Truth and Miracles can readily assent to."

A practical answer was rendered to the question of whether Moses's Pisgah-sight was real or visionary. Recognizing that it is difficult to see for more than thirty miles in England, and that Moses had to see for sixty to view the Promised Land, the editor adduces evidence of Moses's keen eyesight and adds that:

> God Almighty who was pleased to confer that Favour upon him, might at that time strengthen his Eye, and render the Medium of Visibility more adapt for such a Prospect; this we are apt to believe, rather than a Visionary Prospect; for if it had been in a Vision, it might as well have been in a Valley, or in his own Tent, as on the Top of *Mount Pisgah.* (IV.2.3)

To the question of why the name of God was not once mentioned in the Book of Esther, an answer was found where little expected, "in Consulting Authors on the *late difficulty* concerning the *Creation of the World*," in a passage of *"A Ben Ezra's Commentaries thereon,"* concerning the practice of the Hamathites of substituting the name of their own idol for that of "the True God." Hence the Samaritan Pentateuch had the word *Assima* where the name of God should be. By analogy, God in Esther suffered a similar treatment at the hands of the Persians (IV.9.13).

In a number devoted entirely to the subject of baptism, the editors struggled with such questions as whether baptism was an antitype of circumcision; whether there were indubitable grounds for infant baptism; why Christ was not baptized before he was thirty years old; why baptism was necessary for children, since they were "saved," whether or not; and whether children had faith, *"since Faith and Repentance are pre-requisite to Baptism?"* The *Mercury's* answers were aimed at the Anabaptists, or rather, Antipaedobaptists, as the editors fussily insisted. Opposition to infant baptism is explained as stemming from:

> Not knowing the *Customs of Nations, Linguisms,* . . . or *Expressions* only peculiar to such and such Tongues, together with the Ignorance of the Radixes or Original Significations in Languages . . . and by consequence, the unhappy Introductions into many dangerous Heresies and Schisms in the Church. (IV.14.1)

At the end of Volume Five, Number 5, the Athenians promised to answer any further questions from their opponents in the last twelve numbers of Volume Six. This promise was fulfilled, however, even sooner, in Numbers 19–27 and 30 of Volume Five. These numbers were published all at once, only Number 19 having a title, the rest continuing without any break, and concluding in Number 27 with a postscript which promised further reply, "if there be occasion . . . every nine weeks in the twelve Numbers, six of the nine will allow you to make good your Party; but be so ingenuous for the future, as not to say we have not answered such and such questions when we had never seen 'em." Number 30 stands independently, without a title, but the words "*Romarks* [sic] *upon the last Sheet Publish'd by the Anabaptists.*"

To prove not only that children have faith but that "sometimes we have visible Effects of the Faith of Children," the *Mercury* quotes at some length from John Eliot's *Tears of Repentance* (1653), particularly of a little child, dying of "*that grievous Disease of the Bloody-flux*" (pp.46–47), who was sensible of the approach of death and said repeatedly to his parents that he was going to God (IV.14.8).

The editors were gratified by the journalistic result of the number on infant baptism. It had moved the Anabaptists to bring out a set of animadversions upon the subject, in which they exposed their tenets and showed the weakness of their objections to the assertions made in the *Mercury*. To the responses of the Anabaptists the Athenian Society devoted a second entire number, not so much to vex as to convince their adversaries (IV.18).

The Quakers generally found even less favor with the Athenians than did the Anabaptists, and in fact were closely identified with the Jesuits:

The Quakers deny the Plenary Satisfaction of *Christ*, and rest on their own Merits; so do the Papists: they Rail at our Ministers, and deny their Legal Call, or Ordination; so do the Papists: They pretend to a greater strictness and singularity of Life than other People, so it's notorious do several Orders among the Papists, so exactly, that one wou'd think the Quakers only a sort of Lay-Brothers to some of their Societies. Then for Phanaticism, and Enthusiasm, they are most admirably match'd, that and Infidelity together making up the very *Creed* of the Quaker (forgive the Expression!). But to consider 'em asunder, it's true, the Papist holds more than he ought to do, and therefore all the Articles of the Christian Faith; but the Quaker much less: They all deny the Christian Sacraments, both Baptism, and the Lord's Supper; and we wonder how they have the Face to pretend to what they never had, *Christianity,* when they were never *Christen'd*. They are indeed a Compendium of almost all sorts of Heresies; for they not only deny the Merits of *Christ,* as has been said, with the Papists, but even his Satisfaction, Divinity and all, being, at best, no better than meer *Arrians;* if we believe 'em what their late (and present) great Champion has refin'd 'em into: Nay, there have some of 'em who as far as we can understand 'em, deny our Saviour's Manhood too, as well as his Godhead; nay, deny Angels, Spirits, Heaven and Hell, turning all into mean and jejune Allegories; and no wonder after this, they should, all of 'em, to a Man, that e're we met with, in positive Terms, deny the Scriptures to the the *Word* of *God;* and most of 'em deny any Resurrection of the Body, as others the Existence, or Activity and Consciousness (which is all one) of Souls after Death. For these Reasons, we think, as a bad Christian is better than none; so a Papist than a Quaker; though Charity gives us room to hope, that there may be some in both of those Parties who may be better Christians, than those Principles, if believ'd, wou'd permit 'em to be; but then they must be neither good Quakers, nor good Papists (IV.30).

The Quakers, finding that the *Mercury* was not an unprejudiced forum, replied to these unfounded assertions in a publication of their own, the *Athenian Society Unvail'd: Or, their Ignorance and Envious Abusing of the QUAKERS Detected and Reprehended.* The two folio half-sheets, printed for *"Thomas Northcott in Georgeyard in Lombard-street* 1692," resemble the *Mercury* in size and typography.[6] The writer protests the inconsistency between the Athenians' "many Offers at a Reformation," their "publick Pretences . . . to encourage some and advise all to the furtherance of it," and their practice, "no other then the Transcript of the Jesuits Maxim: who you say were they, that by their Disguises and false Pretences were the first Promoters of the many unhappy Differences that are now among us, both in Church and State."

The writer, after demolishing the *Mercury*'s assertions

with logic, demands for evidence, and citation of the Act of 1689 *"for exempting their Majesties Protestant Subjects,"* admonishes the Athenians "That plain and positive Proof must make good your Charge. Repentance must make you honest Men, and the continuance in your Crimes will make you as Incorrigible as those Beasts, which serve for Emblems in your Buffoonry: If you cannot do the first, the way to avoid the last is by the middlemost; which that you may, is the desire of him who can forgive enemies, and is in scorn call'd a QUAKER."

The Athenians, however, showed little sympathy for the peculiarities of Quakerism and gave little evidence of any effort to understand them. Of the Quakers' refusal to take oaths in court they wrote: "If swearing had been a Moral evil, God Almighty wou'd never have *Sworn by Himself,* as the Scripture mentions" (VI.26.7).

They demanded that the Quakers make categorical answers to ten questions, such as whether they believed in the Trinity; whether their light within was the third person of the Trinity or their own natural reason; whether they believed in angels "or any Immaterial Spirits besides the Soul of Man;" and where one could find their creed or an account of their religion. These and other questions must be answered, "not with any equivocating Jesuitish Tricks and Evasions, lest we should the more suspect their Original from that side of the Water . . . cleared, not from their own Word, but the Testimonies of their Authentick Writers —which when done to satisfaction, and they have prov'd themselves Christians, we shall be very ready to acknowledge our mistakes, and call 'em Brethren."

The subject was continued in the *Supplement V,* in a request for the Athenians' opinion of the Quakers' "light within." The response was, "For their *light within,* we wou'd *hope* for their Sakes, 'tis no other but *common Reason,* or *natural Conscience,* which all mankind enjoy as well as them. For our thoughts of them and their Opinions, we have already spoken most of what we know concerning 'em . . ." (p.25).

The Quaker was customarily placed on the scale very

close to the Catholic, sometimes a little below, sometimes a little above. He was placed above the Papist in the answer to a question about a Quaker who had gone through the streets of London in July 1692 crying "Repent, or Fire and Brimstone will be your Portions!" Had he been sent by God? On the contrary, wrote the Athenians, he was most probably a Papist disguised as a Quaker, for it was the Catholics who in 1666, after distributing a printed warning of the event, had fired the city "to defeat the Protestant Predictions, and Expectations of great Revolutions, to befall *Rome* . . . upon the Prophesy of the Fall of Babilon in the Revelations . . ." (VIII.24.1).

Two years later the Athenians answered a question about Quakers who had "tamper'd with" an old man, getting him to change his will in favor of them. The Athenians had "reason to believe that it's an usual thing among those People, who are certainly wise in their Generation, whatever they may be for *Children of Light,* and whom we look upon as the firmest and most politick Body of men that Dissent from our Communion; we know not whether we are to except the Jesuits themselves." Following this there is a peculiar left-handed compliment to the Quakers and their doctrines,

> concerning which we have bin so long indebted to 'em, that it's almost a shame to mention it, tho' shou'd we quite forget it, which we hardly shall, they wou'd, we believe, forgive us—tho' in the mean time we must own, that one or two of their Papers on that Subject, were the civilest, and seem'd to argue the fairest of any we have ever seen from their Party, and we shall endeavour to imitate them in our Answers, without any great Inclination to turn Proselytes neither. (XIII.22.1)

The Quakers' practice looked like Popery to the Athenians, the sort of thing by which the Catholics got most of their monasteries and once held the greater part of England. Yet these Quakers were protestants, and if *they* got the inheritance, it could not fall into the hands of the Jesuits. Because the Quakers sought to establish an open forum in which they could debate with the Athenians, they could not very well be regarded and treated as sinister forces of darkness like the Papists. They were instead an organized opposition, not numerically strong, but certainly loud and vigorous in their expression, and they provided good copy for the *Mercury*.

The Jews in England received a quite different sort of treatment at the hands of the Athenians. Jesuits were not to be tolerated or trusted. Quakers were regarded as wrongheaded but nevertheless protestants and therefore not beyond the pale. But the Jews presented both civil and religious problems, as in the following example: *"Whether a Christian Magistrate can Tolerate the Jews, since their Expectation of a Triumphant Messias is a direct Blasphemy against Jesus Christ whom they reject, and their Ancestors had the presumptuous boldness to brag that they Crucified the God of the Christians?"* (VII.12.6).

The Athenians favored a just toleration, saying that "thô we are no *Jews,* yet as we are *Men,* we will venture for once not only to justifie the Wisdom of the Magistrate, but also take off the false Calumnies that are cast upon that dispersed Nation, . . . under these 2 heads, *Ecclesiack* and *Civil."*

Under the first heading the Athenians argued that the Jews were their elder brethren, that their religion had once been the only true one, and that although the Jews had been "Slaves to *Types, Shadows*[,]*Figures,* &c. yet they had also the same *Eternal Moral Law* for their observation which they carefully observe at this day . . . and if they Crucified the Head of our Religion, . . . yet we are the better for it, for had he not been Crucified, our Religion had never had a Being."

The Athenians cast doubt upon the supposed anti-Christian actions of the Jews—rites using the blood of Christians, their murder, or ritualistic daily cursing of them. Under this head they concluded that "we have no order to treat those ill that are not of our Faith, and if in any Civil Account the disorderly amongst the Jews, offend (as no People in the World is free from such Members) the Laws which they live under, and by which they are maintain'd in their Right and Liberties, will also take Cognizance of their breaches of it."

More than three years later the question arose again of whether it was *"lawful for Christian Princes to permit the Jews to live quiet in their dominions, and to give them a free toleration for their Religion?"* (XVII.28.1, Sat 6 Jul 95).

The Athenians feared no civil problems, provided there was neither communication in religion, nor mixed marriages, and so long as the Jews obeyed the civil power and did not seek public office. They expressed the hope that one day the Jews might all be converted and saw also a possible and more immediate advantage for Christians: "By the Jews living amongst us, we may also be the more induced to acknowledge the goodness of God to us, in receiving us to mercy when he cast off his own people; by the remembrance of which we are taught to fear and tremble at the Judgments of the Almighty." Permitting the Jews to live among them also provided witnesses that the Christians had not themselves "composed and written" the Scriptures but that they were the work of their enemies. Toleration would keep the Jews from becoming atheists. And "all gentle means may be used to bring them to the knowledge of the truth, but violence must be avoided, since faith cometh by persuasion, and not by force."[7]

The anti-Semitism of the time is illustrated by the following question: *"A certain* Jew, *having a violent passion for a young woman who is a* Quaker, *promis'd her marriage, on which she consented to his desires, soon after he fell in Love with another, and by the same promise prevail'd so far with her as to serve her as he did the former; the latter of which now proves with child by him. Your opinion is desired whether of the two he ought to marry, the former having much the advantage both in* Fortune *and* Beauty."

The Athenians showed themselves less prejudiced than the questioner, answering "We shou'd say he had done like a *Jew,* were there not too many who wou'd fain be called Christians, that are often guilty of as ill, or baser actions." His falling in love with both showed "such a Love as Brutes have for the whole Herd, a very Heathen having defin'd Love better, that as often as our mind carries us to that which is good, 'tis Love, otherwise Concupiscence." Of "this *Termagant Israelite,*" they felt that, though he was not a Christian, "he might have had some respect to those of the Country where he lives, at least of common Truth, and Honesty, which is planted in the Hearts of all mankind." They advised that he marry the first, "and since he can't the 2d too without ventring [sic] the swing, to provide for her, whom he has ruin'd, as well as the Child, of which he's the ungracious Father" (XVII.25.3).

There are questions showing an interest in the history of the Jews, in their religious practices, and in the origins and extent of Hebrew learning. Wesley's demonstrations elsewhere of his deep interest in these subjects make it almost a certainty that he was responsible for the extensive answers given to such inquiries. Some questions seem trivial, such as whether the Jews set up a scarecrow on the Temple to keep birds away, but the *Mercury* provided a full column answer referring to Maimonides and Josephus, and closing with a mild reproof to Milton for his assumption in *Paradise Regained* that Christ was set upon a pinnacle of the temple by "the *Enemy.*" "Tho the best is, *Poets* are not oblig'd to be the *best Commentators,* and both he and those whom he follows must of necessity be here mistaken, for otherwise, our Lord had wrought a miracle for his own preservation, which the Tempter all along desir'd, and this miracle had not consisted in his casting himself down from the Temple, to which he advis'd him, but in standing upon it, which he already did" (XVII.14.3).

We learn that the Jews fasted in August because "they lookt upon the Creation of the World to be in *September,* and so make [August] to be the beginning of their year, and believ'd God wou'd come to Judge it about that time" (XVI.14.2).

The Jews' ancient attitude toward redemption was of great interest. Questions about it brought forth some interesting speculations from the Athenians, one of these an attempt to show that the Jews expected a redemption from their sins, and not a temporal Savior. Support for this notion was drawn in one instance from "an antient Jewish book called *Pesikta,* who tells us that God had a dialogue with the *Messiah* . . ." (XVI.10.3). The dialogue, not unlike the exchanges of Milton's Father and Son, settles that the Messiah will undergo pain and suffering on earth *"for a whole week of years"* on the condition that all the Israelites shall be saved, *"all those that have been created until now, or shall hereafter be created."*

"Altho there be many idle fancys in this," concluded the editor, "yet through these fables we may plainly discern that the Jews have not always promised themselves a triumphant *Messiah,* nor expected those temporal advantages from his coming, as they did when he came amongst them."

The *"many odd Laws which were given to the children of Israel"* were treated at great length, taking up an entire number of the *Mercury*. The Athenians could not believe that hard laws were given the ancient Jews merely to test them. Neither could they agree with Josephus, Philo, and "the Platonizing Jews" in the belief that there was something symbolic about all the laws. Rather, they agreed with those who thought the laws were to prevent a reversion to heathen idolatry:

> We say then, as to those *usages* which they had in common with the Heathens, as Temples, Altars, Sacrifices, and many others, much the same that our Divines answer to the *Papists,* and others, when they object that our Common Prayer was taken out of their *Mass-Book,* . . . that with more reason it may be affirm'd their *Mass-Book* was taken out of our Common-Prayer, that is, it *degenerated* from the ancient Liturgys, and we reforming after the primitive *patterns,* cou'd not but have some things Common with 'em, because they had not left *all* which they had receiv'd from antiquity, so here the Heathen Nations had preserv'd some footsteps of the true ancient *traditionary Religion* which they had receiv'd from the *Sons of Noah.* (XVIII.7.1)

The very last question in the entire *Mercury* on the subject of the Jews strongly supports the belief that Wesley was still writing for Dunton early in 1696, or else that Dunton was at that time making use of pieces written earlier by Wesley. In response to the question of whether all learning first came from the Jews, there was printed an answer well over fifteen hundred words long (XIX.25.2) exhibiting the sort of "universal" learning characteristic of Wesley's writing. Its thesis resembles his contribution four years earlier to the *Young Students Library,* where in "A Discourse concerning the Original and Antiquity of the Hebrew Points, Vowels and Accents," he aimed at proving that the points, vowels and accents of Hebrew were in existence before 500 A.D., either "coævous" with the letters, or given to Moses on Sinai along with the oral law, or placed to the law and Scriptures as they were first written.

The moderate religious position of the *Mercury* is well illustrated by two references to the work of Thomas Burnet which appeared eighteen months apart in its pages. The first, in July 1691, was in answer to a question from a reader trying to identify pagan myth and Old Testament chronology with each other:

> Question. *Whether Saturn be Noah, and what is meant by the Golden Ages?*
> Answer. For the Golden Age, the Heathens here too seem to confound the time before the Flood, and Fall of Man: And for those who wou'd see a fine Description on't, let 'em consult Ovid, or Mr. Burnets most ingenious Theory of the Earth, which affords one much finer. (II.18.12)

Near the end of the following year, two entire numbers of the *Mercury* were devoted to a refutation of a number of Burnet's assertions in his *Archæologiæ Philosophicæ,* the original Latin version of which had been published only a month earlier.[8] The editors explained at the outset that they were not going to answer all "the Paper of Questions . . . about Dr. *Burnet's Archiologiæ,*" for some of them related to what was "purely an Innocent Hypothesis, and as such we are willing to acknowledge, that there's a deal of Reading, pretty Invention, sharp Wit, and refin'd Philosophy mingled throughout, and as such the Age is willing to receive it: But all these qualifications want foundation to make the whole Canonical, or fix a Standard for every Reader's Judgment" (VIII.28).

The editors felt obliged, however, to expose the error of those other parts, "rais'd upon the Ruines of Eternal Reason and Religion, and built upon a Contempt (accidentally so at least) and a wrestling of the Scripture. . . ." There was some danger that readers would be taken in by "that Air of Wit and Reading they will find there, or at least with the Authority of the Author himself." They were chiefly concerned with the second book of the work, remarking of the first "that in General 'tis a very useful elaborate Treasury of Ancient Philosophy."

The *Theory of the Earth,* however, Burnet's earlier work, was published in a complete English translation in 1690. The first two books of the original Latin, *Telluris Theoria sacra,* had been first published in 1681, the concluding two books in 1689, but an English translation of the first two, *"Concerning the DELUGE, AND Concerning PARADISE,"* appeared in 1684, dedicated to Charles II.

The complete translation of the *Theory of the Earth,* dedicated to King William, excited considerable comment. In 1690–91, Erasmus Warren, Rector of Worthington in Suffolk, and Thomas Burnet exchanged paper bullets. The entire collection of Warren's criticism, *"All Mr. Warren's Parts, in Answer to Dr. Burnet's Theory of The Earth."* was advertised in the *Mercury* in February, 1693 (IX.20). The most substantial of these was *Geologia: or, a Discourse Concerning the Earth before the Deluge, Wherein the Form and Properties ascribed to it, In a Book intituled the Theory of The Earth, Are Excepted against: And it is made to appear, that the Dissolution of that Earth was not the cause of the Universal Flood. ALSO A New Explication of that Flood is attempted.*

Warren expressed a horror of doing anything "in way

of opposition *to,* depravation *of,* or derogation *from,* any Divine Truth." Rather his "new Explication of the Deluge was made to vie with the *Theory"* (p.359).

The *Mercury* for 3 December 1692 contains four questions concerning *Archæologiæ.* In the answering these, the Athenians express approval of the first chapter of Book II of the *Theory of the Earth* because of its telling arguments against Aristotle's contention that the world was eternal, but opposition to Burnet's sacrifice of the authority of "Moses's Narration" of the Creation:

> [Burnet] calls in question his Authority, endeavouring to prove the Historical part of the Creation a kind of Parable, not considering, that thô it shou'd be so granted, (which we shall never be willing to do) yet the 4*th* Commandment, which is of too great a Moment than to have a Parabolical signification, is express, *That in six days God created the Heaven and Earth,* &c. whereas the Drs. Earthy particles, and liquid Mass must be many years (if at all) in setling to a Consistence. (VIII.28)

Burnet's basic theory was that before the Deluge the earth had a smooth, even surface, free from seas, rocks, mountains, or any sort of prominent relief, its physical nature having been so determined as the fluid and confused matter of chaos gradually blended together into a sphere with fire and earthy particles inside it, and oily and liquid matter on the outside. The earthy particles gradually caused the liquid to dry out and congeal.

The Athenians objected that such a process would have taken far longer than the scriptural six days, and that the scriptural passages which Burnet adduced as evidence,[9] were incorrectly applied, ". . . the Apostles design being not to build a *Theory of the Earth,* but to show the parallel between the unexpected Judgment upon the other World of the Ungodly, and the sudden Coming of Christ upon the new World of Scoffers, the first by a Deluge, the last by a General Conflagration."

Burnet's cause for the Deluge is also rejected: "Our Author would have it a *Tehom-Rabbath, An Eruption out of the Womb of the Earth:* St. Peter calls it a *Flood;* and *Moses* gives you the time and degrees of its Increase and Decrease."

The editors promised more discussion of Burnet's *Theory* in the next number, together with proof of very nearly the exact location of the Garden of Eden and the four rivers which came from it, "which will further shew the Earth did not fall in that Destruction the Dr. pretends." Ironically enough, the next installment was delayed four days by an urgent question about the inconsistency between the Talmudists and others as to the number of angels.

Number 30 of the *Mercury* returned to the subject of Burnet's theory, utilizing copious quotations from the Latin edition of his book to show that he contradicted himself in setting up the notion of a "parabolical" paradise. The Athenians argued that since the rivers of Paradise are mentioned in the Bible after the Flood, "the Earth cou'd not possibly be destroy'd, as the Dr. wou'd have it."

Not only was Burnet's theory criticized but also his presentation. The twelfth question in Number 30 asked: *"What think you of the Dr's Paraphrase upon Moses, and the Dialogue betwixt* Eve *and the Serpent; as also in that betwixt* God, Adam, Eve *and the* Serpent, *in their Examination and Sentence?"*

The Athenians thought it lacked "that Caution and Prudence as a matter of so great consequence might have justly claimed, especially from one of his Character." It was "unjust and unfair . . . to that great Law-giver [Moses] to be ridicul'd, because he speaks not Physically as the Dr. does: Some passages are ludicrous enough and suited to the Style of *Terence's* Comedies, perhaps taken out of 'em, and the whole has such an Air in it, that the Wits of the Town have wish't he'd have gone thro' all the Bible after the same manner; an effect We doubt not but the Dr. will be sorry to hear of."

The final question is a reemphasis of the orthodox interpretation of Genesis: *"The Dr. seems to build his whole* Theory *physically:* Query, *When did Nature arrive to such a degree of Perfection, that any thing cou'd be said to be naturally done?"*

Answ. Nature can't be properly said to be perfect (or consequently a thing done Naturally) before the Essential Laws of Nature are constituted themselves by the Author of it; therefore it appears to us a great Weakness in the Dr. to talk of Physicks, and Natural Effects in a Chaos, which nothing but an Almighty hand cou'd bring into any Order" (VIII.30.15).

In their interpretations of religious doctrine the Athenians also interpreted natural philosophy, for no scientific theory that hinted at the inadequacy of Scripture was allowed to go unchallenged. They were not the only ones who showed in such a way their fear for the consequences if Scripture should become discredited as a source of absolute truth. Although not original thinkers like Newton and Locke, they showed a similar eagerness to test each scientific assertion in its relation to Scripture. The efforts of the Athenians in this direction, however, because they have so much less basis in analytical thought, appear to temporize and to avoid controversy by assurances that doctrine and belief are still safe.

CHAPTER 10

[1] The list included figures both prominent and obscure—Salmasius, Mercator, Jerome, Eusebius, Strabo, Diodorus Siculus, Luitsius, Sanson, Purchas, Hakluyt, De la Valle, Calmet, Pineda, Spanheim, Dr. Hyde, Bishop Cumberland, Greaves, Sandys, Bishop Ussher, Lloyd, Marshal, Ptolemy, Cellarious, Reyland, Maundrell, and many more. Bochart, cited very often in the *Mercury,* Wesley alluded to later, when he was writing his Latin commentary on Job, as "worth all the rest put together" and lamented that he had the use of his major work for only a few days. Adam Clarke, *Memoirs of the Wesley Family,* London, T. Tegg and Son, 1836, p.327.

The effect upon Defoe of the casuistry in the *Mercury* is discussed by G. A. Starr, "From Casuistry to Fiction: the Importance of the 'Athenian Mercury,'" *Journal of the History of Ideas,* Vol. 28 (1967), 17–32.

[2] [Samuel Wesley], *A Letter from a Country Divine to his Friend in London.* London, R. Clavel, 1703, p.5.

[3] A physical aspect of this number of the *Mercury* may be evidence that the piece was not written especially for the periodical. The two columns of the *recto* and the left-hand column of the *verso* are set in

the usual pica size, but a few lines down in the right-hand column *verso* the type size changes to a smaller font and continues so to the end. This is not a unique occurrence in the *Mercury,* although elsewhere the reduction in type size was made in order to accommodate more questions rather than to avoid cutting an article on a single subject. Since the editors were paid by the number, Wesley may have contributed a piece already written for some other purpose, or, in view of the rather loose organization of the piece, he may simply have overwritten.

[4] Although the Athenians never answered the question about the raven, two years later the *Mercury* (XII.5. Tue 7 Nov 93) advertised *"Vox Corvi, or the Voice of the Raven that thrice spoke these words distinctly: Look into Colossians the 3d and 15th . . . for W. B. and are to be sold by Tho. Norris. . . ."*

[5] Samuel Bochart (1599–1667), Norman French protestant preacher and controversialist; studied at Oxford and Leyden. *Hierozoicon, sive bipertitum opus de animalibus sacræ scripture,* 1663.

[6] Citations from Vol. 4 of the *Athenian Mercury* and a reference to the *London Mercury* indicate publication in February or March, 1692. Northcott published George Fox's *Journal,* 1694–98, and many other Friends' works.

[7] IX.29. Dunton did what he could to further the conversion of the Jews by publishing and advertising *"An Account of the Conversion of Theodore John, a late Teacher among the JEWS, together with his Confession of the Christian Faith which he delivered immediately before he was Baptized in the presence of the Lutheran Congregation in the German-Church in the Little Trinity-Lane, London. By John Esdras Edzard, Minister to the said Church, on the twenty-third Sunday after Trinity, being the 31th of October, . . . 1692. Translated out of High Dutch into English."*

[8] An English translation did not appear until 1727.

[9] 2 Ephesians, chaps. 3, 5, 6 in *Theory of the Earth,* London, Walter Kettilby, 1684, I.164.

11

"Fuimus Troes, fuit Ilium. . . ."

The continuing popularity of the *Athenian Mercury* over a period of years cannot be attributed to any single subject treated in its pages. "Athenianism," or the love of novelty as Dunton defines it, required variety above all for its satisfaction. For over six years no other periodical approached the *Mercury* as a purveyor of information and opinion on those subjects that could interest the common reader and perhaps engage him subsequently in coffee house conversation. A typical number of the *Athenian Mercury* at the height of its success demonstrates concretely those qualities for which it was read. The range of the fifteen questions in Volume Eight, Number 2 (Sat 16 Jul 92) is not unusual—from a question about the use of heraldry by the twelve tribes of Israel to a dietary query as to why nuts eaten after fish hinder the gathering of phlegm. The Athenians attributed to Cain the origination of heraldry, when he set up his power in the land of Nod. They sidestepped the question about phlegm, saying "it requires time to know the matter of fact, before it can be answered satisfactorily." They dealt with thirteen other questions soundly and seriously, but not without some wit. Three had to do with religious belief, one called for scriptural exegesis, one for a definition of the millenium, and one for an interpretation of Tertullian's "Certum est quia impossibile est" in allusion to the Creation. Two were on matters of history, past and current.

A querist reported that several histories said of Anne Boleyn *"That her Belly was ripped up, and* Edward the VI, *taken out, by order of* Henry VIII. *who said he could have more wives, but did not know whether he could have more children."* But according to the Bishop of Salisbury, she was safely delivered but died of childbed fever. *"Pray your Opinion as to matter of fact?"* The answer showed that the Athenians and the questioner were bound to deprive Jane Seymour of credit for giving birth to Prince Edward: "The Report might be raised upon some question proposed to the King, that in Case the Queen could not be delivered, whether they might administer that Operation." As to current history, the Athenians were asked to settle a wager over the taking of Namur. Did it mean just the town, which fell on 10 June 1692, or the fortress too? The fortress was still under siege. The Athenians replied that it meant both town and fortress unless the bettors had made a distinction at the time of their wager.

A question from a distressed debtor brought out Dunton's sympathy for such unfortunates. The debtor was instructed that "a weekly tribute to a Jaylor generally is the end of all the cost and charges, and Debt sued for, . . . But if your Friends will neither lend Money, nor be Security, your Condition is as bad as one that wants Money or Friends to procure a Pardon; and therefore if the Creditors will not take your offer, you must live the best you can in the confin'd place you are in, as others do, and you will soon learn the way."

The hand of Wesley, however, is apparent in a question as to where Atlas stood *"When he bore the World on his Shoulders?"* and what the Athenians thought of the poet who first invented the fiction. "The Poet pitched upon this," replied the *Mercury,* "as best to express the vast Comprehension he had in Inventing Astronomy; he might as well have feigned he held it in his Hand, and turn'd it every way to find out its Proportions and Harmonick Distances, and let it go again in a String to observe its Motions; as the Poet thought of the word *Weight,* and so set imaginarily on his Shoulders, which fancy was well enough." The poet never believed that the fancy of Archimedes moving the world, "if he had another World to fix his Betty or Instrument upon," would be taken for actuality, "any more than we fancy an Emperor can hold the Globe of the World, represented by a Ball, in his Hand, as Pictur'd, or a Man guide the World which way he pleased, *as if he had the World in a string,* as we Phrase it." Such an opinion is reminiscent of Wesley's other urgings, in the *Mercury* and in the notes to the *Life of Christ,* that the poet be allowed to picture what he imagined as taking place without being reproved for violating the rules of probability.

A three-part question on tobacco inquires how long the weed has been in use in England, *"whether it does not infect the genuine Purity of the Breath? and . . . whether 'tis not insalubrious if immoderately used?"* In answer to the first part the querist is told " 'Tis about *one hundred and six Years,* according to the best Account we can get concerning it, Captain *Richard Greenfield* and Sir *Francis Drake,* not Sir *Walter Rawleigh,* being those who first brought it hither, about the Year 1586." To the second part, " 'Tis e'ne as you *like it:* Some think it a Notorious Stink . . . others . . . that 'tis the best *Smell* in the World—And for the Querist, we'd advise him to be judged by his Mistress, and to let her Nose rule his, if e're he expects his Lips should be acquainted with hers." To the third, immoderate use is bad for the health, as with everything else. Then, "to make out Measure," the editors "throw in a *little Story* . . . :

> When the Christians first discovered *America,* the Devil began to be afraid of *losing his hold* there among the poor People, tho' by Christianity appearing among 'em, (tho' he was more *afraid* than *hurt,* as the Event made appear) and as Mr. *Dryden* excellently expresses it in his *Conquest of Mexico:* He told some of his *Acquaintance* among the *Indians,* that he had found a way to be reveng'd upon the *Christians* for beating up his Quarters, for he'd teach 'em *Tobacco,* which when once they had tasted, they should be *perpetual Slaves* to it, and never be able to leave it: Which was too true as to a great many *Smoakers,* tho' there are some who have used it this *seven Years,* and yet can as indifferently as ever, either take or forbear it. (VIII.2.14)

The fifteenth and last question in this number demonstrates the cleric's ability to spin out an answer to a scriptural question. Asked for an opinion on Jotham's Parable, Judges 9.13, "Should I leave my Wine, which cheareth *God* and *Man?*" he began by observing that "It either relates to *Princes* and *great Men,* who are frequently enough call'd *Gods* in the Scripture, and then the sence is no more than—Wine *refreshes* both *small* and *great,* or *all sorts* of Men. Or else it refers to *Sacrifices,* in some of which *Wine* was offered to *God,* and is said, after the *manner of Men,* and in Condescension to our *Conception* and *Capacity,* to *chear* the *Heart* of *God,* by which no more is meant than to be *acceptable* to him." A third interpretation "which some may think as probable as either" he based on the knowledge that what is dedicated to God's service is said to be dedicated to God, that which is done to God's servants is done to Him; "those *Offerings* which were under the *Old Law,* brought to the *Priest,* and design'd for his Use, are said to be brought to *God*— And to the *Priest* among other things, *Wine* was presented, whose *Heart* being thereby moderately *cheer'd* and *refresht,* we know not but in a Parabolical way of Expression, as this is here, the *Heart of God* may be said to be so."

Moderately cheered and refreshed by a variety of well-authenticated and carefully reasoned data, the reader could patiently await the next number of the *Mercury,* in the meantime taking part with brisk assurance in coffee-house conversation or, if he lived in the country, feeling a little less remote from the intellectual center. The apprentice and the servingmaid found in this particular number little that dealt with the vicissitudes of their own lives; they would not have had to look far among other numbers.

ii

Why should a thriving business of answering questions anonymously ever have ended? The climate for such an enterprise was in some ways better in 1696, when the *Mercury* suspended voluntarily, than in 1691, when it first began. The failure of Parliament to renew the Licensing Act in 1695 permitted a Whiggish periodical to show its bias with less risk. But Dunton, who had learned to live successfully under official restrictions, did not change the *Mercury* in any way that reflected the greater liberty of the press. His lack of change to meet the new competition of newspapers,[1] besides some personal difficulties, brought the project to a temporary halt in February 1696 at the end of Volume Nineteen, and fifteen months later, after one month's resumption, to a final stop in June 1697 at the end of Volume Twenty, Number 10.

As soon as the Licensing Act disappeared, newspapers began to appear, full of domestic and foreign news, and published with greater frequency than the *Mercury*. George Redpath's *Flying Post,* Abel Boyer's *Post-boy,* Fonvive's *Postman,* and Crouch's *English Post* were among the earliest competitors. The common use of "Post" in these titles indicated that the "Mercurys" had about run their course. To meet such competition, the *Mercury* would have had to publish oftener than twice a week, and provide more timely and exciting presentation of advice and information, both changes that would have required more financial risk. The impending demise of the *Mercury* was announced in a few laconic sentences in Volume Nineteen, Number 30, and in the Preface to Volume Nineteen, but there was an earlier sign that the *Mercury's* circulation was dropping, in the Preface to Volume Seventeen, August 1695, in the form of a letter written by the Society to themselves:

Gentlemen,
These are in the name of the Publick (that cares not a farthing for ye, but to our knowledg has been tired with ye these two or three years). . . .

The letter asks that all *"three or fourscore thousand"* unanswered questions be answered precisely in the next *Mercury*.

But that ye may have fair play, we'll remind you of some of the principal of those Questions *we talk of, and so conclude.*
When will the War with France be ended? How shall we find the Philosophers Stone? I'm an Old-Maid, how shall I do to get an Husband? Were there ever such a

parcel of Blockheads as the Athenians? I owe ten times more than I'm worth, how shall I get it paid? Who were all your Fathers? When ye have once crackt these, you shall not fail of more from

Your faithful Remembrancers, &c.

Answ. From Athens!

You shall not fail to receive reasonable satisfaction in these and the remaining Query's in our next Mercury. Witness our Hands this 12th of Aug. 1695.

Acrop.

Evand. Arch.

The tone of self-deprecation permitted the writer, who used Dunton's whimsical cognomen, to put some blame upon those readers who were accustomed to send in questions. The tone was not altogether new, for the Preface to Volume Sixteen, published in mid-April 1695, makes fun of preface writing as a subject, *"as dry as Don Quivedo's Old Women that were made Matches, and stor'd up in Tinderboxes."* If the readers would not excuse him from writing still another preface, the writer asks that they be doomed to *"compile Volumes upon a Cow's Tail: In short, write Athenian Prefaces till our Bookseller is weary with taking Mony, till our Printer has no Errata's, till the Town asks a wise Question, or we give a proper Answer, till good sense is prefer'd to Love-Stories; in a word, till the Age is Wise and Honest."*

The writer asks the *"Genius of Athens,"* the *"Tutelary Guardian of Areopagus,"* to assist him, *"not with Sense or Reason, for that was never thy Province, but something new and noisy; no matter for design, for thou hast not one Votary guilty of Thinking, nor we a Reader that could understand us if we should blunder upon Reason."*

As in the Preface to Volume Seventeen, the writer lists the common subjects of questions received, but with more emphasis upon puzzling ones, less upon the merely frivolous:

Help us to speak intelligibly of what we are ignorant, as to show the Laws and Manners of the People in the Moon, or of our own Australians, to square the Circle, to reconcile the Antient Historiography, to fix the sense of the Law, to reconcile all Religionaries, to prevent War, or to Conquer; to scandalize Mony, to interpret Dreams, to prove Astrology reasonable, to make the Bully modest, the Town Beaux humble, the Atheist devout; In fine, to perform all things possible and impossible, and please all our loving Querists, cou'd we but be expert in these things, we should work Wonders, and out-do the Delphine Oracles *in our Answers.*

The earlier preface to Volume Fifteen, dedicated "To the Pindarical Lady," refers to the Athenians as *"a Society that has pretended* to too much Honesty *to have many* Friends." The lady was advised to *"despise a Snarling World as much as we do, and then it may* grin on till its Heart Ake." Here, near the end of 1694, was the first indication of a change from the brisk, cheerful attitude of earlier prefaces. The Preface to Volume Fourteen, quoted here in its entirety, represents these well. The writer assumes two roles, the one of the widely read and learned man, and the other of the gadfly who makes people think.

Here's yet another Volume *for you, and indeed he must be a very wise Man that can tell* when we shall have done; *and there's* two very good Reasons for it. *1st. Our* Bookseller *will tell you,* it's part of his Trade, *and he can as well shut up Shop, as be without an* Athenian Volume, *especially since* Athenianism was first the Thought, and *consequently the* Darling of his own Brain. 2. *But to be a little graver, Subject matter is infinite, the* Ocean *before us is as wide as the present* Confines of the Human Mind, *that is in some sense* Infinite; *'Tis no wonder that among the great* Variety of things, *we should still offer something* New, *if we only consider,* That no one thing in Nature won't admit of endless Vanity, *for instance in a* Triangle, *the Base may remain unalterable, and the same, and yet the other two sides may be* infinitely diversified; *'tis certain* that immense Distance *betwixt us, and the utmost* fixt Star *discoverable either by the Eye, or a* Telescope, *bears some certain proportion to the* Semidiameter, *not only of our*

> Earth, *but the least difference we can imagin; therefore a* Triangle *among other* Properties, *with any assign'd Base, may be so intended, as truly and properly to* Design *that yet inexpressible distance;* Volumes might be Writ upon a Triangle, *Nay,* of any one Property of a Triangle; *infinite therefore is the subject Matter of all things that fall under the cognizance of our* Senses *and* Intellectuals. *'Twill then be no wonder if* Athens Resolves new Questions *as long as there are Persons to send 'em, whose Notions of Things do in some respect as much differ as their Faces. Courage therefore* Honest Querist, and never think the Fountain will be Exhausted; *we shan't indeed always promise much* Sense *or* Pertinency *in every* Answer, *but we have worse luck than* Epicurus *his* Atoms, *if we don't hit sometimes, and even our* Errors *may have a good use in 'em, they may set some persons of thinking to cavil, or do better, who otherwise perhaps would never else have been guilty of* Thinking *all their Life-time.*

By the end of 1695, however, Dunton had made his decision to give up the *Mercury* as a semiweekly. Volume Eighteen was published on 10 December 1695,[2] and its preface, using larger type and fewer italics than any of its predecessors, announced that Athens was going to fall:

> The Eighteenth Volume *is now finisht, and still the Subject affords new matter; but* Delphos *had its period, and so must we;* Bodies Politick, Societies *and* Private Persons *run the same fate, they have all their rise, encrease, declension and fall, and sooner or later have a just occasion for the Poet's Exclamation,*
> —Fuimus Troes, fuit Ilium & ingens Gloria Teucrorum,——
> *If we reach the* 20th Volume *we shall have* run a fair stage, and *perhaps* no public paper, except the Gazette, *can pretend to such a standing, for the design was lucky enough, and affected every one, the whole World being nothing else but one* GYGANTIC ATHENIAN; *so that had our own abilities been suitable to the task, or the genius*

of the Age been a little wiser, we might instead of handling so many trifling and impertinent Love Questions, have done something that might have been really serviceable to the Age, but Sense *and* Reason *would not sell, our Bookseller found more* Fools than Wise, *and Interest fixt the* Calculations *the wrong way; not that we have not sometimes treated upon Subjects of the highest Nature, and in spite of* NOISE *and* LOVE, *talkt as gravely and usefully as we cou'd; so that the wiser party has not always been disappointed in reading our Paper; and those that are otherwise, by looking for that which was more adapted to their Apprehensions, have accidentally light* [sic] *upon some things which did 'em more service than they wisht for.*

What remains now, but to tell the chief design of this *Preface,* which is to beg our Querists liberty to be as kind to 'em as we can, in the two remaining Volumes, which, for anything we yet see, will conclude the Design; we have sometime since talkt of A NEW SYSTEM of PHILOSOPHY, which has been often required of us; and if the 20*th Volume* be printed all at once upon that subject, it may be the *best farewel* we can give our Querists, and after all their Questions upon so many miscellanious [sic] Subjects, make 'em at last *Philosophers* into the bargain, as well as *Casuists.*

In the brief Preface to Volume Nineteen, Dunton himself, *"The Proprietor of* the Athenian Mercury," made the announcement that *"whilst the* Coffee Houses have the Votes *every Day, and* Nine News Papers *every Week,"* the weekly Paper would be discontinued, but that he would *"carry on the said Design* in Volumes." Thirty numbers would be speedily printed all together to complete the twentieth volume, *"and after that an* Entire Volume *shall be publisht Quarterly, (provided the Twentieth meets with Encouragement) which* New Method *will answer more* Questions *than formerly, the* Weekly Publication *compleating but* (Three) *and this* (Four) *Volumes Yearly——"*

Dunton intended to resume weekly publication *"as soon*

as ever the Glut of News [was] *a little over,"* but he did not begin again until May of 1697. Number 1 of Volume Twenty appeared on Friday, 14 May, the next number the following Monday; so it went for ten numbers in all, the last being published on Monday, 14 June. Resumption of publication was advertised in the *Postman,* 11 May 1697:

> Whereas, in yesterday's Gazette, and in some other papers, there was mentioned a design of publishing, as upon this day, No. 1, Vol. XX, of the Athenian Gazette, which has been for a considerable time discontinued; some gentlemen of great worth and learning, being sensible of what mighty use such a paper as this might be to the publick, if well performed and freed from those multitudes of trifling questions wherewith the last volumes began to swell, have been with the first author of that paper, who long before it was discontinued threw it up, entreating him to engage in it again, and promising him such assistance as it is hoped may answer the expectations of all lovers of solid learning and ingenuity. This being communicated to the publisher, he has thought it fit to alter his measures, and will publish the new model, in which a very particular account shall be given of the whole design.[3]

There is no indication in any of the numbers of Volume Twenty either that there had been a hiatus of over fifteen months since the end of Volume Nineteen, or that there would be no more of them after Volume Twenty, Number 10. The absence of a title page to Volume Twenty further suggests that the resumption of publication was tentative and that even without the death of Elizabeth Dunton to dishearten John he might soon have given up the project.

Dunton had made provision for the sale of bound copies of Volume Nineteen by advertising in Number 30 that notice of their availability would be given "by *John Dunton* at the Raven in *Jewen-Street.*" In earlier times, Dunton advertised the readiness of a bound volume about six weeks after its terminal date, i.e. the date of Number 30, and the later inclusive date on its title page might be either the date of Number 30 or of Number 1 in the succeeding volume. The title page of Volume Nineteen gives no clue to its actual publication date, for the second date is that of Number 30, 8 February 1696. Neither is there any clue to the date in the ten numbers of Volume Twenty. They contain no advertising of any sets of the *Athenian Gazette*.[4]

The competition of the newspapers was not in itself enough to bring about suspension of the *Mercury*. Dunton's personal difficulties nearly coincide with its cessation. He was deprived through death of his father-in-law, Samuel Annesley, 31 December 1696,[5] and of his wife Elizabeth, 28 May 1697.[6] He quarreled decisively with Wesley soon after the death of Elizabeth; the *Life and Errors* is filled with slurring references to Wesley,[7] and a letter from Wesley in that work shows the parson's wan hope that Dunton would not remarry precipitously.[8] Dunton severed relations with Sault too, not over the hoax of the *Second Spira* but because he could no longer employ him. Heavily in debt, Dunton sought to improve his fortunes by a second marriage, only four months after Elizabeth's death. To Dunton the troubles that arose with his new wife and mother-in-law over money and property seemed monumental, and he felt the need to spread the story of them in several publications.[9] He exchanged the useful occupation of publishing the *Mercury* for the self-indulgent one of writing polemics against his enemies and confessional stories of his life. The value of these later works remains in their copious allusions to members of the book trade, writers, and clergymen.

iii

As one traces the history of John Dunton from 1696 to his death in 1733, it becomes increasingly clear that the most stable period of his life was during the years of the *Mercury*, when he was successful enough to be convinced of his importance and therefore happy enough to laugh off the attacks of rivals.

A legacy he received in 1692 together with the profits from the *Mercury*, the *Compleat Library*, and the *Young Students' Library* had made it possible for Dunton to assume the livery of the Stationers Company that year (LE, p.278). He had arrived, and the most prominent public sign of his arrival was the *Mercury,* the only periodical of that decade to appear as often as the *London Gazette,* but more talked about in the coffee houses than the staid official journal of the Secretaries of State. There was more than lack of competition, however, to account for the unique position of the *Mercury.* Dunton must be given great credit for perceiving the advantage of frequent, regular publication, transforming the periodical from an ephemeral curiosity into a respectable institution.

The manifold services provided by the *Mercury* were also a unique contribution to the development of the literary periodical. Some particular ones among them had their counterparts in books for the young student, but the advantage of a specific answer to a specific question was to be found as a regular service only in the *Mercury.* Although not as rigidly departmentalized as the modern magazine, Dunton's periodical dealt methodically with a variety of subjects rather than making random, unorganized selections. Furthermore, the Athenians made plain the distinction between information and advice, especially under the major headings of religion, natural science, and social questions. In expressing opinion they were at their most personal. These distinctions in attitude together with occasional devotion of whole numbers to particular subjects constituted a beginning of the departmentalized publication. Only the *Gentleman's Journal* of Peter Motteux is comparable to the *Athenian Mercury* in this respect, but the *Mercury,* with its comparatively short pieces and its heavier emphasis upon manners and morals than upon literature and the arts, appealed to a less sophisticated and hence larger audience than did the *Gentleman's Journal.*

The *Mercury*'s views were an amalgam in which Dunton's Whiggish political views, Wesley's liberal Anglicanism, and Sault's technological knowledge, together with their common background in Dissent and their common belief in popular education were mingled with expressions of the business and professional ethics of the day. Wesley, the descendant of Dissenting clergymen and son-in-law of a distinguished Presbyterian, had changed his allegiance to the established Church because of the verbal excesses of his contemporaries in the Dissenting academies, not because he rejected the whole motive of Dissent. He never lost his admiration for Charles Morton, a moderate and an intellectual who believed his most useful role was in teaching. Among the Athenians, Wesley's was the strongest voice for reform, but Dunton furnished a pious echo of his sentiments. Although the Athenians asserted unequivocally that their religion was "Church of England," yet they expressed enthusiasm for the "Reformation of Manners," a movement supported most vigorously by Dissenting clergymen of London, led by Samuel Annesley.

There was little risk involved in publicizing a general need for moral improvement, but the Athenians showed real courage in their treatment of certain other social questions—popular education, especially the education of women, the responsibilities of both marriage partners, honest behavior in courtship, and humane treatment of debtors, especially those who were simply victims of circumstances. The impact of the Athenians' answers to questions on these subjects can be fairly assessed only after one reads them in their entirety. The answers are undeniably repetitive, but their very repetitiveness shows the consistency of the Athenians' view on these subjects. Because the *Mercury* was published before the modern concept of the editorial had fully emerged, editorial opinion does not always stand out plainly. This does not mean, however, that the Athenians disguised their opinions—they are the very essence of their answers to such questions as those on social problems.

In treating other major subjects in the *Mercury,* especially those that called for objective data, the Athenians devoted themselves to providing education for the many. They expressed an eagerness to find the best answers to scientific questions through experiment and maintained a degree of skepticism toward astrology[10] and such zoological wonders as centaurs and mermaids.[11] Concerning witchcraft and apparitions it is true that they were as superstitious as most of their contemporaries. In their rationalizations on these topics they asserted that any reasonable man must believe what he sees with his own eyes.[12] A greater objectivity, however, is amply demonstrated in their answer to questions on mathematics, mechanics, weather, physiology, and natural history. In answering questions on these subjects, they sought to teach.

iv

For Dunton, "Athenianism" never really died. On a separate folio half-sheet bound in between Volumes Nineteen and Twenty is the announcement of "THE NEW METHOD . . . in carrying on the *ATHENIAN MERCURY*" that would continue with questions but would also contain

> those Curious Composures that may be Communicated to us both in Prose and Verse: And further, that nothing may be wanting to render this Paper *an Universal Entertainment,* we shall now and then add *Reflections (in a distinct half sheet,* to be annex't to our *Mercury*) on the *most* Remarkable Events which shall happen from time to time: Neither shall our Querists pay any thing the more for this *Additional half sheet,* that so our *New Prosecution of this Work* may meet with a General Encouragement.

This paragraph occupies the top quarter of the page and concludes with a transitional sentence: "And we think we can't do a better peice [sic] of Service to the Publick, than in the *first place* to give AN IDEA of Mr. *Turner*'s History of the Most Remarkable Providences which have hapned in this Present Age, &c." Subscriptions for this work were invited by means of a full-page advertisement in which it was pointed out that no other work like it existed, save for an incomplete one by "the learned Mr. *Pool,* Author of the *Synopsis Criticorum,*" an authority highly regarded by Samuel Wesley.[13]

Dunton had published Turner's *History of all Religions in the World* in March 1697. It was an encyclopedic work in two parts, most of the first part descriptive of the organization of the Christian church but with a section on Mohammedanism and on heathens, the second part, in imitation of Fuller's *Holy Living,* dealing with such abstractions as knowledge of God, love to the souls of others, good wives, laboriousness, and government of the tongue; the final section of the second part consists of anecdotes concerning apparitions and "wonders." Turner was outspokenly anti-Aristotelian and also found Sir Thomas Browne offensive. In his preface Turner referred to Aristotle as being "a great Philosopher, but little Divine, having an Eagle's Eye in the Disquisition of Nature, but a very Buzzard in Spirituals; insomuch, that it would tempt one to father Religio Medici upon him."

The method adopted for getting together materials for the *History of Remarkable Providences* resembled that often employed for filling the pages of the *Mercury.* The Athenians invited "all men, especially DIVINES, to impart . . . any such *remarkable Providences* as they have recorded, or remember to have befallen themselves, or others, either in *Mercy, or Judgment."* Dunton himself contributed to the work, for he boasted that Turner found the last letters between Philaret and Iris "such a *Rare Pattern of Conjugal Love,"* that he inserted them in the *History of Remarkable Providences* (LE,p.354). Additional bait was held out to attract both contributions and subscriptions by the statement that

> (We have also the promise of a *Folio Manuscript,* written by the Famous Mr. *SELDEN,* containing the most *Memorable Things* which have hapned in this last Age) and we assure all others, that will be so kind as to impart their *Observations* to us, that they shall be received with all *Candor and Gratitude* imaginable, and the *Names of the Authors* published, if permitted, that the publick may know to whom they are indebted for the promoting of such an *useful work.*

Proposals and specimens were to be had at Dunton's shop. Advertising of the subscriptions continued throughout the summer of 1695, and a deadline was set for 1 September, when the first payment of fifteen shillings was due. On 5 October it was promised that the work would be put into the press *"with all convenient speed . . . but at the request of those who live Remote from London,* and have almost COMPLEATED THEIR SETS," the deadline was extended to 20 January. The first volume would be out by Hilary Term (XVIII.24). On 4 February, Dunton was still promising to go to press with all convenient speed, but he had printed the scheme of the entire work on the verso of the *Mercury* of Saturday 1 February 1696 (XIX.28). Although the *Mercury* was to have but one more number before its penultimate suspension of fourteen months, there were enough subscriptions to float William Turner's book; it was published in 1697, its title among the four advertised as "Newly Publish'd" in the first number of Volume Twenty of the *Mercury* (Fri 14 May 97).

Turner's preface characterizes the long-heralded work as containing "the most remarkable Particulars of the visible Creation . . . to rouze and awaken the Reason of Men asleep, in to a Thinking and Philosophical Temper; that . . . they may startle at Extraordinaries, and wind up their Reasons a little higher, upon the sight of Wonders." He attacked as his "greatest Adversaries . . . the Wits of the Age, some of Epicurus's Litter, who deny all Revelation and Scripture-Evidence, and take upon them to Philosophize upon the World, and so professing themselves to be Wise, they become fools."

The design of the collection was, in conclusion, "to glut and satiate the Mind with a Prospect of meer Nature, and to administer a fair occasion for raising of the Soul to Higher, and lofty and Noble Speculations, the Study of Divinity, and the Glories of the upper World, which will please and make us happy, without any Nauseousness, for ever and ever."

The advertisements in Volume Twenty, their small number eloquent of failure, are almost all of books published by Dunton, and of these, chiefly Turner's. One other is of the funeral sermon preached over Samuel Annesley by Daniel

Williams; still another, the first volume of the *Night-Walker*. Besides these, Philomela's *Poems on Several Occasions*, the *General History of the Quakers*, and Dunton's translation of the *Knowledge of the World* rub shoulders in the next to last number (**XX.**9).

So the *Mercury* ended less brilliantly than it began. At the start its attractiveness was in its anonymity, its unique function as a medium for education, and its sensitive reflection of the spirit of the new decade. As the character of the age changed, so did the *Mercury*. Anonymity became the weapon and the armor of the political pamphleteer; there were no more great and mysterious movers behind the scenes. The short answers of the *Mercury* were insufficient to meet the demands for popular education. That sensitivity to its time which a periodical must have, faded from the *Mercury* as life in England became more complex and Dunton's earlier assistants on the periodical, especially Samuel Wesley, bent their attentions upon other more compelling matters. The novelty of the project provided by Dunton had decayed and was supplanted by burgeoning newspapers. The defiant innovator at the Sign of the Raven had used up his skill. He spent the rest of his days trying fruitlessly to regain the initial success he had found in *"concealing the Querist and answering his Question."*

CHAPTER 11

[1] These included *Votes of the House of Commons* (1696–97), *Post-Boy, Flying Post, London News Letter, Present State of Europe, Protestant Mercury, Lloyd's News, London Mercury, Old Post Master, Weekly Survey of the World*.
[2] Advertisement in XIX.13 (Tue 10 Dec 95).
[3] Quoted in *Catalogue of a Collection of Early Newspapers . . . formed by . . . John Thomas Hope, Esq. and presented to the Bodleian Library . . .* (Oxford, 1865) pp. 9–10.
[4] Dunton customarily advertised "sets" of the *Gazette* at the foot of the title page, as in Volume Nineteen:
> Printed for *John Dunton*, at the Raven in *Jewen-Street*, 1696. Where is to be had the *Entire Set* of ATHENIAN GAZETTES (and the *Supplements* to 'em for the Year 1691.) as also the *Entire Set* for the Year 1692, 1693, 1694, and 1695. / (or single Volumes to this Time.) These Volumes are also sold by EDM. RICHARDSON, near the *Poultry-Church*.

[5] At Dunton's request, Defoe wrote the *Character of the late Dr. Samuel Annesley by way of Elegy*, verses that revealed his strong affection for the man who had influenced him so positively.

[6] LE,p.355. In 1698 Dunton had published as a tribute to her *An Essay, proving, We shall know our Friends in Heaven*.

[7] Dunton suggested, in the character he gave of himself, that he held something over Wesley: "*I . . . can be secret if trusted (or woe be to Parson* G R U B)" LE,p.323.

[8] Dated "Epworth July the 24th 97." ". . . . *I wou'd fain have sent you an Elegy, as well as an Epitaph* [for Elizabeth], *but can't get one to my Mind, and therefore you must be content with half your Desire; and if you please to accept this Epitaph 'tis at your Service, and I hope 'twill come before you need another Epithalamium*." LE,p.229.

[9] He married Sarah Nicholas at St. Alban's on 23 Oct. 1697. In 1700 he made public his marital troubles in "the *Case of John Dunton, Citizen of London: With respect to his Mother-in-Law, Madam Jane Nicholas, of St. Albans; and her Only Child, Sarah Dunton, with the Just Reasons for her Husband's Leaving her. In a Letter to his Worthy Friend, Mr. George Larkin, Senior. To which is added His Letter to His Wife.*" London, A. Baldwin.

[10] IX.8 (Sat 7 Jan 92/93) is devoted entirely to a refutation of the defence of "judicial astrology" written by John G[adbury] in his almanac for 1693. In *Answer* 1 it is observed "for the Paralogism which wou'd make *Superiority* in *Altitude* . . . and *Superior in Nature* and Power, to be the same things, 'tis so absurd, that we need not say we deny it; at this rate every chimney is more noble than a Man, because 'tis higher, . . ."

[11] Asked who first *"managed Horses,"* the Athenians replied that the Centaurs, "or rather *Hippocentaurs,* a People of *Thessaly*" had; "when they were first seen upon the backs of Horses, the Neighbouring People thought 'em to be Monsters . . . and hence arose those many Fables about the *Centaurs*." IX.5.3 (Tue 27 Dec 92).

[12] IX.6.1 (Sat 31 Dec 92) answers a question about Mather's *Tryals of several Witches* (a book reprinted in London by Dunton) by quoting from the statement of William Stoughton and Samuel Sewall published in the book: ". . . we find the Matter of Fact and Evidence truly reported. . . ." p.48.

[13] XVII.15 (Tue 22 May 95). This advertisement alternated with full-page lottery advertisements during May.

12

Athenianism: the Final Years

In 1697, when the *Athenian Mercury* ended, Dunton was only thirty-eight and had before him thirty-seven more years of life. He was one of the best known and most experienced members of the London book trade. No other bookseller had advertised as widely as he during the last decade of the century, and in an age when booksellers became the earliest victims of depressions in trade, he had weathered two periods of severe decline, in 1685 and again during the middle years of the 1690's. At thirty-four he had assumed the livery of the Stationers Company. He had a wide acquaintance, most of whom he attempted to record in his *Life and Errors*. He was on good terms with numbers of booksellers, printers, engravers, and bookbinders and took part in congers with some of the most astute among his colleagues.

Yet few of Dunton's undertakings during the next twenty-five years[1] achieved anywhere near the success of those he had engaged in between 1681 and 1697. He earned the label of eccentric and lunatic from his contemporaries and from literary historians by his activities after the turn of the century. Unlike the *Mercury,* the publications he fathered or godfathered from 1697 show a diminishing sense of responsibility and reality.

In his later works Dunton was most often pleading his own case; the gamut of particular subjects running from his quarrels with his second wife and her mother over money, to the unfairness of imprisonment for debt, to injuries received from other booksellers, to attempts by "lewd" women to seduce him, to his unrewarded efforts in behalf of the Whig party and the Elector of Hanover. There is the confessional tone of the *Life and Errors,* with its pious interchapters promising reform; the personal anecdotes of the *Dublin Scuffle* (1699), in which Dunton, always the hero, flaunts "Doing good" as his slogan; the romantic self-pity of the *Art of Living Incognito* (1700); and his curious references to himself in the third person as a scandalously neglected servant of Queen Anne and George I, in an array of political pamphlets—his preoccupation from 1712 to 1723.

The promise of reform was a keynote after Dunton first abandoned the *Mercury.* In the "Idea of a New Life," written soon after Iris's death, he offers *"some Rules to be observ'd, under the Character of an Author."* He admits that he has been "so wretchedly inclin'd to Scribling" that his new life will not be "altogether freed from an ITCH of that kind." He has been "a little unhappy in the *Choice of Subjects*" for the pieces he has written, and he has generally "OVERDONE it, wrought it so, *Back-side* and *Fore-side,*" that he has run it out of breath. He should have polished his style, he should have known more about his subject:

> Reading of Good Authors, remarking their peculiar Beauties, and writing much are the best Means to refine a Man. After all, this Study should take up no more than a Third Part of my Time, the rest I'd devote to the Improvement of my Mind. I cou'd enlarge here with some Pleasure, but these Particulars, well observ'd, *wou'd sufficiently reform me under the Character of an Author.*[2]

He wrote much wherever he was and was never at a loss for projects. Facing a life without the *Mercury* he could observe, *"My Head is pregnant, with agreeable and everlasting Inventions*— 'Tis (only) in a PRIVATE CELL I ha' Time to finish 'em" (LE,p.409).

He became the sort of sick man who outlives all his healthy friends. For the next twenty-five years he complained as much about his health as about his enemies, and in doing so revealed that he threw himself often upon the charity of friends:

'Tis true, my Heredetory [sic] Distemper the *STONE,* often brings me so very LOW, that I am not able to help my self.

At Mr. *Marshals* in *Suffolk,* I could not turn my self in my Bed, for several Months.

At Mr. *Lutwitches,* I was brought to the Brink of Eternity.

At Mrs. *Gardiners,* I was consum'd to a meer *Skeleton.*

At Mr. *Wilsons,* I was given up for a Dead Man.

And I am (often) seiz'd in the Streets with such *Fits of the Stone,* as I can neither stand nor go.

This makes it NECESSARY for me (except I'd perish to save charges) to have the constant Assistance of some Person, and none so fit as those (*for my own Sex make but odd Nurses*) that have been *Indefatigable* in the saving my Life; and as Zealous (nay, perhaps have been OVER RIGHTEOUS) for the health of my Soul.[3]

Dunton plunged into newspaper publication about four months after issuing the last number of Volume Nineteen of the *Mercury. Pegasus with News* was issued three times a week from 15 June through 14 September 1696, forty numbers in all. The first thirty numbers, through 6 July 1696, with a preface, were bound together as Volume I, with a title page dated "1697," printed for John Dunton, to be sold by Richard Baldwin and Edmund Richardson. Volume II contains only ten numbers, 21 August through 14 September 1696, and lacks the "Jacobite Courant," a feature found throughout Volume I.

Dunton's experience in publishing the *Mercury* enabled him to produce a newspaper with some unusual features. *Pegasus,* although frankly political, differs from its contemporary newssheets in containing essays and "novelties" in prose and verse. The "Preface" states the aim of providing "answers to the principal Cavils of the Jacobites against the present Government," and the first number describes the undertaking as "a TRIPARTITE PAPER, of

NEWS—AN OBSERVATOR—*And a* JACOBITE COURANT by three distinct hands. . . ." The news, chiefly from the Continent, is presented in a plain style, each subject identified in the margin within curved brackets. The "Observator" comments upon the news from a Williamite position, and the "Courant," for the first six numbers, consists of a crudely versified dialogue between a Williamite and a Jacobite. The assertion of "three distinct hands" may well have been true, for when in Number 7 the "Courant" switches to prose, its writer remarks that the "Observator" is the "grand master Doctor" who reads a "Physick Lecture," and that the "Courant" is "the *Observator*'s humbler Zany. . . ."

Dunton's presence in the background is shown by the paper's advertisements, as in Volume I Number 1, that advertisements sent in will be inserted at reasonable rates; in Number 2, that the complete set of nineteen volumes of the *Athenian Mercury* can be purchased at the Raven in Jewen Street; and in Volume II, Numbers 1 through 9, advertisement of *Poems on Several Occasions* by Philomela, the Pindarick Lady. Each volume is preceded by an alphabetical subject index.

The "character" of *Pegasus,* too, reveals Dunton's shaping hand. The newspaper has a messenger who can go through the air, riding on Pegasus.[4] He will now and then call at Parnassus "and oblige the lovers of the Nine Sisters with a line from the Muses, *to let the world know* the sentiments of that Speculative and Sublime Society, as to the Publick Transactions" (I.1).

The greatest difference between *Pegasus* and the *Mercury* is in a shift from the role of informant to commentator. Although many of the *Mercury*'s answers really had the form of short essays, they were almost always relevant to the questions they answered. In *Pegasus,* the "Courant" especially takes on a personality, as for example in describing his Williamite bias he writes:

> we do but copy from old *Sir Rogers* fiddle: Only with this difference; his Base was for playing the *Williamites*

Out of their Senses; and our *Trebble,* by a more honest Change of the Note, is for playing the *Jacobites* Into Theirs.[5]

The innovation of the daily essay was yet to come, but *Pegasus* contained occasional ones, such as *"A Short Character of Ambition,"* aimed at Louis XIV.

Like Volume Twenty of the *Mercury,* which succeeded it eight months later, *Pegasus* ceased publication without warning. The topical and propagandistic nature of its material suggests that it was supported by a subsidy which was suddenly cut off, or that its writers deserted Dunton without notice.

It was followed immediately by a more pedestrian publication, a monthly which first came out in September 1696, entitled the *Night Walker or Evening Rambles in Search after Lewd Women with Conferences Held with them etc.*[6] The first number of this publication was old stuff warmed over. The writer's supposed interviews with prostitutes in its first number had appeared as "six *Nights Rambles"* in the *Mercury* five years earlier.[7] The *Night Walker* had eight issues, concluding in April 1697, one month before the brief revival of the *Mercury.*

Dunton had become thoroughly committed to the publication of his periodicals in volumes. With two exceptions, each number of the *Night Walker* has a dedication to some particular group: the first "to the Whore-Masters *of* London *and* Westminster;" the second, "to the Dutchess of—;" the third "to the Whores of London and Westminster;" the fourth "To the Gentlemen of the Society for Reformation;" for February, "To the Magistrates of London and Westminster;" and for April, "To the Youth of both Sexes, in the Cities of *London* and *Westminster,* the Borough of *Southwark, &c."*

The Preface to Volume I asserts that prostitution had been countenanced by the Stuart kings in order to weaken the English and make them prey to "Popery *and* Slavery," an insidious practice likened to that suggested by Balaam to Balak to corrupt the Israelites with the Midianitish women. The corruption of the English had brought upon them heavy judgments of fire, pestilence, and war. The author's design is not to provide food for wanton thoughts or to please "the Prophane Pallets *of the* Beaux *and* Sparks *of the Town, but to display* Monthly *their Abominable Practices in lively Colours, together with their dismal Consequences, in order to frighten or shame them out of them if possible.*"[8]

He admits that he had attempted something of the sort some years ago in "the six nights rambles," but had "for several Reasons" discontinued further search till this year. The new beginning, at St. Bartholomew's Fair time, will continue until there have been revealed "most of the Lewd persons in Town, from the Whoremonger of Quality to the meanest Porter," and "from the Pensionary Miss *to the* Suburb Strumpet." The sparks of the town may find "their own Rambles brought for Instances."

In the first number of the *Night Walker* appears the familiar request for free material:

> *that nothing may be wanting to complete this good work* [of reforming], *we have already setled a very good Correspondence with* Proctors, Apparitors, Justices, Clerks, Constables, Watchmen, Clerks of the Sessions, Church-wardens, *Bridewell,* and with some of the Society for Reformation, *many of which have sent us in Considerable* Lists of such persons of both Sexes, *as have come within their Cognizance, with an* account of their particular Crimes.

The design of the journal was *"to Reform, and not to Expose,"* and therefore the writer of it would refrain from using names, but now and then he would use initials to let the most notorious criminals know *"that we could name them if we please."* The predominant method of achieving a reformation would be that of examining the conscience of the whore.

In the first number, however, the three instances presented were of three men who had been tricked by prostitutes; a clergyman who "reveled" with some wenches at the Fair, had his pocket picked by them, and later tried to buy off the interviewer, who for his part insisted that he only wanted the clergyman to repent; an old gentleman fleeced at the Fair by a whore and her pimping husband; and an overseer of the press whose misdeeds were given away by an informer, "that *Nose-wise Animal* [who] had Gessed about" (I.1, 26).

At the end of each number the subjects for the coming month were advertised. These were almost entirely "exposures" of sexual adventures, in spite of the writer's insistence that his aim was to reform. The only notable exception was the number for February 1697, the shortest of all, consisting of fourteen dreary pages on the pox, its cause and cure.

The last paragraph on the last numbered page of the April number indicated a forthcoming change of authorship:

> Some particular reasons have occasioned the change of the Person concerned in this Undertaking, but 'tis hoped without any disadvantage to it or the publick, tho we must own that Gentlemans Accomplishments to be very great and not easily matched.

On the page opposite is a notice that the undertaking "will be continued Monthly." On 28 May 1697, however, Elizabeth Dunton died. Volume Twenty of the *Mercury* had commenced on 14 May, perhaps in a desperate effort to make a profit and pay some debts. The *Night Walker* was advertised in Volume Twenty, Number 4, the first volume, September through December 1696, and three months of the second volume. Here too it was announced that the undertaking would be continued monthly, but no more appeared.

Dunton seems to have been involved in no other periodical or newspaper publication until 1701, when he started the *Post Angel*. In the meantime he took a new wife,[9] fell out with her and her mother, closed his shop, put his books in a warehouse, and undertook a journey to Ireland to sell books at auction in Dublin. The commercial success of this venture was not great, but in 1699, the year following the trip, he published a book relating his adventures in Ireland.

Of Dunton's major works, the *Dublin Scuffle* has the

most clearly defined shape, distinguishing it from the chaotic rambling of the *Voyage Round the World* and the strange inconclusiveness of the *Life and Errors*. There is plagiarism in it of a distinguished sort, Carew's "Know, Celia" altered to "Know, Clara" (p. 388), and a part of Swift's first published poem, the *Ode* to William III (p. 379), neither one properly identified, both inserted in such a way that the reader would naturally accept them as Dunton's compositions. It is probable, too, that some of the characters of Dubliners and Irish country gentlemen and ladies were lifted from the work of others, as were so many of those in the *Letters from New England*.[10]

The book has a bellicose running title that tells much of the story: "BEING A / CHALLENGE / SENT BY / JOHN DUNTON, Citizen of *London,* / TO PATRICK CAMPBEL, Bookseller in *Dublin.* / Together with the small skirmishes of Bills and Advertisements." A second part of the work demonstrates Dunton's sense of persecution in its erotic dimension: "The *Billet Doux,* sent him by A CITIZENS WIFE in Dublin, Tempting him to Lewdness, / WITH / *His Answers to Her.*" The third and final part of the work, more relaxed and anecdotal, includes character descriptions and travelogue: "Some Account of his CONVERSATION IN IRELAND, Intermixt with particular Characters of the most Eminent Persons he Convers'd with in that Kingdom; but more especially in the City of *Dublin.*" The use of the term *conversation* in the last section of the work produces a fine Duntonian ambiguity that combines business with pleasure; "living or having one's being *in* a place or *among* persons. . . . consorting or having dealings with others . . . commerce, intercourse, society, intimacy" (OED). These senses, now obsolete, relate well to Dunton's extravagant account of his quarrel with a Scottish bookseller over occupancy of an auction room; of the billet doux "both Enticing and Threatening [him] to . . . wanton Embraces"; and of his encounters with the hospitable Irish as he inspected Kilkenny Castle, crossed the Boyne in a curragh and rode in a stage coach with a French officer who stood treats repeatedly for all the other passengers, and whose great generosity led Dunton to quote two stanzas from Swift's *Ode* to illustrate the theme of "doing good." All three sections are in the epistolary form, the first an exchange between Dunton and an unidentified gentleman, the second between Dunton and "the Irish Dorinda," and the third between Dunton and "a Lady of High Birth." In his foreword *"To the Spectators of* the Dublin *Scuffle"* Dunton confessed that the chief thing he sought in writing the book, aside from clearing his innocence with Campbel, Dorinda, and other enemies, was "to find Employment for a Spirit that wou'd *break the Vessel,* had it nothing to work upon" (p. 5).

To those angry at his frequent digressions he answered ". . . (with the ingenious *Montaign*) that *Constancy* is not so absolutely necessary in *Authors as in Husbands; . . .* when I have my Pen in my Hand, and Subject in my Head, I look upon my self as *mounted my Horse to ride a Journey;* wherein, although I design to reach such a *Town by Night,* yet will I not deny my self the Satisfaction of going a Mile or two out of the way, to *gratifie my Sences with some new and diverting Prospect . . ."* (p.5).

The risk of appearing in print was *"worse than hanging;* for the Torture of the Halter is but an Hour or so; but he that lies on the *Rack in Print,* hath his Flesh torn off by the Teeth of Envy and Calumny, though he meant nobody no harm" (p.6).

Only Dunton's polite addresses to the "Honourable Lady" in the third part of this work are reminiscent of the assumed dignity of the Athenian Society. Even though Dunton's travel books may be largely fictional, they suggest that he found travel a stimulating relief from doing business in London. The trip to Ireland was much like his journey to Massachusetts in 1685, when for the first time he was separated from his wife and was risking solvency with a large consignment of books. Upon his return from both trips, he had to dodge the bailiffs. In 1699, however, he could not take refuge among his countrymen in the Netherlands and led a fugitive existence outside London for a number of years; his publications from 1698 through 1700 allude to a life of retirement. The *Art of Living Incognito* (1700), the most explicit record of this period, was dedicated to the same "honourable Lady" to whom Dunton had directed the letters in the *Conversations in Ireland,* and like the earlier work, has the imprint of Anne Baldwin, widow of Dunton's good friend Richard Baldwin.[11] Dunton denied that the lady, "Climene," was but a fiction with which he amused the world. Of doubters he wrote in the "Dedication": *"if they will not believe upon the Credit of an* Honest Man, [he] *can go no farther."* In the lady's thoughts he had discerned the charms of solitude, which inspired him to live incognito. There is no mention of any inspiration added by the bailiffs.

The whole correspondence was to be presented with no assistance from any of his former authors; for he had "a Thousand Maggots *swarming in* [his] *Brain."* The whole was to be published in two hundred parts, "at so easy a Price that the Poorest may purchase 'em" (A2 *verso*), but the volume contains only six letters.

In cultivating his new-found art of living incognito, Dunton found that he scarce had a being till his "Raven went to Roost; . . . 'till it left the Hurries of *Stocks-Market,* for the solitude of Jewen street" (p.4). But now he had left even that out-of-the-way street for the quiet of the country, where with a good landlady he lives like Adam with Eve in Paradise, she tending the garden, he admiring the surroundings.

In "LETTER III. *Of the* (Athenian) *Itch"* Dunton alleges that he has recovered from "that vain desire of knowing more then's reveal'd" (p.26), he has in fact lost the Athenian itch, and has contempt for all who still have it, even for the Royal Society, "tho compos'd of the best, and most Knowing Men in the World." These men can't tell us why the loadestone points North, or why a lion trembles at the sight of a cock; they "have not yet attained a perfect Understanding of the *smallest Flower, and why the Grass should rather be Green than Red?* . . . They have, perhaps, *Artificial Cunning,* but how many Curiosities be framed by the least Creatures in Nature, unto which the Industry of the most *Curious Virtuoso's* doth not attain? But I'le leave 'em in a fond Pursuit of they know not what" (p.36).

The theme is continued in the next letter, "There is nothing New under the Sun." Dunton asks himself if the *Athenian Mercury* wasn't a new project, since it had its first meeting in his brain, and the first *Athenian Mercury* was partly composed by him. But even though it pleased the ingenious by answering any reasonable question, and continued to twenty volumes, it was "far from being a *New Project;* for don't we read some thing like it in the *Queen of* Shebah, *who hearing of the Fame of* Solomon, *came to prove him with hard Questions; and her* Questions, *however* Nice and Curious, (to use the Phrase in my *Athenian* Title) *were all told her by* Solomon; *Neither was there any thing hid from the King, which he told her not"* (p.49).

His female correspondent protests a little at Dunton's contempt for learning. She thinks Solomon could not have extended his dictum as far as to the arts and sciences; to deny them would destroy the foundation of the Port Royal, *"upon the supposition of* new Arts and Inventions, *to prove the existence of God, and that the World is not Eternal."* She valued "the Invention of Printing, of the Sea Card, Guns and Mills, *which . . . must be the* new Inventions of later Ages" (p.58).

ii

Dunton had not yet given up periodical publication, and his attempts in this line do a little to alter the lunatic impression of the self-indulgent, confessional works concerned with his personal problems. Each of his periodicals after the demise of the *Athenian Mercury* has something peculiarly original about it. The *Post Angel* (1701) had an ethereal messenger service; the *Secret Mercury* (1702) was to provide a remedy of reform for an age "dangerously ill"; the *Athenian Spy* (1704), not strictly a periodical, was a love spy for the assistance of lonely hearts; the *Christian's Gazette* (1709–1713) and the *Athenian News* (1709–1710) were to cure the "Athenian Itch" that Dunton had earlier aroused. These periodicals, as the *Mercury* before them, generously offered service of some kind not only to those who bought and read them, but to the whole community.

They were more or less contemporary with the *British Apollo* (1708–1711) and Defoe's *Review* (1704–1713), both of which had imitated the *Mercury* and infuriated Dunton by supplying answers to questions.[12] Although Dunton's own later attempts lacked the incisiveness and sensibility of these rivals, they had something of the same personal quality that distinguished the *Mercury*.

Dunton's first periodical in the eighteenth century was the *Post Angel; or, Universal Entertainment,* which appeared first in January 1701 and continued through September 1702 as a monthly magazine. Plainly, it had its roots in the *Athenian Mercury,* for it was divided into departments: "Remarkable PROVIDENCES"; "The LIVES and DEATHS of the most Eminent *Persons*"; "A New ATHENIAN MERCURY"; "Publick News at Home and Abroad"; and "BOOKS lately Publish'd, and now going to the Press." To these was added "A Spiritual Observator" to provide "a Divine Emprovement of *every Remarkable Occurrence* that happens under the Sun." The "Post Angel" himself, for whom John Dunton was only amanuensis, was to provide "several things worth reading out of the *common Road of News;* for sure a *Post-Angel* is able to *Out-flit a Post-Master, Post-Man, and Post-Boy;* and those lesser *Fliers,* the *English* and *London Post.*"[13]

The *Post Angel* was published by Mrs. Baldwin, but Dunton had apparently maintained his connection with Smith's Coffee House; the second number of the periodical opens with a testimonial letter, of which the Spiritual Observator says: "tho' I'm altogether undeserving of the Praises it gives me, and as ignorant of the Contents of it before Mr. SMITH THE COFFEE MAN DELIVERED IT TO ME, yet being desired by the Writer of it to insert it in the Post-Angel . . . 'tis here printed. . . ."

In the first number readers were asked for contributions to still another projected history of providence, on over twenty suggested topics, ranging from "The Appearance of Good and Bad Angels" to "The confessions of those that are hang'd (if very remarkable) . . . or any thing else they have observ'd in the Works of Creation and Providence."

A correspondence with the shorthand writers of London was proposed, to print "most funeral sermons" in the periodical, but none actually appeared. Dunton explained that his new *Athenian Mercury* would be new to those who had the old, and doubly so to those who didn't, for the latter couldn't have the original "except they encourage the Reprinting of it in this Journal" (I.2,72).

Following the practice begun in the *Art of Living Incognito,* the writer of the *Post Angel* pretended not to be Dunton, and explained that the bookseller had retreated from the world to study living incognito. Yet out of respect for Dunton and in view of the fact that the *Athenian Mercury* had lain dormant for six years, the writer was sure no other bookseller would interfere. Should anyone do so, however, he was promised the same treatment given the Lacedemonians.

None of the old Athenians were participating. The two contributing writers of the periodical were "Fido" and "Incognitus," who provided poems on the creation, the happy man, the soul, Paradise, virtue, and similar topics. Fido's poem on virtue was addressed to Dunton *"on his Re-Marriage,"* that is, the attempted reconciliation with Sarah, and citing a precedent, urged the lady to seek safety with her husband:

> Whilst *Eve* with her Protecting Lord remain'd,
> The blameless Nymph her Innocence retain'd:
> But when alone, along the Grove she walk'd,
> She listened as the Snaky Syren talk'd.
> (II.107)

Among the new books described in the pages of the *Post Angel* was the first volume of John Norris's *Essay towards the Theory of the Ideal or Intelligible World* (1701), described as an essay "calculated for Learned Men of high Notions . . . beyond the Capacity of the Readers" he expected to inform. Although some querists had called it "as unintelligible as Hermes, Jacob Behman, or Pordage's Mystick Divinity; yet whoever reads it with unprejudic'd Eyes, will see that Mr. Norris's Learning sets him above these Reflections." Norris was, in fact, "a Person of extraordinary Sense, and such a universal Scholar, that one told me . . . he believ'd Mr. Norris had learn'd all could be taught him on Earth, and that if he'd know more, he must go to Heaven" (I.383).

In another allusion to Norris's learning, the writer announced that in any question "where, by my own Observations I shall remain dissatisfy'd, I shall give Publick Notice of such Questions, (except Dr. N— continues his Assistance, and then I can never be puzl'd) to desire the Notions of the Learned . . ." (I.451). Norris's friendship had been with Sault, however, who had read Malebranche, rather than with Dunton, and any expectation of help from Norris probably had little basis at this late date.

In June 1702 the undertaker announced that he was going to the country for his health, and that the periodical would be carried on by "A Society of Gentlemen," assisted by clergymen and others. The last number, which appeared in September, closed with the announcement that the October issue was in preparation and that the authors planned to "write off" the numbers "something sooner in the future" (III.180).

That same month Dunton began and ended a weekly called the *Secret Mercury or the Adventures of Seven Days*. Printed as a folio half-sheet, it appeared four times on successive Wednesdays.[14] Little different from the *Night-Walker,* its main design, described in No. 1, was *"to expose the Vanity and secret Lewdness of the Town."* It was presented as a "Ramble" in seven parts, "answerable to the Stages of [the] Journey." The weekly itinerary was to be the church on Sunday, the music house Monday, the cheats of the town Tuesday, the play-house Wednesday, the whores on Thursday, Bridewell and Newgate Friday, and on Saturday the writer would *"Retire into the Country, and spell the Intreagues and Manners of the Clowns and Bumkin's."*

The last number of the *Secret Mercury* closed with the notice that the author was actually going in quest of intrigues into the country so that the next paper would not be published "till the Second *Wednesday."* In its brief life the

Secret Mercury was the most unsavory item in Dunton's entire output.

The rights to questions and answers from the *Athenian Mercury* were sold to Andrew Bell in November 1702 to be published as the *Athenian Oracle.* If the first volume sold well, Bell was entitled to purchase material for three more volumes at the same terms. These were to consist of old material only, however, for Dunton reserved to himself the right to continue the project. Although Dunton was sad at having *"beat the Bush for another to catch the Bird"* (LE, p.263), the relationship with Bell was cordial enough for Dunton to characterize the printer as "not only just, but grateful" (LE,p.282). Three volumes were published by Bell in 1703, a fourth in 1710.[15] But in the meantime the first three volumes appeared in a second edition in 1704 and a corrected third edition in 1706. The publication of all four volumes in 1728 as a "third edition" is evidence of the continuing interest in the encyclopedic contents of the *Mercury.*

The first variation upon the theme of Athenianism appeared in 1704, when a book, the *Athenian Spy,* was published by R. Halsey, one of Dunton's neighbors in the Poultry. The book was sold by Dunton to the highest bidder, for he wrote of Halsey that he knew "how to bid for a saleable Copy, or had never printed the *Athenian Spy*" (LE,p.294). Of Montgomery, a rival of Halsey, he observed that he "bid like a Man, for *The Athenian Spy*" (LE,p.353).

An offshoot from the polite questions on "gallantry" in the *Athenian Mercury* and the debates between ladies and gentlemen in the *Ladies Mercury,* the *Athenian Spy* was not a periodical strictly speaking, but its sequential arrangement, one episode of Platonic courtship developing out of another, gives it the flavor of the *Mercury,* in which questions were kept alive week after week upon the ground that particular readers were interested in their continuation.

The *Athenian Spy* is full of echoes from Dunton's past, especially from the period of the *Mercury*. It is dedicated to the "Pindarick Lady," and its first part is "A Pacquet from Athens," of Platonic love letters between Mr. R— S—,

Mathematician of New Athens, and several ladies, one of them "Madam Laureat," the "Climene" of *Conversations in Ireland,* who is anti-Platonic; another, "Irene," carries on a Platonic courtship with "Philaret," as Sault's letters are signed. This appearance of Dunton's old *nom de plume* suggests his authorship, although the fiction provided is that *"in the last Session of our Society at* Smith's, *'twas carried by the Majority of Voices that* R. S. *the* Mathematician *should make Love to Ingenious* Irene, *according to the Platform of* Plato's Idea" (p.26). In the "Dedication," one participant is introduced as "The Ingenious *Sault,* who at the Age of Twenty was arrived to the Knowledge of a Bearded Philosopher" (A *verso*). In the "Preface" we learn that

> (*even*) *the* Athenian Society *it self* (*with all its Gravity*) *has bin* LOVE-SICK.
> *Our* Reverend Chaplain (*God forgive him*) Stole *a Wife from a Conventicle.*
> *Our* Mathematician WHIN'd (*like a Dog in a Halter*) *for Mrs.* Sault.
> Philaret (*till he considered the matter*) *was* Hanging *himself for the* Pindarick Lady.
> And not a Member of Athens but LOVES an Angel in Petticoats (A9 f).

The "Pacquet" draws upon a poem of John Norris, taken from his *Collection of Miscellanies,* a book that was in its fourth edition by 1699. Norris also plays a role in "Letter XX" where "Philaret *flourishes upon the Ideal advantages of the Platonick State of Matrimony, proposes* Mr. Norris *for the Parson, and sends* [Irene] *the Forms both of Publication and Marriage; of which he desires her thoughts"* (p.66). (The second set of letters, XXII–XXXI, is a correspondence between "Orinda" and Dr. Fido, a Platonic parson.)

> *Our* Mathematitian *Succeeding so well in his* Platonick Courtship, *at the next meeting of the* Athenian Society, *we Propos'd* a Platonick Wife *for our* Rever-

end Chaplain, *the* Lady *we Recommended to him was the Charming* Orinda, (*a Daughter of the Church*) *and* a true Platonick from Head to Foot. (p.76)

"The Athenian Parson" beat an honorable retreat in Letter XXVIII, for he found, after a severe course of mortification, that he could not refine his body enough to venture on a Platonic wedding. He quoted the first two stanzas of Norris's "Seraphick Love," including the lines:

> . . . *I can be no longer thine;*
> *A Nobler, a Diviner Guest,*
> *Has took Possession of my Breast;*
> (p. 101)

This was to show Orinda, "in the very words of the *Seraphick Norris,* . . . [that] had we both kept in the same Mind, he'd never have *join'd us in Platonick Matrimony.*"

A note on the last page of the book informs the reader that

> Most of the Letters . . . were written *ex tempore,* without *Revisal* or *Correction,* and we can't see why any of our Correspondents (*tho' 'twere Madam Laureat her self*) shou'd be displeas'd at their Publication; for the Letters were really sent to the *Athenian-Society;* and we here promise that the Ladies Names shall be for ever conceal'd. In a word, if our Correspondents are ever discover'd, it must be by themselves; and therefore we expect they never upbraid us with publishing such Secrets as had ever been conceal'd; . . . (p.326)

The note perhaps raises more doubts than it allays, since the collection was got together some time after Dunton had parted company with both Sault and Norris, and seven years after he had published anything for the Pindarick Lady.

A third set of letters in the volume, XXXII–XXXV, begins with a request for advice by Charles Wem, who "(*having Kist a Buxome Girl in his Dream*) *intends to venture on a Corporal Wedlock, and desires the* Athenians *to discover to him the several Kinds of Love, that so by knowing a true Passion from a Counterfeit, he may Love so as to be Happy in Marriage"* (p.120). The final one of the set, in which *"The* Athenians *direct him in his whole Amour,"* is dated at *"Smiths* Coffee-House, *Oct.* 20th, 1703."

Four letters, XXXVI–XXXIX, were exchanged between the Society and *"The Young Virgins,"* who asked to be instructed in the mysteries and the arts of love (p.222). Following these is a curious, separately paginated section of thirty-six pages,[16] meant to serve as a sort of marriage market, in which young bachelors and young spinsters in turn are named and described as eligible and desirable mates. Their names and descriptions show that the *Athenian Spy* and the *Life and Errors* were put together at about the same time, for "Mr. *John Wade* in the County of Meath—He is short set, rather Low than Tall," so described in the *Spy* (p.(*6)), lives between dashes in the *Life and Errors* as "—the short-set and spruce *Wade* of *Ireland*—" (p.365). Next in the *Spy,* for ladies who "don't like Mr. *Wade,* (for tho' he is Rich, he is pretty Old)," Mr. Carleton of Hull is recommended; "lovely and courageous *Carleton* of *Hull"* follows Wade in the *Life and Errors.* The two works continue on parallel tracks with Norton of Fleet Street, young Benjamin Harris (p.(*7)), and Mr. Thorncomb, tobacconist, who plays the lute and has "three Virgins in love with him at this time; but two are Red hair'd, and he loves nothing but a brown woman—" (p.(*8)).

Among the number of *"young Ladies that are Uningag'd"* (pp.(*11)–(*18)) are Mrs. Johnson of Kensington, she who wrote the introduction to Philomela's *Poems* (1697), and Mary Astell, "(the young Gentlewoman that corresponded with Mr. Norris)."[17] Two pages are devoted to young women from the Isle of Wight, where "we shou'd scarce meet with a Virgin . . . but what wou'd make an excellent Wife." For a beautiful wife, Madam Tempest is recommended; for polite discourse, "Madam *Sanders* bears the Bell from all the Virgins in *Europe.*" "Were any Fellow in *Oxford* or *Cambridge* inclin'd to marry, we wou'd advise him to Madam *Hollis,* for she is a *nice Philosopher,* and is in the hard and knotty Arguments of Metaphysical Learning, a most nervous and subtle Disputant." Among the ladies of

Dublin is Mrs. Davis, of whom Dunton wrote at length in the *Dublin Scuffle*. Others, of Scotland, Andover, Holborn, and Manchester are also described, and all appear more briefly in *Life and Errors* (p.365). The conclusion is pure Dunton: "were we unnoos'd, we don't know where, within the compass of the Sex, to make a better choice for our selves; (but alas! some of us have been fatally mistaken)."

An attempt at a full-scale revival of Athens occurred also in 1704. *Athenæ Redivivæ, or the New Athenian Oracle*, was published by Sarah Malthus, who published the *Life and Errors* the next year, and was printed by George Larkin. Both of these may have extended credit to the author, Mrs. Malthus because she was then trying to make a success of the business left her by her late husband Thomas, and Larkin because of long friendship for Dunton.

The revival, according to its title page, was made up of three parts:

> I. *The Divine Oracle (or Directory for Tender Consciences)*; Resolving all the Uncommon Cases propos'd to the *Athenian Society,* by Persons under Trouble of Mind, &c.
> II. *The Philosophical and Miscellaneous Oracle;* Answering all Questions in any part of Learning; where we entirely throw off the Rules and Pedantry of the Old Way, and think a New, both for our selves and our Querists.
> III. *The Secret (or Ladies) Oracle:* Giving a Modest Satisfaction to the Nicer Questions, relating to the *Arcana Naturæ,* and such Love Secrets as are privately sent to the *Athenian Society,* by Young Gentlemen and Ladies.
> The Whole, Resolving such *Nice and Curious Questions* in *Divinity, Chronology, History, Philosophy, Law, Physick, Trade, Mathematics, Love, Poetry, &c.*
> As were never Answer'd in the Old *Athenian Oracles.*

Dunton proposed to continue it "in this Method, till the Question-Project is Compleated."

The jibe on the title page at "the Rules and Pedantry of

the Old Way," is indication enough that Dunton undertook the revival on his own, without Wesley's restraining hand and sterner morals. In his "Preface" Dunton observes that the Society was never formally dissolved, although *"Death . . . has taken off our* Algebraick Brother, Mr. Richard Sault, *and our* Reverend Chaplain (*God forgive him*) *is tack'd about to the* High Flyers." There has been a new election of members, however, *"all Masters in their several Faculties; so that the World is now to hear from* New Athens, *in a Supplementary Way* to the Performances of the O L D."

New questions were invited, the rules for them much the same as in 1691: no obscene questions; no riddles or equivocations, "for they are of no use to the Publick;" nothing of scandal to the government or abuse to particular persons; not more than one or two from any person; and lastly, "nothing . . . Destructive to the Principles of *Vertue* and Sound Knowledge, and then let our Querists be as Nice and Curious as they please."

Tirelessly projecting, Dunton asked that querists send *"all their* Remaining Scruples," in order that he might bring out the three volumes of *Athenæ Redivivæ "in* Parts, Six Pence each, . . . *Printed on the same Size and Letter, with the* Old Athenian Oracles." He assured readers *"that we shant meddle* with a single Syllable of the Old Mercuries; *for Truth is* as Infinite and Inexaustible as the Eternal Unity."

Like an aging actor, Dunton asserted that coming back out of retirement was involuntary: *"It is with very much of inward Reluctance that we thus offer our selves, as* Publick Confessors *to the World. Our* Oracle, *had for ever slept in Peace and Silence, had there been no sufficient Reasons to over-ballance us in this Affair, and make us lay aside the dear Thoughts of Solitude and Private Ease"* [A3]. Only in this way could truly scrupulous consciences unbosom themselves freely: it was *"with the most Tender Regards imaginable to such Persons as these"* that he took up once more *"the Mighty Labours, which the Task requires."*

No longer incognito but again servant to the public, Dunton did not wish to usurp the role of the minister, but noted that *"Ministers are forced to deliver their Sermons at Ad-*

ventures, and though now and then they may hit the mark, yet the Sound slides off, and the Memories of an Audience are often Unretentive."* Correspondence with the Athenians, however, would help *"The Children of Light that walk in Darkness and the Shadows of Death. . . ."* [A3 verso]. A last note of warning is sounded to religious querists, however, *"that we wont give them any Groundless Hopes, or Sooth them in their Sin, so we shall be very careful not to terrify them with unnecessary Fears."*

In the philosophical part, the reader may expect *"a free way of Thinking, and as much* Unadictedness *as possible; we shant be over Positive, unless where the matter comes up to Demonstration and Assurance, and we shall be always ready* to own the Obligations that are done us by other hands."

The third part is guaranteed to do no disservice to religion or good manners, but it will relieve those afflicted with love melancholy or *"any Secret of that Nature."* In this department, "NEW ATHENS" was already overstocked with questions, to be answered in their turn unless there were some that needed immediate satisfaction. The Athenians would remain neutral in religion, *"unless where the Essentials of our Christian Faith are Touched, and there we shall chearfully Interpose."* Thus was the Athenian project to rise Phoenix-like from its own ashes, but the three new volumes were *"absolutely Necessary for those Gentlemen that desire an Answer to such Curious Questions as were wholly Omitted in the* Old Oracles" [A3 verso].

In spite of the ponderous announcement, the three "heads" have very little under them. "The Divine Oracle" occupies twenty-five pages, double column, in the quarto volume, and consists of ten questions and answers, two of them in verse, none of them very much different from those already familiar to Dunton's earlier readers. "The Philosophick and Miscellaneous Oracle" occupies only ten pages and answers only five questions, one of them in verse. The first question is from a club formed at Cambridge to meet weekly and think up questions to puzzle the new Athenians, on the ground that there were not enough difficulties in nature "for a vigorous and active Reason" (p.26). The club believed this was "the Age where all Mens Souls are in a kind of Fermentation, and the Spirit of Wisdom and Learning, begins to mount and free it self from those drossie and terrene Impediments, wherewith it hath been so long clogg'd. . . ." They believed the New Athenians to be "the Men that must lay a Foundation of a more magnificent Philosophy, never to be overthrown: That will Empirically and sensibly canvass the *Phenomena* of Nature, as we observe are producible by Art, and the infallible demonstrations of Mechanicks: And certainly this is the way, and no other, to build a true and permanent Philosophy" (p.27).

Dunton agreed with the "ingenious Club" that even *"the Professors and nobler sort of Philosophers,"* when some difficulty arose which they could not solve, asserted the impossibility of any solution. Dunton's illustrations would be familiar to any faithful reader of the *Mercury:*

> Thus came they to upbraid *Chymistry* with the Altahest and Philosophers-Stone; *Geography,* with Longitudes; *Geometry,* with the Quadrature of a Circle; *Stereometry,* with the Duplication of the Cube, *Trigonometry* with the Trisection of an Angle, *Algebra* with the Æquation of three discontinued Numbers, *Mechanicks,* with a Perpetual Motion, Physick with the incurability of Cancers and Quartans. Nay, the Spring and Nepe-tides in *Natural Philosophy,* the Doctrine of Comets in Astronomy, the *Terra Incognita* in *Geography,* the Hearts Motion in *Anatomy,* the forming of Conick Sections in *Dioptricks,* the Various Variation in *Magnetical Philosophy;* are accounted as insuperable Difficulties as the former, whose Causes (they say) defie all Human Industry ever to discover them. (p.28)

The other discouragement to true learning is the fear that the world has decayed to such a point that it is near "to its period." In regard to this fearsome notion, Dunton is optimistic, finding comfort in the analogy between God and His world and a watchmaker and his mechanical creation:

he that made this great Automaton of the World, will not destroy it, till the slowest Motion therein has made one Revolution. For would it not even in a common Watchmaker, (that has made a curious Watch for some Gentleman or other, to shew him the rarity of his Art) be great indiscretion, and a most imprudent act, and argue also a dislike of his own work, to pluck the said Watch in pieces before every Wheel therein had made one revolution at least? Now the *Apogœum* (if it move equally, as it hath hither to done) will not perfect one Revolution under 20000 years, whereof there is but one Quadrant yet spent, [as proved by the scriptures] and 15000 years are yet to come. (p.29)

Dunton debated whether the world was made solely for the use of man, *"or in subserviency unto him and his faculties?"* Modern philosophers have found that the whole orbit of the earth is "but a Point, in regard of the immense distance of the Fixed Stars."

What are we then but like so many Ants or Pismires, that toyl upon this Mole-hill, and could appear no otherwayes at distance, but as those poor Animals, the Mites, do to us through a good *Microscope,* in a Piece of Cheese? Let us not therefore pride our selves too much in the Lordship of the whole Universe. (p.33)

Moving from the sublime to the ridiculous, the philosophical section concludes by honoring a request to describe "once more" the anatomy of the louse, the querist having read in the "Old Athenian Oracle" the question of whether fleas have stings (I.17.1). He would like to know also whether the louse is *"a sanguineous Animal, and hath both an Heart and Auricles?"* (p.34). The editors obliged with references to Dr. Harvey and a transcription of Sir Theodore Mayhern's description in Latin of the louse.

"The Secret Oracle," only three and one-half pages long, attempts three questions: ". . . *whether the Seed of a Plant, or Animal, is essentialy distinct from a young Sprig, or Plant, or a New-born Animal? . . . Whether the Soul of*

Man is created, or produced by Generation?" and *". . . with what Caution and Modesty must a young and unexperienced Couple act, that they might not exceed the sober and lawful Use of the Marriage Bed?"* Dunton believed that "the very Vestals might read" this section, but his next remark raises apprehensions: "We have just now receiv'd several nice and surprizing Questions—concerning *Adultery, Incest, Rapes, Sodomy, Self-pollution,* &c. Which will be proper Subjects for our Secret Oracle, and having some thing very uncommon in them, our Querists may expect 'em in the second Part of the New Athenian Oracle . . ." (p.39).

Although a number of the titles of Dunton's eighteenth-century publications look like the names of periodicals, few of them were in fact. Rather, they were miscellanies in single volumes, complete with dedication and preface. Some relied on the word *Athenian* or *Athenianism* to catch the purchaser's eye, as in the *Athenian Spy, Athenian Oracle, Athenian Sport,* or *2000 Paradoxes* (1707), and *Athenianism* (1710). Others, although published in book form, used some term that suggested periodical publication, as the *Christian's Gazette* (1709).

This last volume, "a Pacquet for the Pious Virtuosi; On SUBJECTS never started before," contains a long dedication to "the Lovers of Novelty"; advertisements for six books, all written by Dunton and sold by John Morphew, at that time Swift's bookseller; and eighty pages divided into eight "Novelties," ranging from *"The Celestial Court, or News concerning that Invisible World we shou'd correspond with"* to *"That the Universe is framed in such a manner as will at length produce a new Sun, Moon and Stars."*

In the "Dedication" Dunton proposed to publish weekly, monthly, or annually *"A Pacquet"* by means of correspondence not only with "Pious Virtuosi" of London, Edinburgh, and Dublin, but also *"with the* Inhabitants of the Invisible World: *So that our GAZETTE may properly be call'd News from Heaven."* He explained that inhabitants of the invisible world were *"all the Spiritual Host of the middle Region, that are employ'd about us, either as Friends or Enemies."* Their news was to be *"Discoveries relating to our future State,"* and the pious virtuosi who received these discoveries were those "Accomplish'd, Virtuous, Ingenious Persons, who enquire after NEWS not as Athenians, but as Christians." Heaven itself was not the outward and visible part *"but* the supreme Imperial Part, the Seat of the Blessed, which is out of Sight, and the Reach of Humane Sense."

Dunton planned to imitate *"Dr.* Brown *in his* Religio Medici," a way he found *"easier and more proper . . . than to pretend to any Form or Method, wherein I might commit a Thousand Mistakes; but in this some of 'em will pass like his,* for uncommon Errors, *and please for the sake of Novelty."* He cautioned readers not to be *"too* Curious *in drawing the Curtain of Holy Mysteries, to see what passes in the* Celestial Court; The Christian's Gazette *dares not give you such News as Heaven wou'd have conceal'd . . ."* (p.ii).

He seems to have had Boyle's *Christian Virtuoso* as strongly in mind as Browne's doubting doctor, for he quotes Boyle in support of his celestial inquiries: " 'There are some Things . . . that are grounded neither upon Mechanical, nor upon Chymical Notices, or Experiments, that are yet far from deserving to be neglected, and much less to be despised, or so much as to be left uncultivated' " (p.v). He would prefer *"the Furniture of* Duck-lane *before the Plate of* Lombard-street, *and . . . had rather have* the Possession of a Library, *than be Master of both* Indies" (p.x). He takes more pleasure *"in One Hour's Retirement with* Lock's Essay, *(or in preparing a Book for the Press) than in whole Days* Attendance on Profit." This is the old Dunton, hymning the praises of learning, but in a new key, for he really had but little choice between poverty and wealth.

The book, he asserted, had been in preparation for six years, *"to gratifie a curious Palate,"* but even though it was filled with novelties, there was nothing not founded *"on Scripture and Reason; for our* Christian Gazette *is not design'd to promote* the Athenian Itch, *but to cure it."* Although his speculations were entitled novelties, all the "Divine News" therein would be "problematical and disquisitive." He had as much inclination to find out the views of others as to air his own, and had made use of *"some* true

Philosophical Arguments, ... *intermix'd* ... *with* Potical Thoughts *on Subjects both new and uncommon"* (p.x).

He presented an ingenious excuse for borrowing the opinions of others:

> *If it shall be* ... *objected,* that I am very frequent in Quotations, and that therefore it may be suppos'd I have said little but what will be found express'd by others—*I shall acknowledge I have wilfully done so, because I had a Desire to get my self strongly seconded in my* New Opinions *by the Determinations of Learned Men: for I verily believe, that* if an Angel himself shou'd avouch any thing singly, and as his own Opinion, he wou'd not be believ'd by some Men. (pp.xiii–xiv)

His use of the reasons of Locke, Boyle, and Glanville might get him a reputation as a plagiary, but how else could an argument be given force and efficacy? Dryden too was accused of using some of the same words and phrases as others used *"who writ before him* ... *but no body blames the frequent usage of Words of Art, or those which the first Masters or Restorers of any Doctrine have been wont to express their Notions by"* (p.xiv).

Those who questioned the truth of his news from heaven or objected that heaven was too perfect to be the source of anything new, would also object to such reasonable notions as the being and providence of God, the possibility of motion, and the certainty of sense.

The glib promises of the "Dedication" were not very well fulfilled in the eight novelties that made up the remainder of the work, and no further celestial news appeared until 1713, when "The Second Edition, corrected and greatly enlarged" was published. The title page, somewhat modified, bore no date, but letters in the text give the year date and all right-hand pages have the heading "January, February, March *and* April" to imply periodical publication. New additions were "The *LAME-POST, Or a History of Providence, Nature, and Art, well attested,"* and *"The COURT-*

SPY, Or a Detection of such secret, odd, and uncommon Transactions in Church and State, as are wholly omitted by other News-Writers: With a Spiritual Observator (or Divine Improvement upon each Occurrence.)"

In his "Dedication" to Anna Sophia, Electoress Dowager of Hanover, Dunton announced that the *Gazette* would publish *"Monthly* Religious News, or a Divine Improvement of every remarkable Occurrence under the Sun" (p.i). His choice of the Electoress for the dedication indicated his Whig and anti-Jacobite position, and he left no doubt of it when he promised to detect "the Treasonable Words and Practices *of the Jacobite Faction (but more especially of Dr.* Sacheverell)."

By 1713, Dunton was extremely interested in the plight of the imprisoned debtor. His own bitter experience dictated the reflections on the subject in the *Christian's Gazette,* as contained in "HUMANE-DICE, *Or a Character of such merciless Creditors that attempt to murder their honest (tho' insolvent) Debtors, by a close Confinement"* and "THE SPIRITUAL OBSERVATOR" on it (pp.23–43).

A letter dated from the Fleet Prison, April 30, 1713, sets forth the reasons offered to Parliament by John Asgill for a more extensive act for discharge of prisoners, and presents the story of "Fido," or Dunton himself, and his struggles with a merciless creditor, an undertaker, "Dice" Hewson, so called because he threatened to make dice of his debtors' bones (p.31). There are frequent allusions to "Dr. Smirk" as one whom Fido had befriended in adversity, the first denoting him as "that *ATHENIAN PRIEST* that owes his very Chaplain's Scarff to FIDO's *Guineas,"* one who *"ought to blush at"* his ingratitude (p.32). The author says of Dr. Smirk and one "Dr. *JOHN's-SON,"* a Welsh divine, "I wou'd have *Fido* threaten to publish their *Secret History* (or at least those *fawning Letters* they sent to him, when they were *courting with empty Pockets*) for what *Lash* can be too severe for ungrateful Men . . ." (p.32). They had been "deaf to the Prison Groans of a *try'd Friend,* . . . but these gentle Lashes will be all the Correction they'l ever have, for not giving him ONE PULL at a

Dead-Lift, when bare lending of 20 *l.* wou'd now set him at Liberty" (p.33).

At this time Dunton had been kept "a close Prisoner for two Years" (p. 42). Almost fifteen years after his marriage to Sarah Nicholas, he was still in difficulties over the marriage settlement, with no hope of release for, "except *JOHN's-SON* and *Smirk* (by calling to Mind *the solemn Word of a Priest*) will voluntarily come and release him, or *Friendly Death* will knock off his *Jointure-Shackle,* he may (perhaps) ride at Anchor in the *Royal Fleet,* 'till his *leaky Vessel* . . . sinks into Native Clay. . . ." (In a note to the phrase *"leaky Vessel"* Dunton explained that it meant his hereditary distemper of the stone "and many other Distempers that he has contracted by Means of *a long and close Confinement."*)

He had not mentioned Wesley in print since 1705, in the *Life and Errors,*[18] although inclusion of Susannah and pointed omission of Samuel Wesley as a friend, in *Dunton's Shadow; or, the Character of a Summer Friend* (1706; 1710) show that resentment had smoldered all the while, kept alive by Wesley's comparative success rather than by any demonstrable slight.

After Elizabeth Dunton's death there was not much reason for Wesley to associate with Dunton. The later journalistic undertakings of Dunton were so short-lived and so thinly financed that probably no other writers were called in to assist, much less to draw up an agreement such as that which guaranteed the regular appearance of the *Mercury.*

The complete roster of Dunton's works numbers nearly a hundred, allowance being made among these for contribution by other hands in the periodicals in such encyclopedic volumes as the *Young Students Library.* Publications before 1711 frequently echoed Athenianism, but thereafter Dunton switched to political pamphlets supporting the Hanoverians, attacking the Tories, and demanding a reward for his services.

Among his sallies into the journalistic jungle warfare that characterized the reigns of Queen Anne and George I, *Neck or Nothing* (1713) attracted the most attention. It was intended to supplement Walpole's *Short History of the Parliament* and reveal the schemes rampant "for bringing in the Pretender, Popery, and Slavery."

In a note to Oxford, Defoe listed *Neck or Nothing* as "a continual rhapsody of scandal and raillery" and observed that six thousand copies printed showed "how pleasing such scandalous things are among us."[19] But it was Swift who used it, in the *Publick Spirit of the Whigs,* his satirical attack upon Richard Steele and the *Crisis.*

"Among the present writers on that side [Whig]," wrote Swift, "I can recollect but three of any great Distinction, which are the *Flying Post,* Mr. *Dunton,* and the Author of the *Crisis.* . . ." *Neck or Nothing,* he allowed, was of all these "the shrewdest Piece, and written with the most Spirit of any which hath appear'd from that Side, since the Change of the Ministry: . . . a most cutting satire upon the Lord Treasurer, and Lord Bolingbroke." He wondered that none had ever undertaken to answer it. To humiliate Steele, Swift wrote that he was "at first of the same opinion with several Good Judges, who from the Style and Manner supposed it to have issued from the sharp Pen of the Earl of *Nottingham,* and . . . still apt to think it might receive his Lordship's last Hand." Steele, he concluded, must yield to both Dunton and Nottingham "in Keenness of Satire and Variety of Reading." In a burst of generosity, he added that Steele was "a writer of a superior class to either; provided he would a little regard the Propriety and Disposition of his Words, consult the Grammatical Part, and get some Information in the Subject he intends to handle."[20]

Royal Gratitude (1716), in which "Philo-Patria" addresses Walpole in behalf of Dunton, repeats Swift's praise as "a True character of Mr. *Dunton* and his Writings" (p.18). But in *Queen Robin: or the Second Part of Neck or Nothing* (1714), Dunton protested that the author of the *Examiner* "was an *abusive Raskal*" to foster his "*poor incorrect Scrawls*" upon so great a genius as the Earl of Nottingham, and that it was done not to compliment him but to debase *"that Glorious Patriot"* (p.64).

An advertisement at the end of *Royal Gratitude* promised *"a Thousand Essays in Prose and Verse"* to be printed by subscription under the general title of *Athenianism,* as well as a periodical, with Dunton its sole author, *"Athenian News; or, Dunton's Packet for the Virtuosi of Great Britain.* In Thirty distinct Parts" [G4 *verso*].

None of these grandiose schemes actually materialized. It was as if Dunton had retained only his peculiar inventiveness without that ability, so impressively demonstrated in the *Mercury,* of carrying out a project.

His practice of self-plagiarism was present throughout, but in his later years, alienated from those who had aided him in timelier and more popular projects, his pamphlets became a repetitious babble of his own characteristic phrases. In the *Mercury* a conservative form held a great variety of information often expressed in witty and cogent ways. In the later works whimsy runs wild, and their content, largely self-promotion, could have been taken seriously only if presented with some measure of humility.

As Dunton became more the political pamphleteer than the educational journalist, he lost much of his skill in presenting a balanced publication. The last exemplar of Athenianism, the *Athenian Library* (1725), illustrates his decay. It has a mere seventy pages of text, nearly all with a familiar cast, but allegedly it had taken eight years for Dunton and his loyal mistress, Martha Jones, to get it together and into print.

The grand announcement of the work, to be "A Universal Entertainment for the *Lovers of Novelty,* Containing Two Thousand Distinct Treatises in **PROSE** and **VERSE**," appeared in 1717 in eleven folio pages with the main title of *Mordecai's Last Shift.* (Dunton had used the name "Mordecai" the year before in *Mordecai's Memorial: or, There's Nothing for him* to denote his role as savior of that modern Ahasuerus, George I.)

The *Athenian Library* was to contain "New and Surprizing thoughts upon all manner of subjects," the listing of which occupies the entire first folio page, with much the effect of a circus poster. Among the contents would be

"Mr. *Dunton*'s *Farewell to Printing*, ... A L S O A *Catalogue* of all the Books this NOVELIST ever writ, (both in Manuscript and such as were formerly Printed).... W I T H Mr. *Dunton*'s *Effigies* (curiously) Drawn and Grav'd to the Life, ... A N D *Two Alphabetical Tables,* the First for the ready finding any N O V E L T Y in this Project, and the other containing the Names of all those *Noble Patriots* who (to Reward Mr. *D U N - T O N ' s distinguisht Service to his King and Country, and hard Study for Thirty Years in Compiling this ATHENIAN LIBRARY*) have Generously Subscribed towards that *G R E A T C H A R G E* 'twill cost in fitting it for Publick View—With a Poem Intitled, *The Generous Subscribers."*

The whole work would be revised, corrected, and approved "by the several Members both of the *old, and new Athenian Society,* and Intermixt, and Compleated, with some of their *Newest and best Thoughts,* and the most refin'd part of their Writings." The detailed catalogue ends with four epigraphs, of which the third and fourth are most relevant to Dunton's own career. From Robert Wild's poem, *"In Nova Fert Animus,* &c. or a New Song to an Old Friend from an Old Poet, upon the Hopeful New Parliament" (1679), came a couplet on Athenianism that Dunton had used previously in scattered places:

We all are tainted with the Athenian Itch
News, *and* New Things, *do the whole World bewitch—*

The fourth epigraph paraphrased some lines of Thomas Randolph:

He lives that Prints *altho' his Glass were run*
(*Porters Immortal grow by* Flesh *and* Bone)
If I a Poem *leave that* Poem *is my Son—*[21]

These are lines that, like Cyrano's white plume, float defiantly above the fray. Dunton had quoted them in many places, but here in his last major attempt to escape the Fleet and found a new Athenian money maker, they have a certain poignancy, for only an announced revival of the

Athenian Spy,[22] and the meager *Athenian Library* came forth to represent the man who had once boasted that his Athenian Project held exclusive patent on questions and answers.

Although the man declined, the *Athenian Gazette and Casuistical Mercury* remains as his best monument. Its five hundred and eighty periodical issues demonstrated for the first time in England the feasibility of a continuing journalistic project as a private enterprise, and the work of its three principals in the benign disguise of "the Athenian Society" constitutes an early example of the kind of journalistic cooperation now taken for granted. Its questions and answers, unique in their time, engaged readers ingenuous and ingenious. Like the coffee houses where copies of the *Mercury* lay on the long tables, its contents refreshed and sometimes edified partakers attracted by its sense of their present, the world in which they lived. For one impatient with books, it provided a brief respite from action, and to one unacquainted with books, it could be a first introduction to reading for the sake of knowledge. For all it served during most of a decade as the best way of "being *resolved in any Question* without knowing their informer."

CHAPTER 12

[1] His last publication in his lifetime, *An Essay on Death Bed Charity*, appeared in 1728. He died in 1733.

[2] LE,p.390. The course of reading was to be preparation for "a Course of Travels," for which Dunton proposed to collect the best travels and voyages published.

[3] LE,pp.236–237 [Sigs. Cc 2^v–Cc 3]. What would be p. 463^v is actually numbered 200, the remaining pages of the volume continuing in sequence through 251. The earlier p.236 is Sig. R.

[4] For the *Pegasus* emblem see Frontis. and Stanley Morison, *History of English Newspapers*, Cambridge University Press, 1932, Fig. 30, p.52.

[5] Vol. I, No. 7. Dunton anticipates Addison in his witty use of the "Sir Roger de Coverly" dance.

[6] The title was not new, for there are examples of it in the preceding twenty-five years using the term as meaning either prostitute or ghost.

[7] See Chapter 9, pp.145–147. As a periodical, Volume I consisted of September–December 1696; Volume II, January and February 1697; and Volume III, March and April 1697.

[8] Dunton gave a somewhat different description of this project in LE, pp.269–277, where he numbers the "Rambles" among the errors of his

life. After the journal had run eight months, Dunton wrote, his author "was quite out at the *Elbows,* for want of Matter; however, to fill up the last, that the publick might not have it imperfect, *Two young Clergymen,* in other Habits, and my self (with the Consent of *Iris*) began the *Rambles,* for neither they nor I before, had ever seen *The Humours of the Town.* I am well enough satisfy'd with the Innocence of our Design, but indeed the *Prudence* of it, I know not how to justify; . . ." p.269. (Nichols silently omitted the details of this project. See LE, 1818, p. 201.)

The encounters described in the pages that follow are not the ones that appeared in either the *Mercury* or the eight numbers of the *Night-Walker,* although Dunton's device of frightening a whore by pretending to be a ghost appears in all three places. Only in *Life and Errors* is there the elaborate provision for the company of some clergymen, "neither both of 'em Dissenters, nor yet both Conformists" (p.270).

[9] This in spite of his extravagant statements in "Philaret's *last Letter to his Wife,*" LE, pp.364–368 [*Aa6^v–8], where he asserted "if I shou'd survive thee . . . I doubt whether I shou'd ever be brought to draw again in the *conjugal Yoke,* except (*Phœnix* like) from thy Ashes another *Iris* cou'd arise. . . ." (pp.364–365); "shou'd you dye First, I shall instead of *seeking a second Wife,* make *Court* to your Dead Body, and as 'twere *Marry again in the Grave*" (p.365).

[10] See Chapt. 1, n.17.

[11] Two other works, the *Case of John Dunton* (1700) and the *Case is Alter'd* (1701), concentrate upon Dunton's troubles with his new wife and her mother. They are highly emotional works, expressing Dunton's need to assuage his disappointment at not receiving money from his mother-in-law, with which he might have paid his debts.

[12] J. R. Moore in *Daniel Defoe, Citizen of the World,* p.232, lists half a dozen topics on which Defoe may have written for the *Mercury.* The *Review,* however, does not resemble the *Mercury* nearly as much as does the *British Apollo.* See William F. Belcher, "The Sale and Distribution of the *British Apollo,*" pp.73–101 in *Studies in the Early English Periodical* (ed. Richmond P. Bond), Chapel Hill, University of North Carolina Press, 1957.

[13] Dunton cites John Aubrey's relation in his *Miscellanies* of the correspondence between one Dr. Nepier and the archangel Raphael. He mentions Elias Ashmole, Henry More, and others as having communicated with angels, and censures Luther for having feared to do so. He praises the usefulness of angels in interposing in human affairs, as in preventing suicide.

[14] No. 1, 2–9 Sep 1702; No. 2, 9–16 Sep; No. 3, 16–23 Sep; No. 4, 23–30 Sep.

[15] The agreement is in Bodleian MS. Rawl. D.72, No. 67. In 1707, Bell was willing to pay Dunton for a fourth volume, to contain Volumes Eighteen and Nineteen of the *Mercury,* the *History of the Athenian Society,* and "An Essay upon all Sorts of Learning," by the Athenian Society. Swift's *Ode* with his letter to the Society, and other material from the Supplements was also included. This volume was not published until 1710, but Dunton was working on it in 1707, for he wrote a

letter on 30 December to Narcissus Luttrell, humbly entreating him to lend him the two volumes and the *History*. He no longer had them himself, and he had "searcht in near an Hundred likely Places" without success. He went on persuasively: "S^r. your Generosity in this Matter will be a Reall Peice of seruice to ye Publick as I know not where to procure them ('tho ye Athenian Mercury was my own Project) and I hope that scarcity will in some measure excuse this Great Presumption." He offered Luttrell a complete set of the *Oracle* when the fourth volume was printed as well as a pledge for the safe return of the three volumes of Luttrell's, even though their original cost was only sixpence. A memorandum in Luttrell's hand but signed by Dunton a week after his first application attests that he received not the separate volumes he requested, but Volumes Eleven through Twenty in a single binding, for which he deposited two guineas with Luttrell, and promising the complete *Oracle*, gratis. Pp. 26–27 in James M. Osborn, "Reflections on Narcissus Luttrell (1657–1732)," *Book Collector*, Vol. 6, No. 1 (Spring 1957), pp.15–27.

[16] Pagination, which had reached 242 before this insert, resumed with a new set of letters on questions of marriage and divorce, with 219 and ran without interruption to the end, p.326.

[17] *Letters concerning the Love of God, between the Author of the Proposal to the Ladies and Mr. John Norris,* London, 1695.

[18] See chap. 11, n. 8.

[19] "Collection of Scandal," dated 10 March 1713/14, endorsed by Oxford. *Historical MSS. Commission, Portland,* V, p.395.

[20] *Prose Works of Jonathan Swift,* Oxford, Blackwell, 1953. VIII. 31–32.

[21]
    Let Clownes get wealth, and heires; when I am gone,
      And the great Bugbeare grisly death
        Shall take this idle breath
      If I a Poem leave, that Poem is my Sonne.

"*An Ode to Mr Anthony Stafford to hasten him into the country.*" *The Poems and Amyntas of Thomas Randolph* (ed. John Jay Parry), New Haven, Yale University Press, 1917. Pp.129–131.

[22] Adv *Flying Post,* 2 Jan 1719/20.

INDEX

Account of the Conversion of Theodore John, An, 190 n7
Account of the Life and Memorable Actions of Father Petre The Jesuit, An, 13
Acta Eruditorum Lipsiae, 50
Advice to a Son, 94
Ælian, 126
Ælius, 175
Aeneid: as best poem, 89; Douglas's translation, 100
Alsop, Benjamin, 10
Anabaptists: *Mercury*'s attacks on, 164, 176, 177. See also Dissenters; Quakers
"Anacreontique on a Pair of Breeches, An," 7
Anna Sophia (Electoress Dowager of Hanover), 235
Anne, Queen (Princess Anne): and James II, 64; mentioned, 62, 97, 210, 236
Annesley, Elizabeth. See Dunton, Elizabeth Annesley; "Iris"
Annesley, Samuel: and Dunton, 5, 7, 8, 208 n5; influence on Defoe, 20 n11; religious position of, 163; death of, 201; and "Reformation of Manners," 203; mentioned, 206
Annesley family, 95
Apocrypha, 166
Archæologiæ Philosophicæ: in *Mercury,* 185–186, 187
Archimedes, 93, 192
Aristobulus, 175
Aristotle, 125, 157, 187, 205
Artaxerxes, 170

Art of Living Incognito: description of, 218–219; and *Post Angel,* 221; mentioned, 210
Ashmole, Elias, 79, 241 n13
Astell, Mary, 226
Astroscopium, 119
Athenæ Redivivæ, 227–232
Athenian Gazette: purpose and beginnings of, 23; soliciting questions for, 26; title change of, 28; mentioned, 200, 201. See also *Athenian Mercury;* Athenians
Athenian Library, 238–240
Athenian Mercury: times of publication, 3; organization and purpose, 24, 27, 46, 103, 219; title change of, 28; readers of, 30, 31, 194; dating and numbering, 32 n1, 49–50, 200, 201; reasons for success of, 33, 84, 191, 202; Swift on, 33, 124; satirized, 36–40, 77, 80–84; history of suspensions, 63, 64, 65, 66, 164, 194, 195–201, 206, 207; *Athenian Oracle,* material from, 223; mentioned *passim.* See also *Athenian Gazette;* Athenians; Supplements
—compared with: *Athenian News, Christian Gazette,* and *Secret Mercury,* 219; *Athenian Spy,* 219, 223; *British Apollo,* 18, 84, 220, 241 n12; *Coffee House Mercury,* 17; *Compleat Library, Young Students Library,* 58; Defoe's *Review,* 84, 220, 241 n13; Dunton's later works, 238;

243

Examiner, Tatler, Weekly Review, 18; *Gentleman's Journal,* 18, 49, 202; *Lacedemonian Mercury,* 84; *Life and Errors,* 15; *London Gazette,* 30, 49, 202; *London Mercury,* 30, 35–36; modern magazines, 202; *New Athenian Comedy,* 85 n17; *Pegasus with News,* 212; *Philosophical Transactions,* 113; *Post Angel,* 219, 220; *Ramble Round the World, A,* 15; *Rambler,* 141; *Second Spira,* 67; *Spectator,* 18, 141, 142; *Voyage Round the World, A,* 15
—contributors to: agreement between writers and bookseller, 24, 25, 26; Sault, 24, 25, 76; Singer, 105, 106; Wesley, 24, 25, 103; *See also* Dunton, John (bookseller); Sault, Richard; Singer, Elizabeth; Wesley, Samuel
—miscellaneous subjects in: Anne Boleyn, 191; Atlas, 192; distribution and types, 3, 25, 29, 30, 46, 58 n2, 103, 114, 191; heraldry, 191; Namur, 192; Norris, 94; propriety of, 28; Singer, 106; tobacco, 275–276
—poetical subjects in: 89–93, 100–102, 110 n1, 192, 193
—political subjects in: 9, 30, 59–62, 106
—religious subjects in: 30, 78, 79, 101, 164, 166–185, 194, 208 n12
—scientific subjects in: 47 n6, 78, 92, 93, 113–117, 125–138, 138 n1, 138 n2, 140 n15, 140 n18, 185–189, 208 n10, 208 n11
—social subjects in: 104, 105, 142–155, 157–160, 167, 192
Athenian News: and *Mercury,* 219; and *British Apollo,* Defoe's *Review,* 220; mentioned, 238
Athenian Oracle: description of, 223; mentioned, 228, 232
Athenianism, 232, 238
Athenians: and rivalry with Lacedemonians, 40–41; attack of Brown, 42–43; Protestant views of, 56, 57; in praise of Singer, 107; feminist sympathies of, 108; and Boyle, 117, 137; scientific knowledge of, 117, 123–124, 203, 204; anti-Cartesianism of, 123; position on science and religion, 135–137, 189; social attitudes of, 141, 160–161; political views of, 142; view of Adam's fall, 144; religious position of, 163–164; and Dissenters, 203; views on social and scientific problems, 203. *See also Athenian Mercury;* Athenian Society
Athenian Society: public image of, 24, 67, 124; emblem of, 27; and Universities, 27; satirized by Brown, 36–40; Settle on engraving of, 86 n20; scientific knowledge of, 113, 114; Dunton on dissolution of, 228. *See also Athenian Mercury;* Athenians
Athenian Spy: compared to other journals, 219, 220, 223, 226–227; description of, 223–226; Dunton's authorship of, 224; on love and marriage, 226–227; mentioned, 232, 240
Augustine, 165
Auzout, Adrien, 130, 140 n19

Baalam, 173, 213
Bacon, Nathaniel, 68, 84 n4
Balak, 213
Baldwin, Anne: and Dunton, 218; mentioned, 220
Baldwin, Richard, 65, 119, 211, 218
Baxter, Richard, 11
Beaumont, Francis, 100
Behman, Jacob, 221
Behn, Aphra, 108
Bell, Andrew: and Dunton, 223; mentioned, 49
Bennet, Thomas, 53, 139 n7
Berkeley, Bishop: on vision, 125
Bibliothèque Universelle, 51, 57
Bishop, Bethia: and Dunton, 9

Blount, Charles: and Gildon, 47 *n*7; work of, 65
Blount, Henry, 116
Bochart, Samuel: as Biblical authority, 172; Wesley's praise of, 189 *n*1; description of, 190 *n*5
Bohun, Edmund: as Licenser, 63, 65; Dunton's description of, 65
Boileau, N., 98
Boleyn, Anne, 191
Bolingbroke, Lord, 237
Boyer, Abel, 195
Boyle, Robert: and *Mercury*, 92, 93, 117; on reason, 136; Athenians' view of, 136–137; on remedies for common diseases, 138; influence on Dunton, 233; mentioned, 45, 57, 94, 113, 123, 234
Brick, Widow ("The Flower of Boston"): and Dunton, 8
British Apollo: compared to other journals, 18, 84, 220, 241 *n*12
Brown, Tom: and *Mercury*, 34, 36–40, 93; and Dunton, 37, 38, 41, 43, 46; criticism of Wesley, 38, 44, 142; criticism of Gildon, 39; and Athenians, 42–43, 45; as writer for *Moderator*, 44; and *New Athenian Comedy*, 84
Browne, Sir Thomas: and *Christian's Gazette*, 233; mentioned, 32 *n*5, 205
"Bunduca," 108
Bunyan, John: and *Second Spira*, 69; mentioned, 45
Burnet, Gilbert, 51, 171
Burnet, Thomas, 185–189

Cain, 191
Calvin, John, 68
Cambridge club, 229, 230
Campbel, Patrick, 216, 217
Canticles, 89
Carew, Thomas, 103, 216
Carleton, Mr. (of Hull), 226
Caroline, Queen, 97
Cases of Conscience, 157

Catholics: in *Mercury*, 173, 180. *See also* Jesuits; Papists
Cato, 78
Cave, William, 57, 58 *n*12
Character of the late Dr. Samuel Annesley by way of Elegy, 208 *n*5
Characters, 20 *n*17
Charles I, 63
Charles II, 158, 186
Charleston (writer on nutrition), 133
Chaucer, Geoffrey, 100
Christian's Gazette: compared to other journals, 219, 220; description and purpose of, 232–235
Christian Virtuoso, 233
Chymia Sacra, 79
Clarissa Harlow, 155
Cleaveland, John, 100
"Climene," in Dunton's works, 218, 224
Coffee House Mercury, 16, 17, 121
Collection for Improvement of Husbandry and Trade, A, 120, 121
Collection of Miscellanies, 224
Compendium Physicæ: influence of, 31, 132; description of, 123, 139 *n*12
Compleat Library: description of, 54–55; compared to other journals, 57, 58; length of publication of, 57; mentioned, 46, 55, 56, 65, 70, 201
Conflict of Conscience, The, 68
Conquest of Mexico, 193
Cooper, Charles Henry, 75
Cornelius, 175
Cowley, Abraham, 98, 99, 100, 109
Crashaw, Richard, 100
Crisis, The, 237
Crouch, Samuel, 195
Culverwel, Nathanael, 27
Cursory Reflections, 94
Cursus Mathematicus, 119
Cutts, Henry: on Wesley, 99
Cyprus, 170

Darius, 170
David, 100
Davideis: and Wesley, 98; mentioned, 100
Davis, Mrs. (of Dublin), 227
Davis, Sir J., 100
Defoe, Daniel: in *Dunciad,* 12; and Annesley, 20 *n*11; scientific knowledge of, 31, 123; Dunton's attack on, 86 *n*21; and *Mercury,* 140 *n*14, 189 *n*1, 241 *n*12; on Dunton's *Neck or Nothing,* 237; mentioned, 28, 42, 69, 208 *n*5
de Fonvive, John, 195
Demoivre, Abraham, 120
Descartes, René: in *Second Spira,* 71; on scientific curiosities, 125; mentioned, 117, 129, 140 *n*15
DeVane, Mrs. W. C., 116
Digby, Kenelm, 116
Diocles, 127
Dion, 175
Dionysius, 165
Discourse of the Light of Nature, A, 27
Discourse of Things Above Reason, 136
Dissenters: academies of, 6, 31, 122–123, 164, 165; and Dunton, 6, 7, 9; in *Mercury,* 30, 164; and millenarianism, 166; and the Athenians, 203; mentioned, 144. See also Anabaptists; Quakers
Donne, John, 100
Doolittle, Sarah, 6
Doolittle, Thomas, 6
"Dorinda," 217
Douglas, Gawen, 100
Dowley, James, 41, 47 *n*8
Drake, Sir Francis, 193
Dryden, John: on Athenianism, 27; compared to Wesley, 99; Singer's praise of, 107; mentioned, 45, 97, 98, 100, 103, 193, 234
Dublin Scuffle: and other works, 216; further description of, 217; mentioned, 75, 210, 215, 227
Dunciad, 12
Dunton, Elizabeth Annesley: and Dunton, 5, 7, 9, 10, 20 *n*12, 109, 149, 208 *n*6; death of, 200, 201, 215, 236; mentioned, 6, 11. See also "Iris"
Dunton, John (?–1676), (clergyman): and Dunton, 4, 6; life of, 19 *n*8
Dunton, John (1659–1733): biographical data, 4, 15, 19 *n*8, 201, 204 *n*1, 209; as bookseller, 4, 5, 7, 11, 124, 209; as author, 6, 14, 15, 16, 20, *n*17, 102, 209–210, 216, 218, 221, 234, 236–238; debts of, 7, 9, 10, 148, 217; travels of, 7–9, 10–11, 215, 216, 217; as satirized in *New Athenian Comedy,* 80–84. See also "Kainophilus"; "Philaret"; "Smart, P."
—opinions of: political, 7, 17, 209, 212, 235, 236; on debtors, 17, 192, 235, 236; on English Jews, 17, 190 *n*7; on morality and personal reform, 17, 210; on education and learning, 17, 218, 230, 233; on religion, 17, 203, 230, 231, 241 *n*13; on science, 17, 125; on Athenians, 27, 204, 228; on poets, 77; on apprentices, 141, 210–211, 236; on appearing in print, 217, 218; on marrying again, 241 *n*9
—relationships with: See particularly Brown, Tom; Defoe, Daniel; Dissenters; Dunton, Elizabeth Annesley; Dunton, Sarah Nicholas; Gildon, Charles; Sault, Richard; Singer, Elizabeth; Swift, Jonathan; Wesley, Samuel
—as author of: *Art of Living Incognito,* 210, 218–219, 221; *Athenæ Redivivæ,* 227–232; *Athenian Library,* 238–239, 240; *Athenian Spy,* 219–220, 223–227, 232, 240; *Case is Alter'd,* 241 *n*11; *Case of John Dunton,* 241 *n*11; *Conversations in Ireland,* 218, 224; *Dublin Scuffle,* 74, 210, 215, 216–217, 227;

Dunton's Shadow, 236; *Letters from New England*, 9, 216; *Life and Errors*, 4, 11, 14–15, 18 n1, 28, 43, 53, 64–65, 73, 75, 92, 95, 102, 103, 209, 210, 216, 226–227, 236; *Mordecai's Last Shift*, 238; *Mordecai's Memorial*, 238; *Neck or Nothing*, 237; *Pegasus with News*, 211–213; *Queen Robin*, 237; *Ramble Round the World, A*, 14–16; *Royal Gratitude*, 237, 238; *Voyage Around the World*, 14–15, 20 n12, 216
— as contributor to: *Athenian Mercury*, 3, 25, 28, 64–66, 164, 198–202, 219; *History of Remarkable Providences*, 205, 206; *Knowledge of the World*, 207; *Night Walker*, 207, 213–215, 222, 240 n8; *Religio Bibliopolæ*, 32 n5
— as publisher of: Dissenters' works, 6, 11; political biographies, 12–13; news sheets and periodicals, 13–17, 219; *Account of the Conversion of Theodore John, An*, 190 n7; *Account of the Memorable Actions of Father Petre, An*, 13; *Athenian Gazette*, 23, 26, 28, 200, 201; *Athenian Mercury*, collected edition of volumes of, 49; *Athenian News*, 219–220, 238; *Athenian Sport*, 232; *Bloody Assizes, The* 12–13; *Christian's Gazette*, 219–220, 232–235; *Coffee House Mercury*, 16, 17, 121; *Compleat Library*, 46, 54–58, 65, 70, 201; *Continuation of News*, 13; Daniel Williams' funeral sermon for Samuel Annesley, 206; *Dying Speeches*, 11, 12, 13, *Essay on Death Bed Charity, An*, 208, n6; *Essays, proving, We shall know our Friends in Heaven, An*, 208 n6; *General History of the Quakers*, 207; *Good News from Ireland*, 14; *History of all Religions in the World, A*, 204, 205; *Irish Courant*, 14; *Joy of Faith, The*, 11; *Ladies Mercury*, 103, 104, 223; *Lord's Last Sufferings, The*, 6; *Maggots*, 6, 94, 95, 96, 164; *Pleasure with Profit*, 118, 119; *Poems on Several Occasions*, 106, 107, 108, 207, 212, 226; *Poetical Fragments*, 11; *Popish Champions, The*, 12; *Post Angel*, 215, 219–221, 222; Sault's translation of *La Recherche de la Verité*, 118; *Second Spira, The*, 67–68, 69, 70–73, 81, 85 n7, 210; *Secret Mercury*, 219–223; *Soul's Return to Its God, The*, 11; *Tragedies of Sin, The*, 11; *Treatise on Algebra, A*, 118, 119; *True Protestant Mercury*, 16; *2000 Paradoxes*, 232; *Young Students' Library*, 27, 46, 52, 53, 55–57, 58, 86 n20, 174, 185, 201, 236

Dunton, Sarah Nicholas: marriage to Dunton, 4, 153, 201, 208 n9, 215, 221, 236, 241 n11

Dupin (writer of religious works), 57

Earle, John, 20 n17
Edward VI, 191, 192
Edzard, John Esdras, 190 n7
Εἰκων βασιλικη, *A true accompt of ye author of . . .*, 63
Eliot, John, 8
Eloisa to Abelard, 107
English Man's Phisitian, The, 64
English Post, 195, 220
Enquiry into the Physical and Literal Sense of Jeremiah viii.7, An, 135
Essay on the Human Understanding: in *Young Students Library*, 57; in *Bibliothèque Universelle*, 57; criticized, 94; mentioned, 233
Essay towards the Theory of the Ideal or Intelligible World, 221
Esther, Book of, 175
Examiner, 18
Ezra, Ben, 176

Fairy Queen (Settle's): description of, 79; song from, 86 n19; mentioned, 77
Fairy Queen (Spenser's), 100
Faithorne, William, 96, 97
Feare-full Estate, 68–69, 71
Fielding, Henry, 148
Flatman, T., 100
Fletcher, John, 100
Flying Post, 195, 237
Fraser, James: as Licenser, 59, 63; Dunton's description of, 64; mentioned, 13
Friendship in Death, 107
Fuller, Thomas, 20 n17, 205

Gadbury, John, 208 n10
Galileo, 93
Gentleman's Journal: description of, 17–18, 57; and *Mercury,* 18, 49, 202; Wesley in, 103; mentioned, 99
George I, 210, 236
Gilbert, William, 113
Gildon, Charles: and Athenian Society myth, 24; on Dunton's use of "Athenian," 27; as writer, 34, 35, 39, 41; in apology to Athenians, 39; Brown's attack of, 39; on *Nuncius Infernalis,* 42; and Charles Blount, and as Dunton's *Atheist,* 47 n7; on *Mercury,* 91; and Sault, 118; mentioned, 43, 106
"Gingerbread Mistress, To My," 7
Giornali de Literati, 50
Glanville, Joseph, 234
Godfrey of Bulloign, 100
Gondibert, 100
Greene, Robert, 147
Greenfield, Richard, 193
Greenwood, John, 68

Habbakkuk, 3, 105
Halley, Edmund, 57
Halsey, R., 223
Hamathites, 176
Hanoverians, 236
Harper, Charles, 96
Harris, Benjamin, 68, 226
Harris, Widow (publisher), 68
Harvey, William, 114, 131, 132, 231
Henry VIII, 191
Herbert, George, 100
Hermes, 221
Hicks, John, 12
High Flyers: and anti-Stuart books, 64; and *Mercury,* 164; mentioned, 30, 228
Hind and the Panther, 35
History of the Athenian Society: publishing of, 41; description of, 42; bound with *Mercury,* 49; on *Mercury,* 91; in praise of Sault, 118; mentioned, 24, 27, 55, 106
History of Learning, 52
History of Old and New Testament Attempted in Verse, 97
History of Remarkable Providences, 206
History of the Royal Society: in *Young Students Library,* 57; mentioned, 125
Hobbes, Thomas, 136, 169
Hollingsworth, Dr. Richard, 63–64
Hollis, Madame (Dunton's "nice Philosopher"), 226
Holy and Profane State, 20 n17
Holy Living, 205
Hooke, Robert, 57, 113
Houghton, John, 120, 121
Huygens, Christian, 57, 130

Independents, 168
"Irene," 224
"Iris" (Elizabeth Dunton): courtship letters of, 5; Dunton's praise of, 8; on Sault, 72; and "Philomela," 108; death of, 149, 210; "Philaret's" last letter to, 241 n9; in *History of Remarkable Providences,* 205; mentioned, 10, 240 n8. See also Dunton, Elizabeth Annesley
Israelites, 213
Isaiah, 89, 166

Jacobites: in *Mercury*, 62; in *Pegasus with News*, 212; mentioned, 164, 211, 213
James II: in *Mercury*, 59–62; and daughters, 59–64 *passim*; mentioned, 7, 10, 12, 13, 96
Janeway, Richard, 14, 16
Jay, Stephen, 11
Jeffreys, George Lord, 12, 17
Jesuits: Athenians' view of, 163, 181; mentioned, 164, 177, 180. *See also* Catholics; Papists
Jews: and Dunton, 17, 190 n7; in *Mercury*, 181–185
Johnson, Elizabeth: on women, 108; mentioned, 226
Johnson, Samuel: praises Singer, 107; mentioned, 134, 141
Jonathan Swift's Relations to Science, 116
Jones, Martha, 238
Jones, Thomas, 42, 44
Jonson, Ben, 45, 100
Josephus: authority of, 171; mentioned, 183, 184
Journal de Scavans, 50
Judges 9.13, 194

"Kainophilus" (John Dunton), 14. *See also* Dunton, John; "Philaret"; "Smart, P."
Kersey, John: Sault's criticism of, 120
Key into the Languages of America, A, 20 n17
King William and Queen Mary Conquerors, 65
Kircher, Athanasius: on sun, 130; description of, 140 n19
Klopstock, Friedrich, 107
"Know, Celia," 216

Lacedemonians: and Athenians, 40–41; mentioned, 46, 221
Lacedemonian Mercury, The: title change of, 39, 46 n5; suspension of, 44; compared to *Mercury*, 84; mentioned, 43. *See also London Mercury*
La Crose, Jean Cornand de: and Le Clerc, 51, 52, 53; and Dunton, 52, 53–54
Ladies Mercury: description of, 103, 104; and *Athenian Spy*, 223
Lake, Mary, 19 n8
Lamentations, 89
Lampridius, 175
La Recherche de la verité, 118, 139 n7
Larkin, George, 227
"Madame Laureat," 224, 225
Le Clerc, Jean: works of, 51, 94; and La Crose, 51, 53; influence of, in *Young Students Library*, 57; and Locke, 57
Lee, Samuel, 11
Leibnitz, Gottfried Wilhelm, 117
L'Estrange, Sir Roger, 7
Leybourne, William: and Sault, 118; writings of, 119
Life and Errors: description of, 4; compared to other publications, 14–15, 216, 226–227; title page of, 18 n1; on *Athenian Gazette*, 28; on Taylor, 43; on Dunton, 53; on the *Mercury*, 64–65; on Sault, 75; poems in, 95; acrostics, doggerel, and verse in, 102, 103; criticism of Wesley in, 103, 201; *Night Walker* episodes in, 240 n8; mentioned, 11, 73, 92, 209, 210, 236
Life of Christ: prefatory essay to, 56; description of, 96; and Queen Mary, 97; and *Paradise Regained*, 98; Christ on pinnacle in, 101; mentioned, 100, 103, 164, 193
Lightfoot, Dr. John, 174
Lives of the Fathers, 57
Lloyd, William, 100
Locke, John: and Le Clerc, 57; and *Young Students Library*, 57; in *Second Spira*, 71; on causation, 131; mentioned, 51, 93, 137, 233, 234
London Gazette: title of, 28; compared to *Mercury*, 30, 49, 202; mentioned, 198, 200

London Mercury: and *Mercury,* 34, 35–36, 93; title change of, 39, 46 n5; mentioned, 42, 84, 92. See also *The Lacedemonian Mercury*
London Post, 220
Lot, 173
Louis XIV: *Mercury's* position on, 30; mentioned, 61, 213
Lovejoy, A. O., 144
Lower, Dr. Richard, 134
Luther, 241 n13
Lutheranism, 166
Luttrell, Narcissus: and Dunton, 241 n15, mentioned, 49

Macrobius, 175
Magdalen College, Fellows of, 96, 168
Maggots: Wesley's humor in, 94, 95; mentioned, 6, 96, 164
Magnalia Christi, 8
Magus, Simon, 175
Maimonides, 183
Malebranche, Nicholas, 85 n16, 118, 222
Malthus, Sarah, 227
Malthus, Thomas, 227
Manship, Samuel, 85 n16
Martyr, Justin, 175
Mary, Queen (Princess Mary): as ruler, 59; and James II, 64; and social reform, 142; mentioned, 51, 62, 97. See also William and Mary
Mary of Modena, 62
Mather, Cotton: and Dunton, 8; mentioned, 208 n13, 133
Matthew 5:32, 167
Mayhern, Theodore, 231
Mead, Matthew, 10
Methodius, Bishop of Tyre, 166
Microcosmography, 20 n17
Midgely, Robert, 52
Midsummer Night's Dream, A (Settle's version), 77
Millenarianism, 165–166
Milton, John: and *Life of Christ,* 97; and Wesley, 97, 98, 99, 100; mentioned, 96, 183, 184

Miscellaneous Works in Prose and Verse of Mrs. Elizabeth Rowe, 106
Montaigne, Michel Eyquem, 217
Moderator: on *Mercury's* poetry, 44, 93
Mohammedanism, 205
Montgomery, Hugh, 223
More, Henry, 241 n13
Morphew, John, 232
Morton, Charles: anti-Cartesianism of, 123; Dissenter academy of, 123; writings of, 123, 132, 133, 135; education and scientific knowledge of, 139 n12; description of, 203; mentioned, 20 n14
Motteux, Peter: description of, 17; on Wesley, 99; mentioned, 41, 42, 57, 103, 202
Moses: Pisgah-sight of, 175; mentioned, 169, 185, 187, 188
Mr. Tate on His New Poem of the late Promotions &c., To, 102

Nashe, Thomas, 147
Natural History of Nutrician, 133
Nepier, Dr. Richard, 241 n13
New Athenian Comedy, The: description of, 64, 77; and *Mercury,* 77, 80–84, 85 n17
Newcome, Richard, 14
New Poem on the Late Illustrious Congress at the Hague, A, 103
New Theory of Vision, 125
Newton, Isaac, 113, 116, 117
Nicholas, Sarah. See Dunton, Sarah Nicholas
Nicholas, J. B., 75
Night Walker: description of, 213, 214–215; compared to *Secret Mercury,* 222; in *Life and Errors,* 240 n8; mentioned, 161 n3, 207
Normanby, Lord, 97
Norris, John: in *Athenian Gazette,* 23; in *Mercury,* 67, 114; in *New Athenian Comedy,* 80, 83; criticism of *Essay concerning Human Understanding,* 94; DeVane's praise of, 116; and Sault's Male-

branche translation, 139 *n*7; relations with Dunton and Sault, 222; in *Athenian Spy*, 224, 225; mentioned, 76, 169, 221
Northcott, Thomas, 178
Norton, of Fleet Street, 226
Nosce Teipsum, 100
Nova Fert Animus, &c., In, 239
Nuncius Infernalis, 42

Observator, 12
Ode to the Athenian Society, 24, 33, 42
"Ode to St. Cecilia's Day, An," 103
Ode to William III, 75, 216, 217
Oldham, John, 100
Old Post Master, 220
Origen, 175
"Orinda": 224, 225
Orinda's, 108
Osborn, Francis, 94
Overbury, Sir Thomas, 20 *n*17
Ovid, 185

Palmer, Samuel, 8, 9
Panarithmologia, 119
"Panegyrick upon the Athenian Society," 67
Panorganon, 119
Papists, and *Mercury*, 180, 181, 184. See also Catholics; Jesuits
Paradise Lost: and *Life of Christ*, 97; mentioned, 100
Paradise Regained: and *Life of Christ*, 98; mentioned, 96, 183
Parkhurst, Thomas: description of, 4; and Dunton, 5, 6; mentioned, 10
Partridge, John, 10
Pate, William, 34
Pausanias, 127
Pegasus with News, 211–213
Pentateuch, 169, 176
Persians, 176
Petre, Father, 13
"Philaret" (John Dunton): courtship letters of, 5; and "Philomela," 108; in *History of Remarkable Providences*, 205; in

Athenian Spy, 224; last letter to "Iris" of, 241 *n*9; mentioned, 10. See also Dunton, John; "Kainophilus"; "Smart, P."
Philo, 184
"Philomela" (Elizabeth Singer): in praise of Athenians, 107; and "Iris," 108; mentioned, 207, 212, 226. See also "Pindarick Lady"; Singer, Elizabeth
Philosophical Transactions: revival of, 46; and Dunton, 57; compared to *Mercury*, 113; mentioned, 122, 134, 139 *n*12
"Pindarick Lady" (Elizabeth Singer): in *Athenian Spy*, 224, 225; mentioned, 197, 212, 223. See also "Philomela"; Singer, Elizabeth
"Pindarique On the Grunting of a Hog, A," 6
Pindarick, to the Athenian Society, A, 107–108
Plato, 127, 136, 157
Pliny: disparagement of, 127; on swallows, 134; mentioned, 126, 175
Plutarch, 127, 136, 175
Poems on Several Occasions: prefatory poem to, 107; significance of, 108; mentioned, 106, 207, 212, 226
Pool, Matthew, 204
Pope, Alexander, 107
Popping, Sarah, 73
Pordage, John, 221
Post Angel, 215, 219–222
Post-boy, 195, 220
Postman, 185, 220
Pesikta, 184
Presbyterians, 168
Prior, Matthew, 107
Psalms, 89, 100, 166
Publick Spirit of the Whigs, 237
Purcell, Henry, 120

Quakers: and *Mercury*, 30, 164, 177–181; mentioned, 182. See also Anabaptists, Dissenters
Quarles, Francis, 45

Raleigh, Sir Walter, 193
Rambler, 141
Ramble Round the World, A, 14–16
Randal, Thomas, 100. *See also* Randolph
Randolph, Thomas, 239. *See also* Randal
Ranew, Nathaniel, 63
Ray, John, 136
Reading, William, 19 n8
Reasons of Mr. Bays Changing His Religion, 35
Redpath, George, 195
Reflections upon Ancient and Modern Learning, 132
Relation of the Feare-full Estate of Francis Spira, in the yeare, 1548, A, 68–69, 71
Religio Medici, 32 n5, 233
Revelation, 165
Review (Defoe's): and *Mercury,* 84, 220, 241 n12; and other journals, 220
Richardson, Charles, 41, 42, 67
Richardson, Edmund, 211
Richardson, Samuel, 142
Rotterdam (coffee house), 46
Rowe, Elizabeth Singer. *See* "Philomela"; "Pindarick Lady"; Singer, Elizabeth
Royal Academy: description of, 120–122; mentioned, 124
Royal Gratitude: Dunton and Swift on, 237; mentioned, 238
Royal Society: compared to Athenian Society, 113; on politics and religion, 117–118; and Dunton, 218; mentioned, 46, 119, 126, 127, 139 n12

Sacheverell, Dr. Henry, 235
Sanders, Madame (in *Athenian Spy*), 226
Sanderson, Robert, 157, 161 n6
Sandys, George, 100
Sappho, 108
Saturninus, 175
Saul, 169
Sault, Richard: and *Athenian Gazette,* 23; and *Mercury,* 24, 25, 31, 50, 76, 114, 115, 118, 202; knowledge and education, 31, 117, 122, 124; and *Second Spira,* 67, 68, 69, 72, 73–75, 76; as teacher, 67, 85 n15, 119, 120–121; and Dunton 75–76, 122, 201; family life, 72–73, 149; as translator, 76, 118, 139 n7; in *New Athenian Comedy,* 80, 81, 83; death of, 85 n10, 228; as mathematician, 115; as writer, 102, 103, 118–119, 122; on mathematics, 119–120; contemporary reputation of, 120; and Royal Academy, 120, 122; and Wesley, 122; and Norris, 222; in *Athenian Spy,* 224; mentioned, 41, 71, 223
Sault, Sarah: description of, 85 n11; in *Athenian Spy,* 224
Scaliot, Mark, 126
Schurman (woman poet), 108
Search after Truth, 85 n16
Second Coming, 165–166
Second Spira: description of, 67–71, 85 n7; 30th edition of, 73; in *New Athenian Comedy,* 81; mentioned, 201
Secret Mercury: compared to other journals, 219, 220, 222; suspension of, 222; mentioned, 223
Selden, John, 205
"Seraphick Love": lines from, 225
Settle, Elkanah: and *Mercury,* 77; on engraving of Athenian Society, 86 n20; mentioned, 64
Sewall, Samuel, 208 n12
Seymour, Jane, 192
Shakespeare, William, 100
Short History of the Parliament, 237
Shower, John, 10
Silent Woman, The, 27
Singer, Elizabeth: as author, 90, 91, 100, 105, 106, 107, 108; praised, 107, 108; poetic subjects of, 109; mentioned, 94, 103. *See also* "Philomela"; "Pindarick Lady"
Slater, Samuel, 11

"Smart, P." (John Dunton), 24, 32 n5. *See also* Dunton, John; "Kainophilus"; "Philaret"

Smith, James: and Dunton, 26; in *New Athenian Comedy*, 80; mentioned, 74

Smith, Mary, 26

Smith's Coffee House: and Dunton, 26, 220; mentioned, 46, 102, 224, 226

Socrates, 136

Solomon, 136, 219

Spademan, John, 10

Spectator: compared to *Mercury*, 18, 141, 142; mentioned, 108

Spenser, Edmund, 100

Spinoza, Baruch, 169

Sprat, Bishop, 125

Stationers Register, 14, 57, 64

Steele, Richard: Swift's attack of, 237; mentioned, 108

Stoughton, William, 208 n12

Stuarts, 64, 213

Suetonius, 175

Supplement I, 52

Supplement III, 52, 94

Supplement IV, 53

Supplement V: contents of, 54; on Quakers, 179

Supplements (to *Mercury*): contents of, 51; as part of *Young Students Library*, 55; mentioned, 49, 50

Swift, Jonathan: and *Maggots*, 7, 95; on Dunton, 12, 34, 124, 237; and Athenian Society myth, 24; views of Athenian Society, 33, 34; and *Mercury*, 124, 138 n3; as satirist, 237; mentioned, 10, 69, 91, 103, 107, 148, 216, 217, 232

Swift, Thomas, 33

Synopsis Criticorum, 204

Tacitus, 175

Tale of a Tub, A: satire of Dunton in, 12, 124

Tasso, 100

Tate, Nahum: on Wesley, 99; mentioned, 41, 42, 100

Tatler, 18

Taylor, Thomas: on Wesley, 99; mentioned, 139 n7

Telluris Theoria sacra, 176

Tempest, Madame (in *Athenian Spy*), 226

Temple, Sir William: and *Mercury*, 33, 34; on blood circulation, 132; mentioned, 174

Tennyson, Alfred, 10

Terence, 188

Term Catalogue, 6, 11

Tertullian, 191

Thales, 127

Theory of the Earth: in *Mercury*, 186–189; mentioned, 185

Thorncomb (tobacconist), 226

Tonson, Jacob, 97

Tories, 236

Tranquillus, 175

Tryals of several Witches, 208 n12

Tully (Cicero), 136

Turner, William: on Aristotle, 205; on *History of Remarkable Providences*, 206; mentioned, 204

Turner's Coffee House, 46

Tutchin, John, 12

Tyrconnel, Richard Earl of, 13

Universal and Historical Bibliotheque, 52

Universal Bibliotheque, 50, 53

Usher, Bishop, 174

Veal, Edward, 6, 20 n14

Virgil, 89

Voyage into the Levant, A, 116

Voyage Round the World, A: compared to other works, 14–15, 16; on Dunton and Elizabeth, 20 n12

Wade, John, 226

Walker, Anthony, 63, 64

Waller, Edmund, 100

Waller, Richard, 46

Wallis, John: Dunton's elegy to, 75, 76; mentioned, 117

Walpole, Horace, 237

Warren, Erasmus: criticism of *Theory of the Earth*; 186–187

Watts, Isaac: and Singer, 107; influence of scientific instruction on, 123
Weekly Review: compared to *Mercury*, 18
Welsh's Coffee House, 46
Wem, Charles, 225
Wesley, John: criticism of, 111 n13; mentioned, 96, 149
Wesley, Samuel: and *Mercury*, 6, 24, 25, 49, 50, 93, 94, 101, 114, 115, 164, 167, 168, 185, 202; and Dunton, 6, 95, 103, 201, 236; education of, 6, 20 n14, 27, 31, 95, 96, 123, 124, 139 n12, 164, 165; as author, 6, 7, 23, 55, 57, 58 n9, 67, 94–97, 102, 103; qualifications of, 24, 164, 189 n1; areas of knowledge of, 31, 122, 124; Brown's attack of, 38, 44; as clergyman, 56, 95, 97, 115, 165; family life, 56, 95, 109, 149, 155, 161 n5; on Hebrew, 56; religious and political views, 96, 111 n10, 203; and Milton, 97–100; on Lucifer, 98; on poetry, 98, 100, 192; and Christianity, 101, 171; compared to Singer, 109; on remarriage, 141; and Dissenters, 165; on millenarianism, 166; on Jews, 183, 185; on Atlas, 192; on poetic license, 192, 193; and Morton, 203; on Elizabeth Dunton, 208 n8; mentioned, 77, 169, 204, 207
Wesley, Samuel Jr., 111 n13
Wesley, Susannah: description of, 109; political views of 111 n10; marriage of, 149, 161 n5; and Dunton, 236

Westfall, Richard S., 135
Whigs, 237
Whipping Post, 87 n21
Wieland, Christoph, 107
Wild, Robert, 239
Wilkins, Bishop John, 124, 135, 136, 139 n12
Wilkins, Richard: and Dunton, 9
William III (William of Orange): as ruler with Mary, 59; French defeat of, 59; Swift's *Ode* to, 75, 216, 217; Singer's poem on, 90, 91, 106; mentioned, 10, 11, 12, 17, 51, 142, 186. *See also* William and Mary
William and Mary: in *Mercury*, 30; oaths to, 168; mentioned, 11, 52
Williamites, 212
Williams, Daniel, 207
Williams, Roger, 20 n17
Wolley, R., 70
Woodes, Nathaniel, 68
Woodford, Samuel, 100
Wooley, Richard, 55
Works of the Learned: title change of, 52; and Dunton, 53, 54
Wotton, William, 132
Wycherley, William, 100

Young Students Library: and Athenian Society, 27; translations in, 53; and *Mercury*, 55, 58; contents of, 55, 56, 57; publication of, 55; on Hebrew, 56; on Protestants, 56, 57; scientific attributions in, 57; Wesley's contributions to, 185; mentioned, 46, 52, 86 n20, 174, 201, 236

Zenobia, 108

THE ORACLE OF THE COFFEE HOUSE

John Dunton's *Athenian Mercury*

by Gilbert D. McEwen

A periodical that would resolve "all the most Nice and Curious Questions proposed by the Ingenious," while concealing the identity of the querist—the idea came to John Dunton, a London bookseller, one day in early 1691. He lost no time in transforming inspiration into reality, for the *Athenian Mercury* began publication in March of that year, and continued to appear on Tuesdays and Saturdays almost without interruption until June 1697. Although the *Mercury* was not in the literary tradition of its great successors, Defoe's *Review* and Swift's *Examiner,* its unique format engaged the interest of a wide variety of readers, from the coffee houses of London to the stately country homes outside the city.

This book is a history of the *Athenian Mercury,* and of John Dunton, as well as the other people associated with it: Samuel Wesley, Dunton's brother-in-law and father of John Wesley; Richard Sault, mathematician, scientist, and atheist; the "Pindarick Lady," Elizabeth Singer, whose poetry was a feature of many of the later volumes of the *Mercury.* Working with the two sets of the *Mercury* in the Huntington Library, the author gives us extensive quoted material from the periodical, covering such subjects as courtship, marriage, religion, science, and a variety of other topics. The result is a rare and highly entertaining view of the interests, beliefs, and prejudices of seventeenth-century England.

Gilbert D. McEwen was born in Mason City, Iowa. He received his doctor's degree from Yale University, and has been Professor of English at Whittier College, Whittier, California, since 1955. He has published several articles on early English journalism.

THE
Athenian Gazette:
OR,
CASUISTICAL MERCURY,

Resolving all the most

Nice and Curious Questions

PROPOSED BY THE

INGENIOUS

Of Either Sex:

From *Tuesday*, *Octob.* 29. to *Saturday*, *Feb.* 8. 1696.

The Nineteenth Volume.

TREATING

On the several Subjects mentioned in the CONTENTS, at the beginning of the Book.

• .
LONDON:

Printed for *John Dunton*, at the Raven in *Jewen-street*, 1696.
Where is to be had the *Entire Set* of Athenian Gazettes (and the *Supplements* to 'em for the Year 1691.) as also the *Entire Set* for the Year 1692, 1693, 1694, and 1695. (Or single Volumes to this Time.)
These Volumes are also sold by Edm. Richardson, near the *Poultrey-Church*.